PCs made easy

STAGE 8

A PRACTICAL COURSE

Microsoft® Windows®
xp
edition

PCs made easy

STAGE 8

A PRACTICAL COURSE

Microsoft® Windows®
xp
edition

PUBLISHED BY THE READER'S DIGEST ASSOCIATION LIMITED
LONDON NEW YORK SYDNEY MONTREAL

PCS MADE EASY
MICROSOFT® WINDOWS® XP EDITION
A PRACTICAL COURSE – STAGE 8

Published by the Reader's Digest Association Limited, 2003

The Reader's Digest Association Limited
11 Westferry Circus, Canary Wharf, London E14 4HE
www.readersdigest.co.uk

We are committed to both the quality of our products and the service we provide to
our customers, so please feel free to contact us on 08705 113366, or via our Web site
at www.readersdigest.co.uk
If you have any comments about the content of our books, you can
contact us at gbeditorial@readersdigest.co.uk

®Reader's Digest, The Reader's Digest and the Pegasus logo are registered trademarks
of The Reader's Digest Association Inc, of Pleasantville, New York, USA

For Reader's Digest
Project Editor: Caroline Boucher
Art Editor: Julie Bennett

Reader's Digest General Books
Editorial Director: Cortina Butler
Art Director: Nick Clark
Series Editor: Christine Noble

PCs made easy – Microsoft® Windows® XP Edition was fully updated for
Reader's Digest by De Agostini UK Ltd from *PCs made easy*, a book series created and
produced for Reader's Digest by De Agostini from material originally published as the
Partwork *Computer Success Plus*
The new edition was adapted by Craft Plus Publishing Ltd

© 2003 De Agostini UK Ltd

Printed and bound in Europe by Arvato, Iberia

ISBN 0 276 42759 9

CONTENTS

6

Windows

The Stand By command

Switching off your computer means you have to wait for it to start up each time you use it. But you can safely leave it on for long periods – and save time and energy – by using power-management options.

In an environmentally conscious world, the way you set up your computer can help to minimize unnecessary energy consumption. We've seen how to use Windows' screen saver options (see Stage 6, pages 12–13), which reduce power usage, but you can cut down usage even further by using Windows' Power Options feature to specify an idle time, after which the computer will switch the monitor into a low-power sleep mode. This minimizes the power consumed by the monitor when you are not using the PC.

However, even though a dormant monitor uses only a fraction of the power it consumes when in use, the computer itself is still fully operational and the computer's internal components – the hard disk, the processor

and memory chips, for example – still consume power at the same rate as if you were working on the computer.

● The Stand By mode
Windows' special Stand By mode drastically reduces the amount of power used by the computer itself. Its processor chip slows right down when this mode is activated. With the screen saver options, the computer keeps track of how long it was since you last pressed a key or moved the mouse before it switches the monitor into low-power mode. In contrast, to switch the computer into Stand By mode, you must click on the appropriate button in the Turn off computer dialog box.

● Instant action
Once you have selected the Stand By option, the screen goes blank and the hard disk stops spinning. To all intents and purposes, the PC appears to be switched off. But as soon as it detects input, such as movement of the mouse, the computer will burst back into life – exactly at the point you left it earlier – to enable you to continue working.

If you use Windows' power management options to put your computer in stand-by mode when it's not being used, you will save on both power consumption and time.

NOTEBOOK POWER

Windows provides extra options that allow you to squeeze the maximum life out of your computer's battery. For example, all modern notebook PCs have an extra tab called Hibernate in the Power Options Properties window. This lets you switch on a special feature that can save time and battery power. If you tick the Enable hibernation option, your notebook will go into a deep sleep. When you close the lid, Windows copies data from memory to the hard disk and shuts down automatically.

When your computer comes out of hibernation, Windows restarts and copies the data back into memory – so you're exactly where you left off without having to start up and reopen files. Many desktop PC's also have this feature (see Stage 7, page 15).

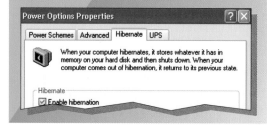

WAKING UP

With some PCs, you may find that moving the mouse doesn't wake the PC from Stand By or Hibernate modes. Don't panic – just press any key on the keyboard and the processor will detect the key-press and wake the PC up.

Power-saving options for Windows

Using the Stand By command instead of Shut Down saves power and leaves your PC in a state where it can get back into action more quickly than when starting up from cold.

1 To see how the Stand By command works, first select Turn Off Computer from the Start menu.

2 In the dialog box, click on the Stand By button. After a moment, the screen goes blank. Inside the PC, the hard disk has also stopped spinning and the processor chip is operating at a lower **clock speed**.

WHAT IT MEANS

CLOCK SPEED

This is the rate at which a chip processes data. For example, when you're using a 2GHz computer, it's making two billion data operations each second.

3 However, the computer isn't totally dormant – it's still waiting for any input from you. Move the mouse a little and the PC starts up, with the screen exactly as you left it.

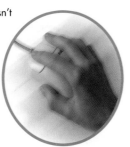

4 Windows keeps all information in the computer's memory intact, so any documents you were working on are exactly as you left them. However, any loss of power to the PC will cause all unsaved changes to your documents to be lost, so it's safest to save or close any documents you are working on before switching to Stand By mode.

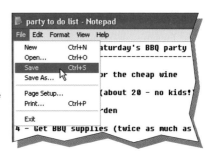

1 If you don't want to use Stand By mode, but do want to save power, you can still fine-tune Windows' power options on the Control Panel. Click on Control Panel in the Start menu and then double-click on the Power Options icon.

WATCH OUT

A computer that is left in Stand By mode can look as if it is switched off. If you forget you have left it in that mode and then try to switch it on, you will lose any data that is still stored in the memory. Always move the mouse or press a keyboard button first to check if the computer is just 'asleep'.

2 On the Power Schemes tab, you can change the settings that control how long a period of inactivity lasts before Windows shuts down the monitor and the hard disk. On this PC, the monitor switches off after 15 minutes of no mouse or keyboard input, but the hard disk never switches off.

3 You can experiment with different settings. Bear in mind that each time the monitor turns back on and the hard disk spins back up to full speed, you are kept waiting. Short settings can prove frustrating, so try to find the right balance between environmental friendliness and inconvenience.

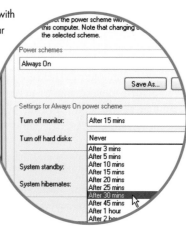

Monitoring PC performance

Windows is a collection of several hundred files and individual programs, all working together to provide a seamless interface. The Performance window lets you see what's happening under the surface to help you diagnose performance problems.

Monitoring your PC's performance can give you an insight into the way that Windows works and thereby help to solve problems. By checking to see how busy the many different parts of Windows are, you can spot bottlenecks and take the appropriate action.

Windows provides several tools to help you, the most basic being the Windows Task Manager (see page 12). This gives an overview of the way that resources on your PC are being used as well as a simple graphical display that you can check at any time with a few clicks.

If you want more detail when measuring the performance of your computer's component parts, it's best to use the System Monitor in the Performance window (see page 13). This can be used to predict when the computer is becoming over-worked and to log the performance of a variety of different devices. So, if your hard-disk drive is working slowly, you can measure its performance with the System Monitor.

● Processor usage

When you first run the System Monitor, it starts by measuring the amount of processor time that is spent idle – specifically, the amount that is not in use by the kernel. This information is displayed as a line graph, which is constantly updated (by default, every second), thereby allowing you to measure exactly how much effort it takes for the computer to carry out certain functions. A number of different resources can be monitored at the same time, so you can check the effect on several resources when you perform one particular action.

System Monitor has a range of customizable features, including many display options. The Histogram display is very useful if you find the overlapping lines

of the Graph option are making it hard to watch a large number of actions simultaneously. You can also edit the axis of any graph, as well as its colour, to make System Monitor as user-friendly as possible.

● Paging and performance

One factor that greatly affects the performance of your computer is paging. Your computer uses both physical and virtual memory to store its data. Physical memory takes the form of memory chips on the PC's motherboard (RAM) but while Windows uses your PC's physical memory for most of its storage, it also treats a section of the hard disk as if it were memory. This virtual memory lets Windows handle bigger files and larger programs than if it used the memory chips alone.

However, Windows cannot work directly upon data while it is stored on the hard disk

WHAT IT MEANS

KERNEL

The kernel is the central core of Windows. Once loaded, it remains in your computer's memory for as long as the computer is switched on. The kernel is responsible for vital basic tasks, such as memory, process, task and disk management. It is a relatively small and tightly programmed piece of code and so doesn't take up too much valuable memory.

Windows is built around a kernel and the Performance tool allows you to monitor how this kernel and many other fundamental parts of Windows are running.

so it needs to be able to swap data between the memory chips and hard disk – this process is called paging.

● The effects of paging

Although most PC users don't realise it, everyone will have experienced the impact of paging at some stage. When Windows starts to copy data to or from the paging file – the part of the hard disk that stores the data being paged in and out of the computer's memory chips – other Windows tasks are delayed. This is one of the common reasons why Windows sometimes seems to stop responding to your input. A program may freeze for a moment, the mouse pointer may change to an hour-glass figure or its movement may become sluggish for a second or two. You may also receive a warning that Windows is running low on virtual memory and that while it is automatically responding to the

problem by increasing the size of your paging file, you may experience problems running some programs.

This delay happens because paging has a higher priority than your own instructions, and Windows diverts its attention to the higher-priority task. When the paging is complete, Windows picks up where it left off, and handles your instructions.

Paging is also the reason that you will occasionally hear the hard disk working away even when you haven't opened or saved any documents, or launched a new program. This is

If you have many memory-hungry programs open at once, Windows may display a dialog box warning of low virtual memory.

When Windows is busy moving data to and from the page file, the mouse pointer disappears completely and the hour-glass cursor appears instead.

simply Windows handling your computer's memory requirements and is no cause for alarm.

● Dealing with delays

If you experience unexpected delays while you are working, you can use the Windows Task Manager to check on the amount of paging taking place (see page 12, Step 6). You may find a more in-depth analysis is required, in which case use the Performance window in the System Monitor, as described on page 13, to keep an eye on the rate at which Windows is swapping data in and out of the paging file. If you find you often have problems with slow performance caused by excessive paging, you should consider adding more memory to your computer (see Stage 1, pages 100–101), particularly if you are still using only 128MB of memory – the minimum requirement recommended by Microsoft for normal use of Windows XP. Adding memory is one way in which you can make significant improvements to your PC's performance.

How programs use memory

Your PC's performance is greatly affected by how much paging takes place. This depends on the programs used and the commands run.

THE AMOUNT of paging that Windows does depends on the programs you have open and the number and size of the files being used. On PCs with 256MB of RAM, you may be able to start a dozen programs, all of which easily fit within your PC's memory chips, without Windows needing to use virtual memory. However, as you use these programs, they often request more memory. For example, if you use your photo-editing program to open a 64MB scanned photograph, Windows must find space for the photo in the PC's physical memory. To do this, it may have to shunt other programs to virtual memory.

Some commands also impose heavy memory demands on Windows. For

The best way to improve PC performance is to add more memory – Windows XP can work within 128MB of memory, but a minimum of 256MB allows Windows to work much more efficiently.

example, in many photo editing programs, if you adjust the colour balance of a scanned photo, the program temporarily creates a second version of the photo in memory to calculate and store the new colours. You don't see this second photo, but the program requests space from Windows for it, and it can cause Windows to do even more paging of other programs.

PC TIPS

Fragmented page file

The page file is central to the performance of Windows so it's vital that it isn't fragmented. To get the most out of your PC, the page file must occupy a continuous area on the surface of the hard disk. This is why it's vital to defragment your hard disk regularly (see Stage 3, page 10).

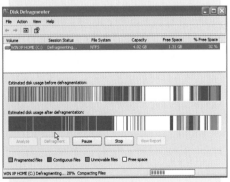

Monitor performance with Windows Task Manager

Normally, the Windows Task Manager is used to shut down programs that have stopped responding, but it also provides an overview of Windows' performance.

1 Close all documents and programs. Then right-click on an empty area of the Taskbar and select Task Manager from the pop-up menu. When the Windows Task Manager dialog box appears, click on the Performance tab.

2 The top of the Performance tab shows four graphs. With a system switched on but no programs in use, the CPU Usage indicates how much of the processor's time is being used. After a very brief blip – caused by the process of loading the Windows Task Manager itself, this figure should drop quite low – 5% or less. The CPU Usage History panel shows the blip.

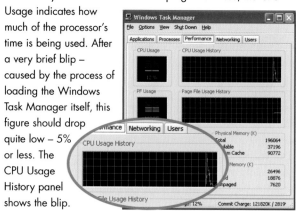

3 Use the Start menu to open two or three programs. The Windows Task Manager stays on top of the program windows, so you can monitor the graphs. You'll see peaks in usage appear as red and green lines. After a few moments, the CPU Usage settles down again.

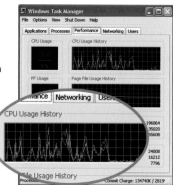

4 You can't make the Windows Task Manager fill the screen, but if you double-click on any of the graphs, the two CPU graphs expand to fill the Windows Task Manager window. You can now see the red and green portions more clearly: the green lines represent overall Windows usage of the processor (or CPU) and the red represents the amount in use by the kernel.

5 Double-click on the CPU graphs to return to the normal display. You can ignore most of the figures in the lower half of the Performance tab, but it's useful to compare some of the figures. Open some more programs from the Start menu.

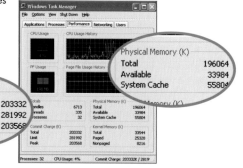

6 If the Commit Charge Total figure becomes higher than the Physical Memory Total figure (as shown here), Windows starts to use the paging file to swap some information from memory to the hard disk. As the Commit Charge Total figure approaches the Commit Charge Limit (which is the sum of the physical memory and the size of the page file), the PC slows down markedly.

STRANGE FIGURES

The memory figures in the Windows Task Manager are given in kilobytes (KB, abbreviated to K in the dialog box) and not megabytes (MB), which can lead to confusion. The important point to remember is that 1MB is equal to 1024KB. In our example, our PC has 192MB of physical memory, or 196,608KB (192 x 1024). Even then, a Windows calculation anomaly means that the number displayed is slightly lower – around 500KB. You can safely ignore these minor differences.

Using System Monitor

The System Monitor goes into more depth than the Windows Task Manager and is more useful in finding performance bottlenecks.

1 Close down all programs and then select Control Panel from the Start menu. Double-click on the Administrative Tools icon. If you can't see this icon, click on the Switch to Classic View link on the right of the Control Panel window to display it.

2 In the Administrative Tools window, double-click on the Performance icon. The Performance window opens, with the System Monitor selected in the panel on the left. To the right is a graph, which is empty to begin with.

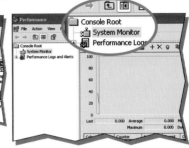

3 The three lines on the graph are: % Processor Time in green; **Page/sec** in yellow and Avg Disk Queue Length in blue. Try starting programs to see how these vary according to the demands you place on Windows. In this example, the Avg Disk Queue Length spent some time at maximum, while % Processor Time was much lower. This indicates that the hard disk was the bottleneck at that moment.

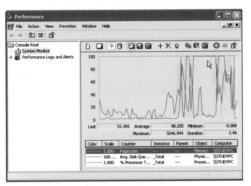

4 To add other indicators, click on the Add button on the toolbar just above the graph. In the Add Counters dialog box, click on the Performance object box and select Paging File (see Unfamiliar terms box, below).

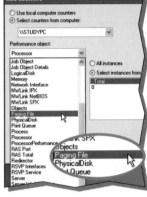

5 Next, select one of the counters in the list. To see a brief description of the counter, click on the Explain button. When you have decided on a counter to add to the display, click on the Add button.

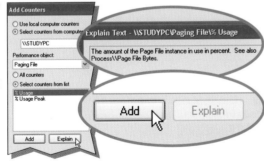

WHAT IT MEANS

PAGE/SEC

This is an indication of the rate at which Windows can move data to and from the paging file. It's one of the default settings for the Performance window because it's a useful indicator of delays caused by lack of physical memory.

6 This counter is added as a yellow line, which is confusing. Right-click on this counter at the bottom of the Performance window and select Properties. Use the Data tab of the dialog box to choose a contrasting Color, Width and/or Style.

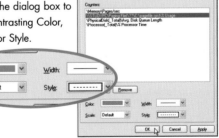

7 Now you can see this counter more clearly. In this example, it shows that our paging file usage hardly dips below about 75 percent.

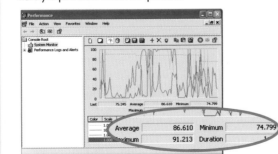

UNFAMILIAR TERMS

The Add Counters dialog box covers many detailed technical aspects of Windows. It's best to ignore most counters initially and simply concentrate on Memory, Paging File, Physical Disk and Processor.

Customizing the Windows Taskbar

The Windows Taskbar is almost infinitely customizable. You can, for instance, add shortcut buttons for your favourite programs and documents, and even set up quick access links to Web sites.

I f you haven't yet experimented with the extra features of the Windows Taskbar, you might have missed some very useful options. With a few adjustments you can add extra toolbars for faster access to programs, documents and even Web sites.

● **Extra toolbars**
There are several ready-made toolbars that you can add to the Taskbar. The first on the Toolbars menu is the Address toolbar, which demonstrates how closely Windows is integrated with the Internet. This toolbar allows you to type an Internet address into a text box on the Taskbar; Windows then starts your browser, dials up your Internet service provider and takes you to the Web site. You can also use an AutoSearch feature that links to an Internet search engine by typing Go, followed by a word or phrase (see Stage 2, pages 136–137).

The Links toolbar gives you easy access to your choice of Internet links. Instead of listing the addresses in a text box, you add buttons to the toolbar for each link, which you can click on to access the site.

The Desktop toolbar offers quick access to everything stored on your Desktop. With a single click, you can open any icon, document or folder stored on the Desktop itself.

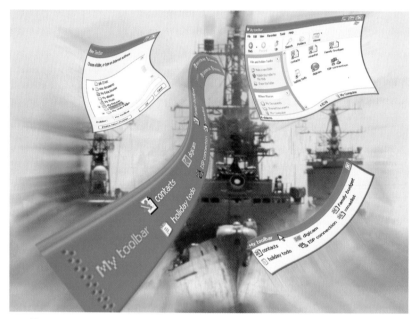
By adding your own shortcut buttons to the Taskbar you can make your most commonly used applications quickly accessible.

The final ready-made toolbar is Quick Launch. This is probably the most useful of all, but by default is switched off when Windows is first installed (when activated, it appears as a set of icons at the bottom of the screen, next to the Start button).

On some PCs, a Language toolbar is also available. If the installed programs use more than one language, this allows you to switch between languages and use different, language-related keyboard layouts.

● **Customizing toolbars**
Depending on how you use your computer, you can add some, none or all of the toolbars. You can also make your own toolbar using shortcuts of your choice, such as documents, programs or Web links. With some thought, you can create a single toolbar that includes all of your favourite aspects of your computer without unnecessary clutter.

Right-click on the Windows Taskbar, select Toolbars, and you'll see several standard options for Taskbar toolbars. Select the ones you want to use and they will be added to the Taskbar.

PC TIPS

Floating toolbars
Once you have added a toolbar, you can drag it off the Taskbar. Click and drag the toolbar on to the Desktop and it appears as a floating window; you can position it wherever you find convenient.

Adding a custom toolbar to the Taskbar

Here we show you how to get more out of the Windows Taskbar by creating your own toolbar containing some shortcuts to documents and programs.

1 Start by creating a folder and adding shortcuts to your favourite programs and documents (see Stage 4, pages 10–11). Give your folder an obvious name – we have called ours My toolbar.

2 Right-click on a clear space on the Taskbar, select Toolbars from the menu and then New Toolbar from the sub-menu.

3 A New Toolbar window lets you locate the folder that you created in Step 1. Select this folder and click on OK.

PC TIPS

Space constraints

The more icons you add to the Taskbar, the more likely you are to run out of space. When you do, small arrows appear to indicate that there are other items in the toolbar.

You can click on the arrows to see the additional items but this defeats the quick-access purpose of toolbars, so don't add too many. Once you have unlocked the Taskbar (see Step 5), you can drag the edge of the Taskbar up to create a double-depth Taskbar.

4 Your new toolbar appears as a small arrow button on the right of the Taskbar. Click on the button to make the pop-up menu of programs and documents appear. Then click on any of the menu items to open them.

5 This toolbar is locked into place, but to customise it you can unlock the Taskbar. Right-click on an empty part of the Taskbar and click once on Lock the Taskbar so the tick next to the option disappears.

6 Now a small vertical marker appears just to the left of your toolbar. Drag this marker to the left to resize the toolbar – the individual buttons for the items start to appear.

7 The items take up a lot of space on the Taskbar, but you can hide the names to save space. Right-click on the My toolbar heading and click on the Show Text command to remove its tick. Now only the button icons appear; to see the name of a button, simply hold the mouse pointer over it.

Housekeeping utilities

Just as your home needs a regular 'spring clean' to remove dirt and junk, so does your computer. Housekeeping utilities help you keep your PC neat and tidy so that it runs quickly and smoothly.

The world of Windows utilities has much to offer. In Stage 5, on pages 8–9, we covered the extensive range of low-cost, or even free, high-quality software that is available. Some of these utilities add extra functionality to Windows itself whilst others let you customize Windows to make it work better for you.

The usefulness of utilities varies greatly from program to program, but there's one group of software that is consistently the most popular and successful: housekeeping programs. These can be simple one-function programs or complete suites of programs, each of which handles a specific task. The common factor is that they are dedicated to keeping your computer well organized. Your computer needs a regular clean-up to keep it running smoothly and the housekeeping utilities do just that. The more you use your computer – especially as you install more programs – the more important a housekeeping utility becomes.

● Removing drudgery

Housekeeping utilities are popular because they remove the drudgery of tidying up, leaving you free to use your computer for the activities it's designed to tackle, such as creating documents, using the Internet, playing games and so on.

Windows already includes a handful of basic housekeeping programs. For example, the Disk Defragmenter (see Stage 3, page 10) helps to ensure that your hard disk doesn't slow down by searching for data and parts of programs that have become scattered all over the disk's magnetic surface. And if you use

Windows XP's error-checking tool (see Stage 3, page 9), your hard disk is checked for errors, particularly chunks of data or programs that have become detached and whose origins can no longer be traced.

These built-in Windows housekeeping utilities are fine as such, but for many people they don't go far enough. The most popular housekeeping suites include more advanced versions of these Windows utilities, and cover other functions not featured on them. Norton SystemWorks is by far the most successful and popular suite (see Stage 5, pages 10–13). It lets you recover a file even if it's been overwritten, or if something you have been working on decides it won't open any more. By running the Norton Utilities component of the suite, you should be able to fix the problem quickly.

CleanSweep, another program in the suite, is similar to Windows' own Add or Remove Programs utility, but is more powerful. For example, it logs all changes made when you install software so that it is more thorough when you later remove unwanted software.

Maintaining Windows can be a time-consuming job, but there is software available to help you.

SHAREWARE

Many housekeeping utilities are available as shareware. If you have an Internet account, you'll find that many can be downloaded from the software developer's Web site. Complete suites can be large (up to 45MB), whereas the simple one-function programs are small, typically less than 2MB and thus quick to download.

Which utility?

There's a wide choice of utilities, whether you want a whole suite of programs for every need or just one.

QuickClean 3.0
McAfee

This program is a much more comprehensive and advanced version of the simple Disk Cleanup and Add or Remove Programs utilities built into Windows XP. It offers many more options to help you keep your programs and documents in order. For example, if you want to clean up your files, simply create a list of the type of files you want to remove and QuickClean will do the job for you. You could tell the software to remove all files over 90 days old from your downloads folder, for instance. The program also offers privacy features, including a Shredder to completely eradicate old data, and a tool that automatically clears the most recently used document lists in your programs.

DirSize
Crystal Software

Monitoring the usage and contents of your hard drive is another useful function that many people wish Windows did itself. It can be very difficult to keep track of what is using up the most space on your hard drive, without having to check individual files and folders using Windows Explorer.

DirSize, like many programs of its type, shows a graphical representation of your computer's hard drive and all its contents. This program is perfect for working out just which programs or files to remove to free up more space on your hard drive. It gives the size of folders and files, as well as the percentage of hard disk space they take up.

EzDesk
EzWareTech

EzDesk is typical of a small but useful housekeeping utility. It manages the layout of your Desktop icons so that they don't obscure each other, which can often happen when, for example, switching between screen display resolutions (see Stage 3, pages 12–13). To prevent this, you can configure EzDesk so that it automatically reorganizes your Desktop layout if you switch to a higher or lower resolution. EzDesk organizes the Desktop according to your specification and can save an arrangement so that it can be restored later.

A further function allows you to choose a keyboard shortcut so that you can make changes just by pressing a button.

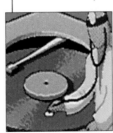

Norton SystemWorks
Symantec Corp

In contrast to utilities like EzDesk and DirSize, which focus on only one element of housekeeping, Norton's SystemWorks is an entire suite of programs. The main program, Norton Utilities, aims to find and fix system problems before you notice them. There's also an anti-virus program and a clean-up tool similar to McAfee's QuickClean.

SITES TO @ VISIT

You can download many utilities, either as shareware or for a trial period:

QuickClean
www.mcafee.co.uk
DirSize
www.crystalsoftware.com.au
EzDesk
www.ezwaretech.com
Norton SystemWorks
www.symantec.co.uk

Don't forget to search shareware sites, such as:
Tucows
www.tucows.com/
C:NET
www.download.com/

Windows' printing options

Using Windows' centralized printer settings means that you can control the way your printer works, both for all the programs you use and for all the documents you want to print out.

Most computer users think about printing only just before they print out a document. Not surprisingly, therefore, the most common approach to adjusting printer settings is through the Print dialog box of the program used to prepare the document.

While there's nothing wrong with this, it can be wasteful of both time and paper because it changes the settings for that printing only. If you need to change these settings often, you might find that a document doesn't print correctly if you forget to check. Sometimes the paper will be the wrong size, or perhaps the page might not appear in your preferred print quality.

● Paper problems

Some printers are initially set up to print on a popular American size of paper – US Letter. This measures 11x8.5 inches (279x216mm) as compared with A4 (297x210mm), which is the European standard. The difference seems small, but a mismatch here can cause several types of problem, depending on the printer. For example, on some laser printers the page might not print at first. Instead, an error message appears on the display asking for US Letter size paper to be inserted. With some software and printers, the page might print but with different margins from the ones you specified in your document. Depending on the software that is being used and the way the document was set up, you might find that the type at the bottom of every page is truncated, affecting the whole of the print job.

Save time, trouble and expense by setting printer options centrally in Windows. Default settings will then apply across your programs.

By using Windows' own centralized method of setting the printer options, you can avoid these and similar printer problems, thus saving time and money.

● A question of quality

There are other benefits too, for example, if you use a 'Best' or 'Top' print quality for most documents, it's tedious to have to change the setting from Normal to Best every time you print. By changing the default to Best in the Printers and Faxes window, you can print all documents at the same high quality, without needing to alter the settings of each one.

You can use this technique to save money, too. If you use a colour printer, changing the default quality setting to draft will mean that you never accidentally waste ink printing a rough copy of a document at too high a quality. Once you've finalized the document, you can then print it at the highest quality setting (see Print Properties box, right).

PC TIPS

Print Properties

When you use Windows' centralized print settings, you can easily tweak settings for individual documents from any Windows program. First, bring up the program's Print dialog box, but don't press the Print button. Instead, press the Properties button to see the full range of printer settings.

● Sharing printer resources

Windows also lets you share your printer if you have a home network (see Stage 5, pages 96–97). In fact, if you used Windows XP's Network Setup Wizard to connect your home PCs, you may already have linked any printers attached to the individual PCs. However, if you added a printer after networking your PCs, it may not be shared by default – in which case you can share it manually (see page 21). Once the printers are shared, any of your PCs can use any printer on your home network. Windows simply routes the image of the page along the network cable to the relevant PC. This PC then sends the page image to its printer. This networking-sharing method works seamlessly, with no interruption for the person using the other PC. As long as both the PC and its printer are switched on, the printed page will appear in the output tray within a few seconds.

UNSAVED SETTINGS

Unlike many other aspects of your documents, such as layout and margins, the printing settings controlled through the Properties dialog box aren't saved with your documents – they apply only to the current session of the program you are using. If you close and restart the program, these settings will revert to the settings in the printer's Properties dialog box (see page 20).

Printer capabilities

There are hundreds of different models of printers, and many different printing technologies as well. Windows reflects the capabilities and limitations of each printer through the Properties dialog box.

WHEN YOU open the Properties and Advanced Options dialog boxes for your printer, don't be surprised if the options and settings you see listed differ from those shown in the following examples. Although Windows presents the settings, they are based upon the printer driver – a small piece of software specifically written for each printer.

The printer driver tells Windows about the capabilities of the printer, including its colour options and paper handling features. This means that some settings are missing from these dialog boxes for certain models – for example, the print quality settings for a black and white laser printer have no adjustments for colour. Similarly, printers which cannot produce banner pages do not have a Continuous print option. If you want to fully explore the features of your printer, browse the Properties and Advanced Options dialog boxes using the printer's manual as a guide. Many printers come with very slim manuals; if you can't find a detailed explanation, look for a user guide on the printer's software CD-ROM.

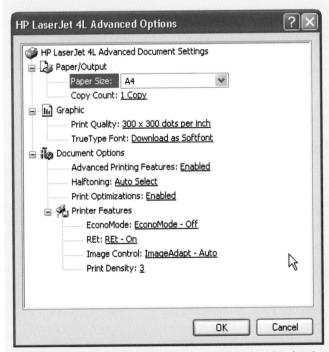

This dialog box – for an older model of laser printer – shows a limited number of advanced settings, reflecting the basic capabilities of the printer.

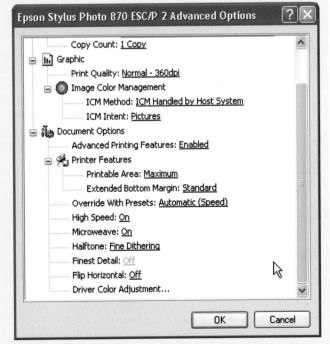

This newer model of colour inkjet printer has far more settings, including Halftone, which allows you to adjust the way colour photos are printed.

Using the Printers and Faxes window

Windows offers a simple way to adjust print settings consistently for all your programs and documents.

1 Click on Control Panel in the Start menu. Then double-click on the Printers and Faxes icon.

2 The window that appears has an icon for each printer (see Phantom printers box, below, if your PC has more than one printer). The printer with a tick next to it is the default printer – the one that Windows uses unless you specifically choose another. Right-click on this printer and select Properties from the pop-up menu.

3 In the Properties dialog box, click on the General tab. In this example, the Paper available shows that this printer driver is set to use Letter size – a US standard. To change this and other settings, click on the Printing Preferences button at the bottom of the dialog box.

4 In the Printing Preferences dialog box, click on the Advanced button to bring up the Advanced Options dialog box. This lists the many default settings for your printer.

5 Click on the Paper Size box – initially containing 'Letter' – and select another setting from the drop-down menu. In the majority of cases, A4 is the appropriate setting for most documents used in Europe.

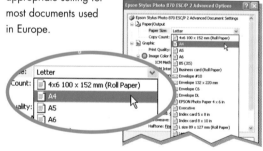

6 Alter any other settings in this dialog box to suit your printing needs. For example, if you only use this printer for printing colour photos, selecting a Photo quality setting means you won't have to set it for every photo you print. Click on the OK button when you are finished.

PHANTOM PRINTERS

Don't worry if your computer's Printers and Faxes window shows that you have an extra printer. It's not unusual for 'phantom' printers to appear. The most common explanation is that your fax software has installed an extra printer driver for its use.

If this is the case, you can send a fax from any program that has a Print command – you select the phantom printer in the Print dialog box and the software sends it using your modem (see Stage 5, pages 26–27).

7 Click on the Apply button in the Printing Preferences dialog box and then click on the OK button. Finally, do the same for the Properties dialog box to return to Windows.

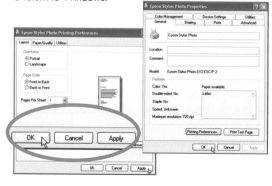

8 Now, whenever you print a document from a program, it will use your new settings. You can check this by bringing up the Print dialog box in a Windows program and clicking on the Properties and Advanced buttons to see its settings.

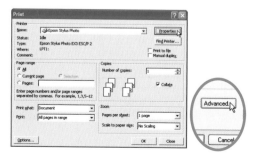

Sharing printers

If you have several PCs networked together at home, you can save money by sharing a single printer, or use any PC to access any printer on the network.

1 Open the Control Panel and double-click on the Printers and Faxes icon. In the Printers and Faxes window, right-click on the printer you want to share and select Sharing from the pop-up menu.

2 The Properties dialog box for this printer appears, with the Sharing tab already selected. If the printer has not already been set up for shared access by other computers, the Do not share this printer option is selected.

3 Select the Share this printer option and then type a descriptive name into the Share name box. Next, click on the Apply button.

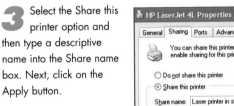

4 Windows pops up a warning that people using MS-DOS PCs may not be able to see the name. MS-DOS is an old PC operating system so you can safely ignore this warning. Click on the Yes button and then click on the OK button to close the Properties dialog box.

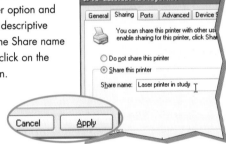

5 In the Printers and Faxes window, this printer icon has changed. The hand indicates that this PC is now 'serving' this printer to other computers.

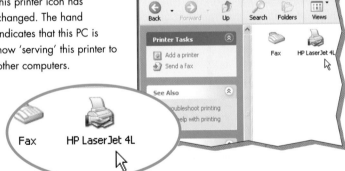

6 Now go to another PC on your network and open its Printers and Faxes window. In addition to any printer attached to this PC, you'll now see an icon for the printer that you've just shared. Look closely and you'll see that this icon includes a cable, indicating that it is on the network. Windows adds its location (on STUDYPC in this example).

7 Repeat the process to share any other printers on your network. You can select any of these printers from any program's Print dialog box. Click on the Name box and all available printers appear, again with a tiny cable indicating the networked printers. Select a printer and click on the OK button to print out the document.

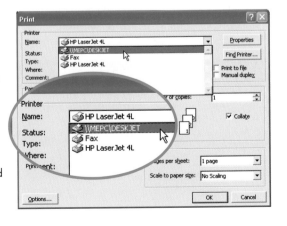

PC TIPS

Sharing and caring

While sharing printer resources is a great idea, bear in mind that printing to a printer attached to another PC imposes a slight burden on that PC's processor. Make sure that other people using the PCs are aware of this. On most print jobs on fast, modern PCs the effect is negligible, but it's possible that full-page colour photos sent via older PCs will cause the PC to slow considerably.

Changing Desktop icons

Windows lets you choose colours, sounds and backgrounds to help personalize your computer. However, to add an extra touch, you can even change the icons representing programs, documents and other elements of your PC.

Icons are the tiny pictures that you see on the Desktop and in folders (when you have Icons or Tiles selected from the folder's View menu). Despite the small number of pixels they use (typically 32x32 pixels), icons are very effective and it's surprising just how detailed some of them can be.

But first it's important to understand how Windows uses icons. When displaying icons for files, Windows looks at the file's three-letter extension. If a file has a .doc suffix, for example, Windows knows it's a Word file and automatically gives it the right icon. The same applies to .xls files for Excel and .cdr files for CorelDRAW documents.

However, you can change the icons used for these documents and folders to ones that you have chosen (see Changing file icons box, below right). You could even switch the Excel icon for the Word document icon, although it's unlikely that you would want to.

● **Desktop icons**

You will probably prefer to customize the more frequently used Windows icons, such as My Computer or the Recycle Bin. While there are some basic icon changing commands within Windows, the range of alternatives is quite limited, and the procedure quite involved. For this reason, many people prefer to use one of the shareware programs which are freely available on the Web to

manipulate and save icon files. You can normally use these programs on their own or in conjunction with a simple bitmap editor, such as Paint.

● **Creating and editing icons**

One of the most comprehensive icon manipulators is called Microangelo, a suite of icon and Desktop editing tools. Although available as shareware, it will expire after 21 days if you don't register. The Explorer feature lets you view all the icons on your PC, and other tools allow you to create icons from scratch and manage icon files.

Make your Desktop unique by substituting icons that are different from those that Windows selects for you. You can use icons you've designed yourself or ones that have been downloaded from icon galleries on the Internet.

Change your icons with Microangelo

It's easy to change your Desktop icons. Windows itself contains some substitute icons but you'll find a wider range in special icon libraries such as Microangelo.

1 To download Microangelo, visit and search a download library, such as www.download.com. Download the Microangelo file to your Desktop. Double-click on the icon and follow the on-screen instructions to install it.

2 Once Microangelo is installed, it integrates with Windows, allowing you to change icons directly from the Desktop. To start, right-click on a Desktop icon that you want to change, such as My Computer, and then select Appearance from the pop-up menu.

3 The dialog box that appears shows that, at the moment, the Windows' System Default icon is being used. Click on the Custom option. You can also use this dialog box to revert back to this icon at any time in the future.

4 An Open dialog box appears, allowing you to choose a file. Microangelo comes with several libraries of icons for you to try, organized into related styles. Select the gold icon file and click on the Open button.

PC TIPS

Customizing your icons

We have already showed you how to customize one of the standard Windows icons to your own specifications using Paint (see Stage 1, page 73).

To use this icon, cut it out to measure 32x32 pixels using any art program, such as Corel PHOTO PAINT (see Stage 3, pages 74–77. Then save it as an icon by adding .ico after its name. Now you can use Microangelo to replace any of your standard Desktop icons with this customized icon.

5 The Change Icon window lets you choose which of the icons within the library to use. Some libraries contain only one or two icons, others may contain hundreds. Select one and click on the OK button.

6 The icon appears in the Display panel, replacing the System Default icon. Click on the OK button to go back to the Desktop.

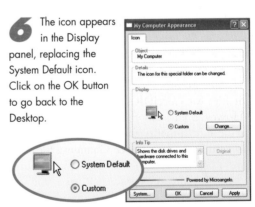

7 Your My Computer icon is now displayed on the Desktop with the icon image you selected.

8 Repeat the process for any other Desktop icons you want to change.

My Network Places

If you have two or more PCs that are connected together at home, or if you use a network of PCs at the office, the My Network Places icon provides a gateway to the shared resources on your network.

Office PC users will probably find that their computer is part of a network – a number of computers connected together. If so, you can access files and folders stored on other PCs that are on the network. You can also share hardware devices such as printers that are connected to the network.

It's not just businesses that can make use of networks though; an increasing number of homes have two or more PCs. Connecting them creates a home computer network, so you can share printers, Internet connections and documents. Even if you only have one PC, networking is an important feature of Windows and is worth learning about as it is widely used in the working environment.

● The components of a network

A network can consist of anything from three or four computers to literally thousands of PCs. The basic components are a network adaptor, some network cable (see Home network options box, right) and Windows' built-in networking software. Network adaptors cost from £15 and come in several versions. Some must be fitted inside your PC, but other external versions simply plug into a USB socket (see Stage 4, pages 102–103).

Larger networks have special, powerful computers called servers, which are used to store files in a central location. All the devices are connected

HOME NETWORK OPTIONS

Many families have several PCs and networking helps them get the most out of their investment in PCs and printers. However, in most homes, the PCs are in different rooms and the cost and bother of installing the network wiring may be off-putting. If this is the case, you could consider adding a wireless network instead. The network adaptors cost a little more, but installation is far easier and the network operates in exactly the same way as shown on the following pages. The wireless signal travels through walls and the range is enough to allow you to use your network while using a notebook PC in the garden.

via a hub. Smaller networks, such as those at home or office networks with only four or five computers, rarely use a central server. Instead, the individual computers might share part of their hard disks, thereby allowing other users to work on their documents.

● **Advantages of networking**
Businesses use networks because it makes collaboration much easier. In addition to enabling staff to communicate by email and to transfer work documents easily, networks also allow people to share folders on their PCs. This helps to increase productivity.

The biggest advantage of a network with a centralized file server for storage is that it's a lot more efficient to back up the business's data. It is unwise to rely on individual computer users to back up important data because this task tends to be left until a convenient moment or, worse still, overlooked completely. A central server, however, can be

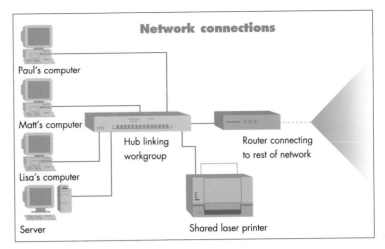

Network connections

Paul's computer

Matt's computer

Hub linking workgroup

Router connecting to rest of network

Lisa's computer

Server

Shared laser printer

set to run backups automatically overnight. Another major benefit is that it is a simple matter to share expensive hardware, such as a laser printer, across a network. If six people can share one large £1000 printer between them, this makes significant savings in efficiency and space.

The diagram above shows a typical small workgroup that shares a laser printer and a server. The workgroup is also connected to a larger network.

How Windows deals with networks

When a PC is attached to a network, a My Network Places window becomes available and provides access to all the other devices on the network.

ONE OF the major features of Windows is its ability to handle networks. This usually happens through a Desktop icon or a Start menu entry, both called My Network Places. Selecting either allows you to browse through the PCs in your workgroup and other computers on the network.

It's possible that neither the Desktop icon nor the Start menu entry for My Network Places is present. This indicates either that the computer is not connected to a network, or that Windows has not yet been properly set up to access the network.

● **My Network Places functions**
The My Network Places icon provides a gateway to any other computers on the network. When you click on this icon, a pop-up window appears, which works in a similar manner to the My Computer window, performing much the same functions except that it is concerned with network devices instead of local hardware. You will see other resources shared by the network listed in the Network Places window. To connect to any one of the other resources listed, you simply double-click on

it. Windows then does some checking to see if you have permission to use the network device. Most offices use passwords and strict authorization systems to protect confidential information. This takes just a few moments.

Once you are connected, you'll see a window that shows the shared area of the other computer. This works just like a window on your own computer. You can drag and drop files and folders from window to window, and even open and save files on the remote computer's hard disk.

● **Managing files**
It is useful to set up special shared folders or drives on each computer on the network so users can keep part of their hard disks for private use and part for shared files that everyone else can see and use.

On page 26, we explore some of these principles. The same basic techniques apply for home PC networks and for those in an office.

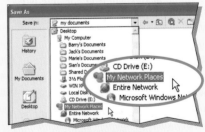

When computers are networked together you can save and open files from any location on the network. In this example, the Save As dialog box includes an entry for My Network Places in the Save in list, allowing us to choose a computer on the network to store our document.

Exploring My Network Places

If your computer is connected to a network, you can try this process for yourself. Otherwise, just read through the steps to understand the principles.

1 If your PC is part of a network, double-click on the My Network Places icon on the Desktop, or select My Network Places from the Start menu.

2 What you see in the My Network Places window varies between networks. In this example, two shared folders appear. To see all the network resources, click the View workgroup computers link in the Network Tasks box on the left of the window.

3 One of the computers shown is your PC (in our example it's the Studypc on the right). Double-click on one of the other icons to see the resources it has shared.

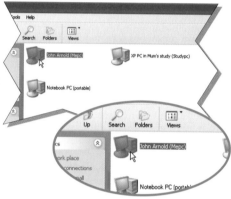

4 The title bar of the window changes to include the name of the PC you selected, and the contents reflect the devices or folders that you can use on this PC.

5 Look through the folders to find some documents. Double-click on one of them and it will open up exactly as if it were on your own computer.

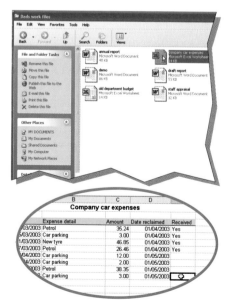

6 You can also copy files and folders between computers, using the same commands and menus as if the data were on your own machine. Here we are copying the company's logo from the remote computer to our own Desktop by simply dragging it onto our Desktop.

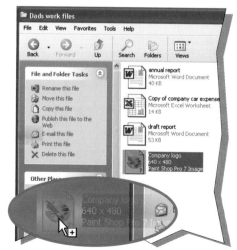

PASSWORD PROTECTION

In many large-scale office networks, network items are protected by permissions set up by the IT department. When you log on to your computer with your Windows password, your access to other computers, files and folders is managed centrally. However, for many smaller networks, permissions are not handled centrally, but are instead set by the people who use the individual computers: they can set a password for any folder.

If you are working on another PC and try to open a password-protected folder, you will be prompted for the password. On some networks, you may have to type in both a user name and a password. In our example, we need only supply a password, previously chosen by the person who uses the Mepc computer.

Finding and mapping a computer

Windows enables you to find remote PCs on your network and then explore their contents using the Map Network Drive command.

1 On large networks, you can search for a particular computer instead of browsing through the My Network Places window. To do this, first select Search from the Start menu. Then click on Computers or people when the Search Results window appears.

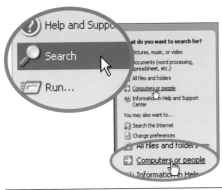

2 Click the A computer on the network link on the next screen and then type in part of the name of the computer you are looking for in the next dialog box. Click the Search button.

3 If the computer is on the network (see Missing names box, below), you'll find it listed on the right of the dialog box. Double-click on it to access its shared resources (see Steps 3–6, page 26).

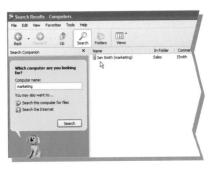

1 Windows has a command called **Map Network Drive**. You can use it to access a folder that is stored on a computer on your network. To do this, first right-click on one of the folders and select the Map Network Drive command.

2 A dialog box appears, asking you to give a letter to this folder. Accept Windows' suggestion by clicking on the Finish button.

3 Instantly, a window appears displaying the contents of the folder. The icon at the left of the title bar shows that this window is a network drive (inset).

4 You can also see your new drive in the My Computer folder on your Desktop. Notice that its icon and name make its network status obvious.

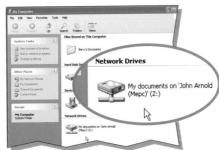

WHAT IT MEANS

MAP NETWORK DRIVE

This is a simple means of using a folder on a remote computer as if it were an extra hard disk on your own PC.

Once you have mapped a network drive, you will see it appear in the Open and Save As dialog boxes alongside your hard disk (C:) and your floppy disk (A:) with a new drive letter.

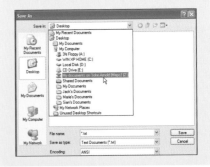

MISSING NAMES

If you use a network a lot, you'll notice that you don't always see the same PCs and devices on it. This is because some other machines might be switched off or someone might have disconnected from the network.

Software

Microsoft® FrontPage®

Introducing PowerPoint

If you want to produce stylish and persuasive presentations, try enlisting Microsoft's flexible PowerPoint program to help you put across your ideas.

Word processors, spreadsheets and database programs are all essential office software, upon which many computer users in business and at home rely. Completing the set of business programs are presentation programs. These programs are packed with special features dedicated to helping you communicate information to an audience in a slick and effective way.

● On the approach

All presentation programs have the same basic approach: you create a sequence of slides, which usually contain text (often in bullet-point form) to convey the themes of the presentation. You can also add pictures, charts and graphs to help get the point across.

In many areas of life, the ability to put across a proposal or an idea in a convincing and well-presented way is becoming increasingly important. Anyone from teachers

to self-employed business people can benefit from using a presentation program. It's not just a sales tool – it's also useful for training and education.

PowerPoint is by far the most popular presentation program in all these areas. On the following pages we'll show you how to create effective and stylish presentations using this powerful piece of software.

WHAT IT MEANS

SLIDES

The pages you create with a presentation program are known as slides. This derives from their original application: creating transparent films for display on an overhead transparency projector. The term is used for all types of pages, including paper pages you'll print out and even 'pages' that will only be seen on the computer's screen.

INSTALLING POWERPOINT

If you have Microsoft Office installed on your computer, check on the Start menu to see if PowerPoint has already been installed. If there's no PowerPoint entry, you need to install it. Put the Office CD-ROM into the CD-ROM drive and follow the on-screen instructions that let you add the individual Office programs. You can buy PowerPoint alone, but at around £280, it's only slightly cheaper than the complete Office package.

● Print and display

There are two ways of using a presentation program: you can create slides with the aim of printing them out, or you can use the computer to display the slides to your audience. Most people will print out the slides and hand out paper copies to their audience. You can also print them on to transparent sheets and use an overhead projector to display them to a larger group of people.

However, for a really slick presentation, many sales people travel with a notebook PC (see Stage 6, pages 108–109) and use PowerPoint to display the slides directly via the screen. Even presentations to larger groups can be done this way, by connecting the notebook to a large external monitor.

One big advantage of giving a presentation directly from the computer is that you can use the computer's Multimedia capabilities in your presentation. Printed slides are static but slides that are displayed on the computer screen can be dynamic, using sound effects, video clips and animations. Among the most commonly used dynamic effects are special transitions between slides. This is a feature of

the presentation program that allows you to make information appear on the screen in attention-grabbing ways. For example, when switching slides, you can make the next slide appear as if through vertical blinds. Also, each piece of information on a slide can be made to slide in from the side of the screen – complete with sound effects. Used with care, these transitions can add professional polish to a good presentation.

Making a start

Each time you want to construct a new presentation using PowerPoint, you must go through these initial steps.

1 Click on the Start button and when the menu appears click on All Programs. Like other Microsoft Office programs, PowerPoint is listed in the first sub-menu. Select it from the list of software that appears.

2 Within a few seconds, the PowerPoint window opens and displays its main workspace. PowerPoint shows a default slide layout in the centre of the screen. To see alternatives, click on Blank Presentation in the Task Pane on the right of the window.

3 The Task Pane now displays small previews of all the slide layouts available. Click on the Title and Text slide layout.

4 The blank slide in the centre of the screen is replaced with one you selected. You are now ready to start working on the slide. See page 32 for a full explanation of the rest of the PowerPoint workspace.

The PowerPoint workspace

Like any new software, PowerPoint includes some familiar tools and some new features. Here, we introduce the workspace.

ONCE YOU have started PowerPoint and chosen a new presentation layout (see Making a start, on the previous page), you'll see a window similar to that shown below. In our case, the blank slide resembles a Word document in landscape form.

There's a typical collection of menus and toolbars as well as a Task Pane. Explore the menus and you'll find that many are almost identical to those in Word and Excel. If you're experienced with using either of these programs you'll find it much easier to learn PowerPoint.

The page looks spartan at the moment because there are no colours or effects. This lets you concentrate on the task of inserting your information on the page. You can add any visual elements or special effects that you require later, when the text has been added and positioned on the page.

THE DISAPPEARING WORKSPACE

When using PowerPoint to display slides directly from the computer screen, the workspace disappears and the slide occupies the full screen. This helps maximize the impact of the presentation. Use the Slide Show button at the bottom of the screen to preview the effect, and press the [Esc] key to return to the editing view.

Toolbars

This strip of buttons holds the Standard toolbar and the Formatting toolbar, placed one above the other for convenience. The buttons cover general document commands such as Open, Save and Print, as well as commands for formatting the content of your slides, such as font and text colour.

Title bar

This displays the program and document name, together with buttons for maximising, minimising and closing the window.

Menu bar

The nine menu options provide access to the complete set of commands available in PowerPoint, and the single document icon at the far left lets you minimize and close the document you're currently working on.

Document

The document area shows the current slide; here it still contains pre-set text boxes.

Text boxes

The text in these boxes indicates where to type your own information. You can choose a different slide layout for different arrangements of information (see Step 3 on page 31).

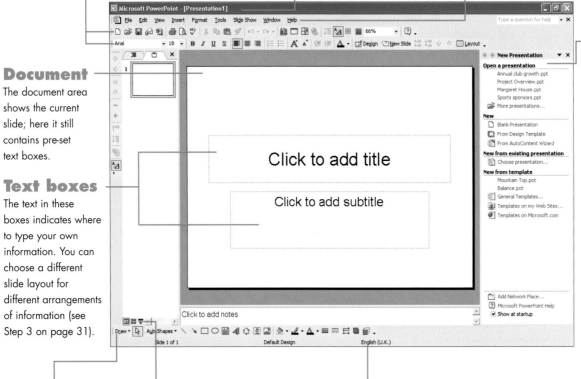

Task Pane

This panel has several pages, each providing a different set of point and click options. For example, the New Presentation Task Pane lets you select templates or presentations you have previously saved, as a template for your new presentation. You can switch Task Panes by using the downwards pointing arrow at the top of the Task Pane.

Drawing toolbar

PowerPoint documents offer the same graphical objects as Word and Excel. Using the Drawing toolbar, you can add objects such as WordArt, lines and boxes.

Mode buttons

These buttons let you conveniently switch between various PowerPoint view modes, including a Slide Show, Slide Sorter View and Normal View.

Status bar

Three areas on the Status bar provide confirmation as to which slide you are working on and any design settings you have applied, and also alert you if there are any incorrectly spelt words in your slides.

Editing slides with PowerPoint

The most basic task in PowerPoint is adding your own information to the slide layouts. Here we've started an election candidate's manifesto presentation from a blank slide.

1 If you have already followed the steps shown on page 31, you will have a suitable blank slide already. If not, select the Title and Text slide layout from the Slide Layout Task Pane.

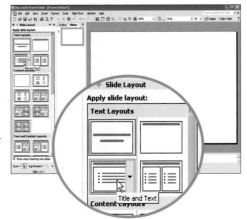

2 The first slide appears; it's not entirely blank, but has placeholder text for the title and for the first bullet point.

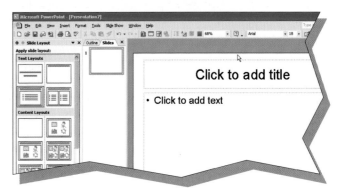

3 Click on the title: you'll see the placeholder text disappear, leaving a flashing text cursor in the centre of the text box.

4 Type in your slide title. Here, we've used our election candidate's name – it appears in the same text format as the placeholder.

5 Now click on the second of the text boxes. Again, the text disappears, but a greyed-out bullet point remains so that you don't have to create it yourself.

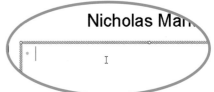

6 Type the first point for this slide of your presentation and press the [Enter] key. A new bullet point appears for the next point.

7 Type as many bullet points as you need. Note that if one of the items is too long, it wraps on to the next line with the correct indent, just as in Microsoft Word.

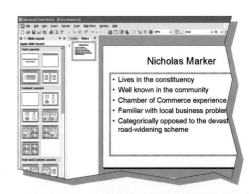

8 Select the Save option from the File menu, give your first presentation a name and save it.

PC TIPS

Formatting basics

Use the text-formatting commands on the toolbar to change the typeface, size and alignment of the text in your slides. The Font dialog box, accessed via the Format menu, provides other text options, including embossed effects.

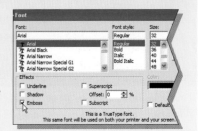

The AutoContent Wizard

If you haven't created a presentation before, it's worth spending some time going through PowerPoint's AutoContent Wizard. It contains tips and advice from presentation professionals.

For many people, presenting formal information is hard work, primarily because it's usually an infrequent task compared with using a word processor or spreadsheet. Even before the potentially nerve-racking experience of presenting the information to an audience, the most basic task of getting the information into order can prove to be no easy job. And, without logical and easy-to-follow information, any presentation is unlikely to hold the audience's attention for long. However, there's plenty of advice provided by PowerPoint itself.

Even though the individual needs of each presentation are likely to be unique, PowerPoint's AutoContent Wizard can help with most presentations. This leads you through a series of choices that cover many common types of presentation. This wizard can be helpful for many different presentations because the logical sequence of information is often the same, regardless of the specific details.

In explaining a new business project, for example, a slide presentation will introduce the concept, describe its details, cover its competitors and outline its launch schedule. You can use the slides as a reminder or guide as to what to cover in your presentation. You might even get useful ideas for elements that you might otherwise have missed.

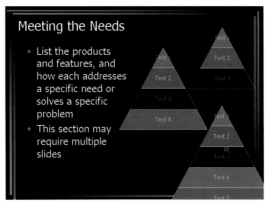

You don't have to create layouts like this from scratch: if you use AutoContent's Selling a Product or Service option, you can simply replace the dummy information on the ready-made slide.

● Options and advice

PowerPoint's AutoContent Wizard covers a wide range of presentation tasks. At the simplest level, the Certificate creates a three-slide presentation that you can also use to make printed certificates. At the other extreme is the Marketing Plan with 17 general purpose sales and marketing slides that would be hugely time-consuming for you to create from scratch.

Some AutoContent Wizard options also include advice and tips from American business guru Dale Carnegie's range of business aids.

Once you have used the AutoContent Wizard to create a 'shell' presentation, you can replace the placeholder information and/or pictures with your own.

Creating an announcement presentation

Using the AutoContent Wizard is easy. By choosing from a range of presentation tasks and telling PowerPoint how you'll be making the presentation, you can get your computer to do most of the work.

1 Start PowerPoint and choose From AutoContent Wizard from the New Presentation Task Pane.

2 Now the AutoContent Wizard dialog box appears. Click on the Next button.

3 In the next screen, select Company Meeting from the panel. Click the Next button to proceed.

4 On the next screen, make sure you tell PowerPoint that you're creating a presentation for display on screen.

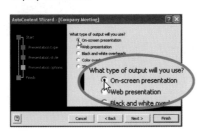

5 The first slide usually includes some basic information about the presentation. Click on Next and type the appropriate text into the boxes on the next screen. Click on the Finish button in the final screen.

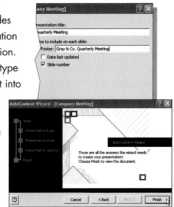

6 The first slide appears in the main part of the PowerPoint workspace, and an Outline panel on the left displays a text outline of all the slides that the AutoContent Wizard has created for you. Click the Slide Show button at the bottom of the screen.

7 The first slide appears, taking up the full screen. Check the spelling and the information and then press the [Esc] key to return to the outline.

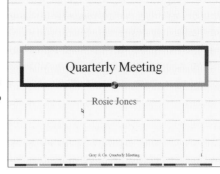

8 Now edit the information on the other slides to suit your presentation. As soon as you click on any text in the Outline panel, its slide appears on the right. Simply select and change the text as necessary, using the placeholders as a reminder of points to include. As you add the information, the current slide will change to preview any alterations.

9 Use the Slide Show button again to review your work and see the effects of your changes. If you spot any errors, press the [Esc] key to stop the slide show and edit the relevant slides. Then save your presentation.

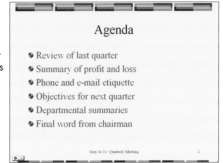

Re-ordering slides

To get your point across, it's vital to present information in a clear, logical order. PowerPoint helps you organize your ideas by making it easy to sort your slides.

When you are setting up any document, it can sometimes be difficult to see how to present the information it contains in the best way. As you put your thoughts together while writing a letter, for example, you might need to move some paragraphs around to make the logic easier to follow.

The same principles apply for presentations. You might discover that certain slides need to be moved to make a point clearer or to hold the attention of your audience. Remember that with a letter, readers can re-read earlier sections if they lose track of the thread, but in a live presentation, the audience can't skip back a few slides to remind themselves of what you were saying.

For this reason, it's vital to run through the order of a presentation and ensure that none of the slides is out of place. Fortunately, re-ordering any number of slides is easy, and there are several ways you can do this.

● The wrong way
Importantly, the most obvious way isn't necessarily the easiest. In most Windows programs, if you want to move items from, say, page three to page five, you can select them, use the Cut command (either from the Edit menu or by pressing [Ctrl]+[X]) and then go to page five and use the Paste command.

There are two main reasons why this isn't the best approach in PowerPoint. Firstly, it is easy to leave a text box or picture behind by accident. Secondly, there are so many steps involved that the job can become very arduous and time-consuming – especially if you need to re-order several slides to do it.

● The right way
For these reasons, PowerPoint includes an easy-to-use Slide Sorter View mode (see PC Tips box, right), which is designed to let you move complete slides around by dragging and dropping them. There's no risk of leaving an object behind, and the task is performed with just a single action. Even better is the fact that you can select more than one slide, so you can

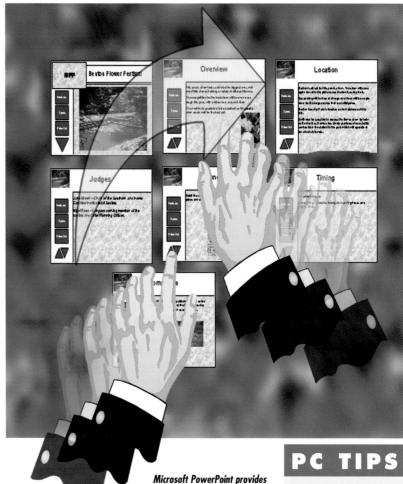

Microsoft PowerPoint provides the tools to help you get your slides into the optimum order quickly and easily.

move whole sections of your presentation around very quickly. This is far harder to do without mistakes in Normal mode.

You can also move your slides around by clicking on the Outline tab in Normal View. In this mode the contents of the slides are shown as an indented array of text bullet points. By dragging the slide icon that appears on the first line of each slide, all the objects on the slide will move, too. This makes it much easier to edit your slides.

In the exercise opposite, we show you just how easy it is to use these different views so that you can manage your presentations much more effectively.

PC TIPS

Switching views
Use the mode buttons at the bottom of the PowerPoint window to switch quickly from one view to another. The Slide Sorter View is the button showing four small rectangles. On its left is the Normal View button, and on its right is the Slide Show View.

How to re-order a presentation

Switching between view modes makes it easy to move slides into whichever new position you want them.

1 Start with a presentation using around half a dozen slides. We've made a short presentation about an imaginary flower show.

2 Click on the Slide Sorter View button at the bottom of the PowerPoint screen.

3 The PowerPoint window changes to show all the slides together. This gives you an overall feel for how your presentation progresses. The order is shown by a number under each slide and the current slide is outlined in a thick border (inset).

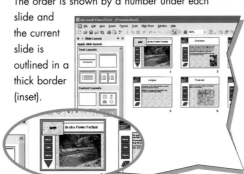

PC TIPS

Space saving

When using the Outline panel to re-order slides, you will often find it useful to reduce the amount of information on the screen. By clicking the Expand All button on the toolbar, you can switch the detail on or off. The first click hides the contents of the slides. You'll see just the title of the slides, which makes it easier to move slides around, especially on long presentations. Click on the Expand All button again when you want to see the full contents.

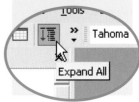

4 In this example, the Timing slide is at the end but it ought to appear earlier. Click once on the slide to select it and drag the mouse pointer to an earlier position (we've chosen to put it just before Location, slide 3). The thin grey line between slides 2 and 3 indicates where the Timing slide will go.

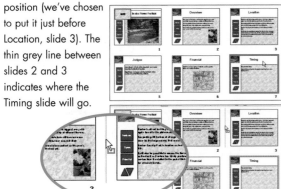

5 The Timing slide appears in its new position and all the subsequent slides are re-sorted and renumbered.

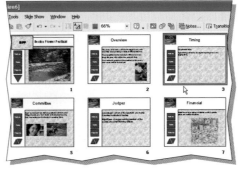

6 You can also move slides using the Outline panel in Normal View. Looking at the new order, we find that we want to move the Financial slide (which is currently last, slide number 7) ahead of the two slides covering personnel (5 and 6). Select the slide, click on the Normal View button at the bottom of the screen, then click on the Outline tab.

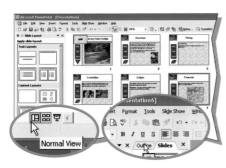

7 The Outline tab shows the Slides as text only, with a numbered slide icon to the left of each heading. The current slide is selected (its icon is highlighted in blue), so simply drag its slide icon up to the correct position – in our example it goes before the Committee slide, currently numbered 5 (inset).

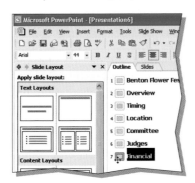

8 When you release the mouse, the Outline updates to show your changes, with the Financial slide now at number 5. If you switch back to Slide Sorter View, you can see that all the objects that make up each slide have also moved, including the picture on the Financial slide.

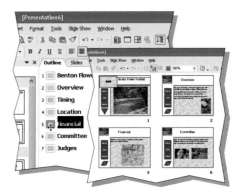

Introducing the Slide Master

PowerPoint's Slide Master provides an easy way to give your presentation a uniform style by adding standard elements to every slide and providing a background template for you to add your own data.

As well as actually coming up with the most persuasive information for the slides in your presentations, it's important to get the look and feel of the presentation itself right. By choosing a design (colours, typefaces, repeating graphics and so on) that complements the slide information, you can help make the presentation more effective.

Although it is up to you to create a good design, PowerPoint helps by providing a background slide called a Slide Master to save you time and effort. It works in a similar way to Master Pages in Microsoft Publisher (see Stage 6, pages 90–91). When designing, you often want headings, picture boxes and text columns to appear in the same position on every page, and PowerPoint allows you to take the same approach with the slides in your presentation. If you edit the special Slide Master page (see PC Tips box, right), adding, removing and altering items as required, these changes will appear on every individual slide.

● **Adding logos and design styles**
If you have a logo which you want to use in the same position on every page, for example, it's much more efficient to add it to the Slide Master than to add it to every slide in your presentation. Firstly, you only have to import the logo once. Secondly, if you add slides later, you don't have to remember to add the logo to them – it appears automatically. Finally, if the logo has to be changed, you only need to go back to the Slide Master and re-import it once to update all the slides automatically.

The overall design of the Slide Master also helps to set the tone of the presentation. For example, it can be sober, with corporate blue shades and a company logo, or lively, with fun graphics, bright colours and unusual typefaces. In fact, you may possibly be using this feature without realizing it when you

Slide Master will help you to approach the design and creation of individual presentation slides in a disciplined way.

create a presentation with one of the PowerPoint templates. Each of these templates is set up so that you overlay your information on a ready-made Slide Master created by Microsoft. This means that whenever you use a template, you can try out different approaches without having to do a lot of extra work. Simply create your presentation and then edit the Slide Master design (see PC Tips box, right, and opposite) to see what it would look like with another design.

PC TIPS

Editing the Slide Master
When editing a slide, if you try to edit an object that resides on the Slide Master, the Office Assistant automatically gives you more information about the Slide Master and offers to take you to it (see inset left). Select the first option to edit the Slide Master.

Using the Slide Master

Here's an easy way to set up an effective presentation incorporating colour, formatted text and graphics for a school sponsorship bid.

1 Start up PowerPoint and create a simple text-only presentation (see pages 31–33). We've set up a few slides about sports sponsorship.

2 Click on the View menu, select the Master option and then select Slide Master from the sub-menu.

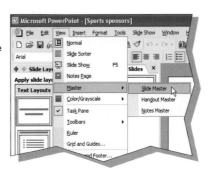

3 The PowerPoint window now shows what lies behind your slide. At the moment, it's merely a collection of text boxes, with little formatting and no colour.

4 Use the mouse to select all the text in the title box and then use the text-formatting list box to choose a new typeface.

5 Now you can format the other text in the slide. Here we've selected the main text and made it bold using the toolbar button.

6 The next step is to add a coloured background and some graphics to the Master Slide. Click on the Rectangle button on the Drawing toolbar at the bottom of the window and drag a box from the top left corner of the slide to the bottom right. At first, a default blue box will obscure all the other slide items.

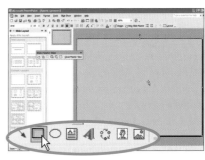

7 Right-click on the box, select Order from the pop-up menu and then Send to Back from the sub-menu. The other boxes reappear. While the box is still selected, use the Fill Color button on the Drawing toolbar to add your choice of formatting. Here, we've chosen a black on beige colour scheme.

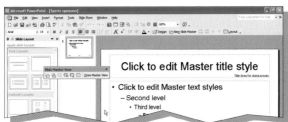

8 Add other graphics objects using the Drawing toolbar. Here we have drawn circles in our school's colours and moved them to overlap only the top left-hand corner of the slide. We have also added a clip-art picture in a black panel.

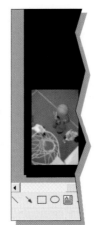

9 Click on the Slide Show button to see how the style of the Slide Master has been applied over the text you set up. As you go from one slide to the next, you will see that the same style applies to all the slides in your presentation.

Introduction to printing

Many presentations need to be printed out at some point. Here's how to use PowerPoint's print commands to ensure that the printouts of your slides are as impressive as the on-screen version.

Slide shows and presentations take many forms and have many different types of audience. A necessary result of this is that presentations often have very different print requirements. Some presentations are intended to be printed and posted or faxed to other people; at the other extreme, others are designed purely for live on-screen slideshows. Many slides have to be created with both types of uses in mind.

● Flexible printing

To cover all the choices, the print options in PowerPoint have to be very flexible. One very obvious example is that you don't want a slide show that has been designed to fit a computer screen with a 4:3 width and height ratio to look silly when you print it on A4 paper's 210mm by 297mm dimensions. Fortunately, PowerPoint takes care of this subtle difference so that you can concentrate on the content of your slides, rather than the technicalities.

Even if you always plan to deliver your presentation from the computer screen and never to hand out paper copies, it's still often useful to print it out. Many people find it easier to proof-read their documents on paper, rather than directly from the PC screen because it's easier to spot spelling and grammar errors. You can use PowerPoint's handy text-only printing option (see PC Tips box, right) to do this.

● Time-saving options

Some slide shows are best printed with one slide to a page; for others, though, this would be impractical. Imagine that you have designed a 40-slide presentation to be given live from a computer screen. If you wanted to hand out a hard copy to every member of a large audience, it would be both time-consuming and wasteful of paper to print and hand out one slide to a page. In

It is very useful to print out the PowerPoint slides you have created. Not only can you carefully check them for errors but you can also hand them out to accompany your presentation.

such circumstances, PowerPoint lets you print two, three or six slides to a page, which is much more manageable.

The right number to choose depends on the design of your slides and the amount of information on them. For example, slides which contain a handful of sentences and a plain background should print well at six per page. In contrast, slides that include tables of figures or charts may be almost useless unless printed considerably larger – perhaps two to a page. If in doubt, err on the side of caution and print fewer slides per page.

● Print preview

PowerPoint has a Print Preview feature similar to Word and Excel (see Stage 1, page 44 and Stage 2, page 56). It also has a command to switch between colour, black and white or greyscale views, so you can check how your slides will look when printed without colour before committing them to paper.

PC TIPS

Text-only printing

To make a quick check of the text information on your slides, bring up the Print dialog box and select Outline View from the Print what drop-down list box. PowerPoint will print a text-only page that looks just like the one you see when using the Outline panel in Normal View (see pages 36–37).

Printing a slide show

Make use of PowerPoint's flexible printing capabilities to get hard copy printouts of your presentation slides.

1 Open a presentation with a large number of slides. We've used the project overview template to generate a slide show of 11 slides quickly. They are shown here in the Slide Sorter View (see page 37).

2 Click on the Pure Black and White View option on the toolbar. You can now design your slide show with a good idea of how it will look when it is printed.

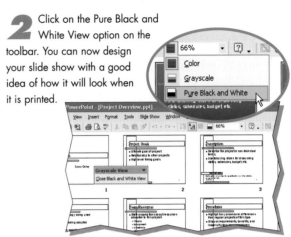

3 Select the second slide by clicking on it once, then press [Ctrl]+[P] to bring up the Print dialog box. Make sure the Current slide option is selected in the Print range area and select Pure Black and White from the Color/grayscale box before clicking on the OK button.

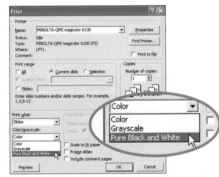

4 The printed page contains the slide's black and white content only, stretched to fit the maximum area of the page, without distortion.

Project Goals
- Ultimate goal of project
- Relationship to other projects
- High-level timing goals

5 Bring up the Print dialog box again. This time select All in the Print range area and Handouts in the Print what area. Then go to the Handouts area and in the Slides per page list, select 6.

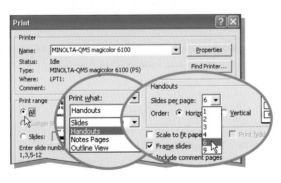

6 Make sure that the Frame slides option at the bottom of the dialog box is ticked. If you have a colour printer, select the Color option in the Color/grayscale box, then click on the OK button.

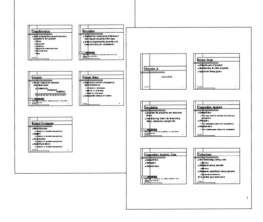

Microsoft® PowerPoint®

OVERHEAD DISPLAY

If you have a colour inkjet printer, you can buy special transparent film to create slides to display on an overhead projector (OHP). When light from the projector shines through the coloured ink on the film, it produces a coloured image on the white OHP screen. Make sure you buy the right type of film for your printer and also select the appropriate print setting (the printer manual will give you the necessary details for both) so that the computer automatically adjusts the amount of ink deposited on the page to suit the film.

7 The entire slide show fits on two pages but the large amounts of information on these slides are still quite readable. The frame around the slides ensures that the text information looks like the slide that the audience sees and isn't just floating on the page.

Clip art and charts

Presentations come alive when you include graphics to illustrate the text in your slides. Here we show how to add eye-catching images and useful charts to your slide shows.

If your presentations are made up entirely of text, your audience will probably get bored very quickly. Your slides might contain all the information that's required, but without any images they will be missing a vital and powerful element.

Illustrations can be used in two main ways: you can use them either to catch the audience's attention, or as charts that provide information themselves.

● Art for art's sake

To make your presentations more appealing, you can use the huge amount of themed clip art that comes on the CD-ROM provided with the PowerPoint package. You can also use the clip art supplied with other programs or even buy selections on CD-ROM.

The size of existing clip art can be altered to fit your exact requirements, or you can create your own graphics with a program such as CorelDRAW or Paint Shop Pro. In fact, any pictures that can be transferred to your PC can also be inserted into your PowerPoint slides. For example, if you want to liven up a presentation about a local club or society event, you can add photos taken with a digital camera.

● Presenting numerical data

Graphics can also help you put across numerical information, but this type of data needs much more careful treatment. Suppose you want a slide to show financial details such as the turnover of a home-run business or a breakdown of business expenditure. You could list this information as a table of numbers, perhaps in rows and columns, but you will be missing a very useful presentation tool: the graph or chart.

It's much easier to spot an overall trend at a glance by looking at a simple bar graph than by comparing figures in a table – as you

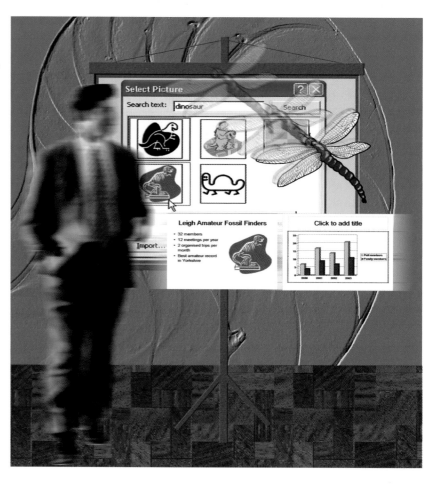

Your presentations will improve when you add some pictures. You can use just about any form of graphics, from photos to bar charts.

will see in the exercise opposite, where we've used a bar chart to show the growth in club membership numbers for a fictional fossil-hunting society.

● How to add graphics

It takes only a few moments to add graphics to liven up your presentations. PowerPoint comes with ready-made slide layouts that include graphics placeholders; you need only double-click on one of these to bring up the appropriate dialog box or window containing a selection of graphics for you to choose from.

Graphics can also be combined with other PowerPoint features. If you want a graphic such as a clip-art logo to appear on every page, add it to the Slide Master (pages 38–39). You'll then be assured of consistent size and positioning on every slide.

PC TIPS

As well as graphics, you can insert other kinds of objects into your slide shows, depending on your software. Inserting objects works in much the same way as with Excel (see Stage 5, page 59). To see the full range of objects you can insert into your presentation using PowerPoint, click on the Object command in the Insert menu.

Illustrating your presentations

It takes just a few seconds to add a sprinkling of pictures and graphs to your slides and you'll be rewarded with a more effective slide show.

1 Start with a blank presentation and choose the Title, Text and Clip Art slide in the Slide Layout Task Pane.

2 You'll see a simple layout appear with placeholders indicating where you add your material. Double-click on the clip-art placeholder.

PC TIPS

If you need to alter the size of a piece of clip art or a chart, just click on it once and then drag one of the eight tiny handles. A dotted line appears indicating the new size of the object. Release the mouse button and the object is redrawn.

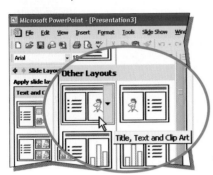

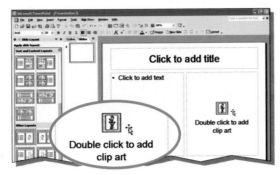

3 The Select Picture dialog box appears (the pictures you see depend on the Microsoft programs installed on your computer). Select a suitable picture for the presentation and click on the OK button.

4 The picture appears on your slide. Add the text for your slide in the title and text panels provided.

5 Now we'll set up a bar chart on another slide. Select New Slide from the Insert menu. Choose Title and Chart from the bottom of the Slide Layout Task Pane.

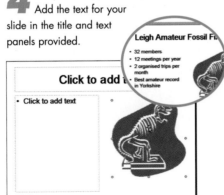

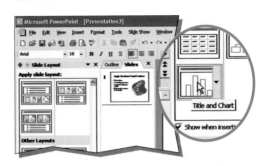

6 When the new slide appears, double-click on the chart placeholder (inset). A spreadsheet-like window pops up, with dummy information.

7 Type the information you want to see displayed as a bar chart into the cells in the table and then press the X button to close it.

	A	B	C	D	E
	1st Qtr	2nd Qtr	3rd Qtr	4th Qtr	
...ast	20.4	27.4	90	20.4	
...est	30.6	38.6	34.6	31.6	
...rth	45.9	46.9	45	43.9	

Click to add title
Double click to add chart

		A	B	C	D
		2000	2001	2002	2003
1	Full members	7	17	14	21
2	Family members	4	9	7	1?
3					
4					
5					

Close

SHORT CUTS

A quick way to insert a new slide is to press [Ctrl]+[M], which saves you having to click your way through the menus. A new blank slide appears, and PowerPoint switches to the Slide Layout Task Pane so that you can choose the best layout for your presentation.

8 You'll now see the chart in place on your slide. Add suitable title text.

9 Change to Slide Sorter View (see pages 36–37) to view both slides side by side.

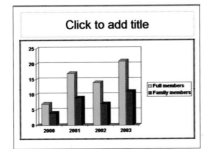

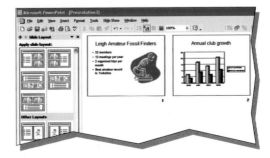

Microsoft® PowerPoint®

Animated slide shows

When giving a presentation directly from your computer screen, you can make use of extra tricks to hold your audience's attention. Here's how to use animated effects for maximum impact.

When professional presenters give a computer-based slide show, they use several tricks of the trade to make sure that their audiences are both entertained and informed. By adding animation and special effects, it's possible to add sparkle to a presentation and ensure that the information is put across in exactly the right way for maximum impact.

You can take advantage of such professional ideas yourself. Any computer that can run PowerPoint can apply special effects to the slides in a computer-based presentation. These make it look more dynamic and interesting than simply being an on-screen version of a paper-based slide show.

There are two main ways to apply animation in a presentation. The first is by animating the way objects appear on an individual slide; the second way is by making animated transitions from one slide to the next (see Transitions box, opposite).

● Animating objects on a slide

When you're giving a slide show, you may not want to present all the information on a slide at the same time. For example, suppose that you are talking your way through a slide show and you come to a slide that contains five bullet-point items, each of which you want to introduce with a sentence or two.

Normally, PowerPoint will simply show all the information on each slide in one go. But, in a case like this, if your audience sees the complete set of points as soon as the slide appears, they are likely to start reading ahead and might not listen to your argument properly. To avoid this problem, you could put each bullet point on a new slide, but that would be unwieldy and create lots of slides with very little information on each one.

A better, and more simple, solution is to keep all five bullet points on one slide but make them appear one by one, telling PowerPoint when you want the next item to be displayed. This puts you in control of when the bullet points appear, so that your audience's attention follows your lead. This technique mimics the way that most TV news programmes present text summaries during a news story: for example, the main features of a government budget plan are commonly listed on screen as a series of bullet points, which are timed to appear in step with the reporter's narration.

● Synchronizing your animation

With PowerPoint, you don't need to time the appearance of items on screen. You simply tell the program which items on the slide you want to animate and the type of animation to use, and you then trigger the changes with a click of the left mouse button. The next item is revealed with each successive click until there are none left; another click then takes you to the next slide in the presentation. But if

When used properly, animation can dramatically improve your audience's appreciation of your presentation.

you want a more regular, automatic animation style, you can time the animation instead (see Self-running slide shows box, below right).

● Moving pictures

The need to control when objects appear doesn't just apply to text; you might also want to control other objects in your slides. For example, suppose you have a slide containing text about finance, together with graphs that show past performance and projected figures for the coming year. Your audience might become so distracted by the attractively coloured graphs that they don't fully take in the text that they are meant to read alongside it. However, you can prevent this by making the graphs appear only after you have outlined the other basic data.

Of course, there could also be times when the text relates directly to the graph. In such cases, it makes more sense to show the graph first, let the audience digest it, and then make your text points appear.

● Choosing animation options

PowerPoint's Custom Animation settings (see page 46) give you plenty of choices for the way that objects appear on your slides. One of the most simple ways is one of the most

effective – by making each item slide onto the screen from the left-hand side. There are many other options you can apply, however. For example, you can make text appear one letter at a time, make new text appear through a checkerboard-style grid or make a graphic drop in from the top of the screen.

Many animations include sound effects as standard – the sound of a typewriter, for example – but these should be used in moderation (see PC Tips box, left).

SELF-RUNNING SLIDE SHOWS

You can use PowerPoint's animation effects to create self-running slide shows, just like those you can see at exhibitions and museums around the world. By adding a transition (see Transitions box, below) and using the time option in the Advance slide section of the Slide Transition Task Pane, a slide show can run without any intervention from you. The only requirement is to give viewers enough time to read the information on the screen.

Transitions

Animating a transition – where one slide swaps for the next – is a good way to liven up a presentation without detracting from the content.

THE ANIMATION effects that you apply to text and graphics on your slides can help make your presentations more effective by controlling the way information is presented. But transition animations that change one slide for another simply add sparkle to the visuals. By making the transitions a little more original, you can help make your slide show stand out from the rest.

Usually, each slide in a PowerPoint presentation appears immediately and fills the screen. There's no delay, no sound and no drama. But PowerPoint's built-in transition effects make the changeover of slides more entertaining. Many mimic the way in which TV shows dissolve from one scene to the next, where you might see a scene fade to black and then a new scene blend in from the darkness, or a new scene might slide in from the right of the screen, covering the previous scene.

PowerPoint has plenty of transitions to try out, including some that look like chequerboard patterns, and horizontal and vertical blinds. You can apply transitions to individual slides in your presentation, or to the complete slide show with a few button presses. Each transition can trigger a sound effect, too. Experimenting with transitions can be fun, but you'll

soon realize that too many can become very irritating if used in long presentations. Take a tip from the TV experts: they, too, can add flashy scene transitions at the click of a mouse button, but audience research has shown that these can have a negative effect. In particular, there are some transitions which simply take too long and it's not very helpful to make your audience wait for the next set of information.

Here is PowerPoint's checkerboard transition pattern at work. The butterfly appears square-by-square from a black screen until the picture is complete.

Animating text in your slides

Ensure that your audience's attention doesn't wander ahead of what you are saying by animating the appearance of text items.

1 Open up a presentation and locate a suitable slide for animation. We've chosen a slide where we want our audience to consider each point in turn, without moving on to later items before we're ready.

Margaret House
Management and services committee

Lift renovation plans

- Estimated cost: £10,000
- 48 flats in Margaret House
- Around £210 per flat (if shared equally)
- Between £160 and £430 (if based on size

2 In the Task Pane, click on the downward pointing arrow and select Custom Animation to display the Custom Animation Task Pane.

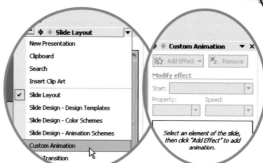

3 Click on the text box that contains the list of items you want to animate then select the whole line containing the first bullet point. Click on the Add Effect button, select Entrance and then Fly In. Change the options for positioning and speed as required. Repeat this step for each of the bullet points.

4 To see how this effect works, you need to change to the Slide Show View. The quickest way to do this is to click on the Slide Show button at the bottom of the PowerPoint screen.

5 When your slide appears, all the text from the bullet-point list seems to be missing from the slide. Click on the left mouse button once.

Margaret House
Management and services committee

Lift renovation plans

6 The first item slides in from the left. In a live audience presentation, you could now talk about this item, safe in the knowledge that the audience can't yet be thinking about the text that follows.

Margaret House
Management and services committee

Lift renovation plans

Estimated cost: £10,000

7 Click on the left mouse button again and the next item in the text box slides in.

Margaret House
Management and services committee

Lift renovation plans

- Estimated cost: £10,000
- 48 flats in Margaret House

8 Continue clicking to bring up the remaining points. Once there are no more items left to animate in the text box, the next mouse click will lead to the following slide in the show.

Margaret House
Management and services committee

Lift renovation plans

- Estimated cost: £10,000
- 48 flats in Margaret House
- Around £210 per flat (if shared equally)
- Between £160 and £430 (if based on size of flat)

Dynamic slide transitions

When switching between slides, give them a professional look with transitions.

1 Open up a PowerPoint presentation that contains several slides and go to the first slide.

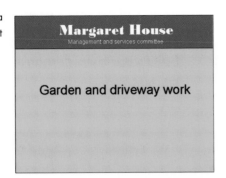

2 In the Slide Layout Task Pane, select the Slide Transition command. This brings up the Slide Transition Task Pane from which you can select one of many special effects.

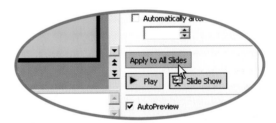

3 Select one of the effects from this drop-down list box. As soon as you choose one – we've opted for a vertical blind effect – the current slide of the presentation previews the transition.

4 Once you have chosen a transition effect, click the Apply to All Slides button in the Task Pane and return to your presentation.

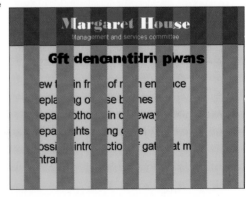

5 Click on the Slide Show button at the bottom of the PowerPoint window and your first slide will appear in the style of the transition you chose in Step 3. This first slide appears from a blank (black) background and you can see the vertical blinds clearly before the transition finishes.

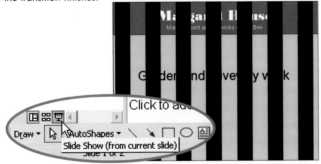

6 Click again and the first slide will turn into the second, with the same transition effect. This time the change is more subtle as the slides are similar. (Note: for clarity, we have darkened the visible parts of the first slide so that you can see the vertical blind pattern clearly.)

7 After just a second or so, the whole of the second slide becomes visible as the transition finishes.

Margaret House
Management and services committee

Garden and driveway

- New turf in front of main entrance
- Replanting of rose bushes
- Repair potholes in driveway
- Repair lights along drive
- Possible introduction of gates at main entrance

PC TIPS

Keep it simple

While the transition commands are very useful, you should, wherever possible, choose one type of transition and stick to it. Be very wary of mixing too many eye-catching transitions that could undermine your carefully composed presentation by distracting viewers from its essential content.

Introducing FileMaker Pro

Databases are the way most information is stored and analysed on computers. Here we will show you how simple it is to build your own databases with FileMaker Pro.

H ave you ever wondered how the people at directory enquiries are able to find the telephone number you want so quickly, even when you give them just the person's name and town? The secret is that they type those details into a computer, which then searches a huge database for the correct number.

A database is simply a collection of information – the data. What makes it so effective is that the information is carefully organized to be as accessible as possible. We all use databases in everyday life, even if we don't realize it. For example, your address book, diary, card file indexes and filing cabinets are all types of database.

Databases stored on computers, however, are especially powerful. You can search for particular items, sort the information and then print it out just the way you want. In many cases, databases consist of one file that contains all the information you need. For example, an address book might hold all your friends' names, addresses and telephone numbers. Sometimes, though, databases are made up of several files. An example of this might be a database for a leisure centre that has different files for bookings, membership and payments.

A database file typically consists of two parts. The first part contains information about the structure of the database, while the second, much larger, part contains the data itself. This data is split into structured sections called records. Each record is, in turn, split into smaller elements called fields.

In the case of an address book, a record would contain all the information associated with one person – name, address and telephone number. Each one of these smaller elements would be stored in a field. You

FileMaker Pro is a powerful and versatile database. In this section you'll discover how to get the most out of this useful program.

SHORT CUTS

Like most other applications, FileMaker Pro makes extensive use of keyboard shortcuts for commands on the menu bar. For example, there are quick ways to open and close a file in FileMaker Pro. The Open command on the File menu can be performed by pressing the [Ctrl]+[O] keys and the Close command by pressing [Ctrl]+[W].

might even choose to break these fields down into smaller ones. For example, the person's name might be broken down into separate fields for first name and surname.

FileMaker Pro is one of the most flexible and easy-to-understand database programs on the market. The version we are using is FileMaker Pro 6 from FileMaker Inc (available from www.filemaker.com). Over the next few pages, we'll show you how to create your own database files in FileMaker Pro, how to enter data into those files, and how you can manipulate that information. First, we'll start with the basics.

● Using FileMaker Pro

Installing FileMaker Pro is a simple matter of inserting the CD-ROM into the computer and following the on-screen instructions. As part of the process, FileMaker Pro will ask for your name and the program automatically adds this information to the databases where this detail is relevant.

After installation, you can create a new database by choosing New Database from the File menu. One of the benefits of FileMaker Pro is that it comes with a range of templates for home, educational and business database files. These templates are ideal for beginners as they avoid the chore of setting up a new database structure from scratch (see Making a start with FileMaker Pro box, below).

You can view your database file in several different ways, known as modes. The one that you'll use most is called the Browse mode: this is the view that lets you search through records in your database, add new records, edit existing ones and delete unwanted ones. In Browse mode, you can view the database as a list of records or as a form. As a list of records, the database looks a little like a spreadsheet (see Stage 3, pages 56–57). Under the form view, the database displays the contents of one record at a time on a form that you can design or customize yourself. Most database users prefer to enter data using forms instead of the cramped spreadsheet-style view, as it is easier to see information.

If you want to add a new record to your database, click on the New Record button on the FileMaker toolbar and type information in the boxes that represent the fields. You can click in each box in turn and type in the information, or use the [Tab] key to move from field to field.

● Automatic saving

Unlike most other programs, including Word and Excel, there's no need to save your work as you go along. Each time you add a new record to your database, or change an existing record, FileMaker Pro saves the information automatically. This is a standard procedure in all database programs.

When you've finished working on your database file, close it by going to the File menu and selecting the Close option. You can return to FileMaker Pro and reopen your file at any time in the usual way by using the Open command on the File menu.

MAKING A START WITH FILEMAKER PRO

Once you have installed FileMaker Pro from the CD-ROM, the program will be added to your Start menu (below). Click on the FileMaker Pro program and you'll see the New Database screen that lets you choose which database you want to work on (right).

The first option, Create a new file using a template, allows you to use one of FileMaker Pro's ready-made, but empty, database templates. If you select this option, a panel on the right lists the templates available. These cover many popular tasks, from storing an inventory of your home contents to handling business expenses.

If none of the templates suits your needs, you can start with a new, blank database instead. You can define the fields you want to use to record information and design the layout of the form in which you will insert it.

If you have already created a database, there will be a third option below the two create options (see dialog box below). Choose this option to open an existing database.

FileMaker Pro workspace

Although the work area of the FileMaker Pro window differs from that of a word processor or spreadsheet program, many elements are similar to those in other Windows programs.

WHEN YOU start FileMaker Pro, you see the New Database screen. Select the Inventory template from the Home template list and then click on OK. When prompted, save the file in a convenient folder. The database shown below will appear. Currently, the database is blank, but it displays all the different elements of the default FileMaker Pro screen with which you should become acquainted.

The first time you open the database, it appears in Browse mode, showing one record per form – as illustrated below.

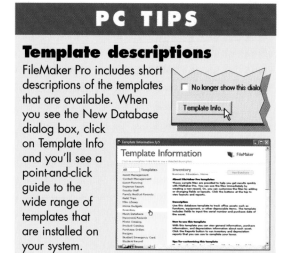
Title Bar

This confirms the program name and the name of the database file you're working on (it is called Inventory in this example).

Menu Bar

The full range of FileMaker Pro commands is available through the standard Windows Menu Bar.

Book

This card index icon, together with the record indicator underneath, allows you to move through the database by clicking from one record to another.

Toolbar

The toolbar looks and works like the toolbars of other Windows programs, such as Word and Excel.

Field

Each record in a database is made up of individual elements called fields. Each field contains a specific piece of information relevant to that record. Here, for example, the record for an item in the inventory includes fields for its date of purchase, cost and age in years.

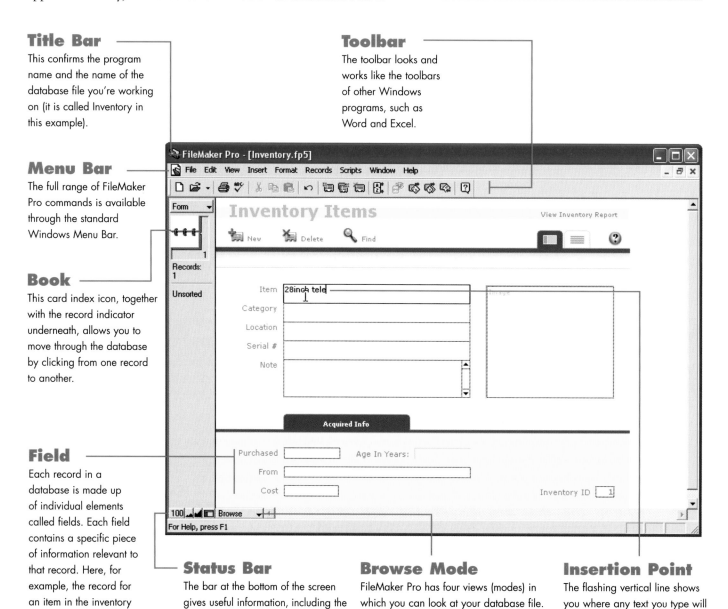

Status Bar

The bar at the bottom of the screen gives useful information, including the mode in which you're working, and contains buttons that allow you to zoom in and out of the screen.

Browse Mode

FileMaker Pro has four views (modes) in which you can look at your database file. The one you'll use most frequently is Browse mode, which lets you edit the information stored in the database.

Insertion Point

The flashing vertical line shows you where any text you type will be added.

Creating and editing a database

We all have something in our lives that could benefit from better organization. Here we show you how a database can help to keep track of your daily tasks.

1 Start FileMaker Pro and select To Do List from the list of Home templates. Click on OK.

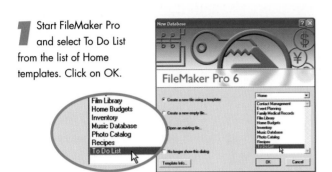

2 FileMaker Pro asks you where you want to create your database. Choose a suitable location on your hard disk, type a name for the database and then click on Save.

3 Your database appears. If you want to view a short explanation of the template click on the question mark button near the top right corner of the database screen. Return to your database by clicking on the left-most of the two tabs near the top of the database screen.

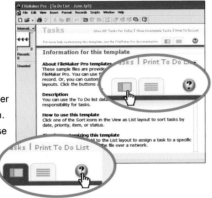

4 FileMaker Pro displays the database with a blank form (this form template is stored together with the To Do List structure in the template). Note that the Records indicator on the left of the screen (inset) shows that there are no records in the database.

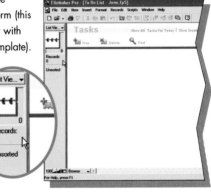

5 To add the first record to your database, click on the New button. When the record appears, you'll see that several fields are filled in for you: the Priority field contains the word Normal and Windows has automatically entered the date. If the US date format is showing, you can change to the British format by selecting Use System Formats from the Format menu.

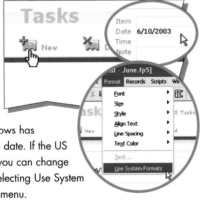

6 Fill in or alter any of the fields, using the [Tab] key to move from one to the next.

7 When you have completed all the fields, click on the New button again and add another record to your To Do List. This database also has a List View option that displays the records in a more compact and neater-looking list – click on the second tab near the top of the database screen to switch to this display.

8 When you've finished entering new records, select Close from FileMaker Pro's File menu. Note that there's no Save command as FileMaker Pro automatically saves your work as you go.

Modifying a database

FileMaker Pro's business, home and educational templates make ideal starting points for building your own database files. Here's how you can customize them.

O n pages 48–51, we saw how to create a database using one of the ready-made templates provided with FileMaker Pro. But what do you do when none of the Filemaker Pro templates matches your exact needs?

The answer is to create your own database file. One way to do this is to create a brand new database from scratch, but you can save time simply by modifying one of FileMaker Pro's templates to suit your precise needs. If you choose a template that contains most of the fields that you plan to use, this will cut down on the work you have to do.

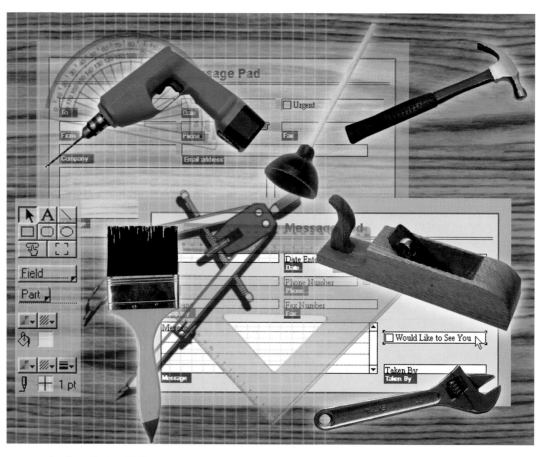

Creating a brand new database file from scratch can take quite a long time. With FileMaker Pro, it is much quicker to customize an existing database.

● Planning your fields

Before you start, it's wise to identify the pieces of information you want to store in each record of your database (you'll usually use one field for each piece of data). Then you will need to choose the right type of field for each separate piece of information.

FileMaker Pro lets you use several types of field. For example, you would use the Text type for a surname field, the Number type for an age field and the Date type for a date-of-birth field. If you try to insert the wrong type of data into a field (text into a date field, for example) FileMaker Pro will ask you for the right type of information.

● Deleting and adding fields

After working out which fields you need, you must then choose a FileMaker Pro template that is closest to the type of database you want. Next you create a new database file, using the basic template but adding and removing fields to customize it.

Removing fields is a two-stage process. First, you remove the fields from the form that you use to edit records. Then you remove the unwanted fields from the database itself. It's vital to understand that the second action permanently removes data in the deleted fields. To avoid losing data in this way, you should do all your customizing before you type information into the database records.

Adding new fields to your database involves the same two steps as removing fields. You have to add each new field to the database and then add it to the forms you use to edit the records.

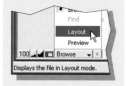

Customizing a database template

Although FileMaker Pro's templates are extremely useful, you may not find one to suit your needs precisely. Here we show you how simple it is to customize a template.

1 Modifying an existing template is the easiest way to create a new database file. Start up FileMaker Pro. On the New Database screen select Create a new file using a template. Then choose Event Planning from the Home list of templates. Click on the OK button and the Create Copy dialog box will appear.

2 Now use the Create Copy dialog box to save your new database. Here we've saved it as 'Party' in a folder called My Databases.

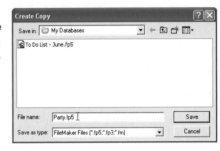

3 When the Template form appears, select Layout mode from the View menu or click the button on the Status bar (see Quick mode switching box on page 52).

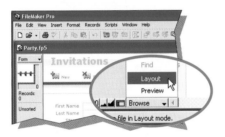

4 To remove a field from the form, click on it and press the [Del] key. Here we're deleting three fields and their labels that are grouped together at the bottom right of the form.

5 You must also remove these fields from the database itself. Otherwise, these unwanted fields will still be present, occupying disk space and slowing the database down unnecessarily. Select Define Fields in the File menu.

6 The Define Fields dialog box lets you add and remove fields. Select each of the fields you have removed from the form in turn and click on the Delete button for each one. Click on the Delete button when FileMaker asks you to confirm each deletion.

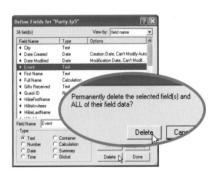

7 You add a field using the same dialog box as in Step 6. Type 'Email address' into the Field Name box, select Text in the Type area and click on the Create button. Then click on the Done button to go back to your form layout.

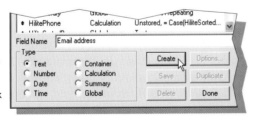

8 The Email address field automatically appears at the bottom of the layout. Use the mouse pointer to drag and drop your new Email address field into position below the Phone field.

9 Here's the new database ready for adding your data. On page 57, we'll show you how to apply formatting to fields in order to get the look you want.

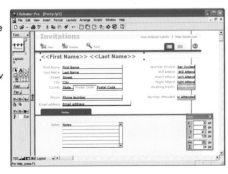

PC TIPS

Different field types

The Type area of the Define Fields dialog box (see Step 7) lets you select other field types as well as text fields. We'll show how to use other field types on pages 56–57.

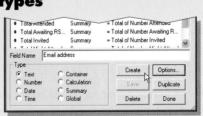

Creating a new database from scratch

Templates provide a quick and easy way to build databases, but they won't cover all your needs. Here's how to create the database you want by building it from scratch.

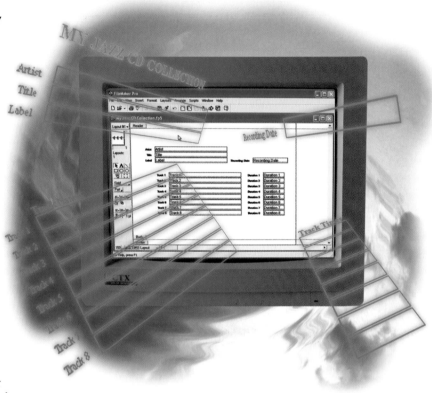

So far, we have discovered how to create a database using the templates provided with FileMaker Pro. We found that we could use the templates as they stand or customize them to suit our own purposes. The advantage of customizing is that it's quick and simple to do. However, if you want to build a database file that doesn't bear any resemblance to the built-in templates, FileMaker Pro lets you create database files from scratch to deal with such situations. While this is a more complex process, it does give you far greater freedom to create exactly the sort of database you want.

● Planning makes perfect
The first step in creating a completely new database is to plan what you want. You need to think about the same things as you would if you were customizing a template: what information do you want to store in each database record and what type of field should you use to hold each item of information?

You'll probably have text information, such as names and addresses, that you can hold in text fields. It's also wise to use text fields rather than number fields to hold data such as telephone numbers because this ensures that zeros at the start of long-distance numbers are displayed and allows for spaces, for example. However, numerical data is best stored in a number field and FileMaker Pro has special types of fields for items such as dates and times (see FileMaker Pro field types box, opposite).

In addition, you'll need to think about how you want your database's layout to look in Browse mode. When you define your new database, FileMaker Pro will automatically create a very simple layout. However, this is not much more than a list of the field names with a box for each data entry. We'll show how you can change the style of your layout using these fields on pages 58–61.

● Designing a layout
It's a good idea to sketch out on a piece of paper a rough idea of how you want your layout to look. That way, you'll be able to make sure your information is clearly presented and easy to understand. You can add headings and you can also group together several fields that hold related information (for example, address, telephone number and postcode fields).

Creating a database file can seem a little complicated at first, but with some forward planning you can ensure you have a database that is perfectly suited to your needs.

Once you've completed your planning, you're ready to define the fields for your database. The process starts in the same way as creating a new database using a template, except you select the Create a new empty file option in the New Database dialog box.

● Define your fields

You define the fields one by one, choosing a name for the field and deciding what type of field it is. Don't worry if you make a mistake – you can always delete fields if you find you don't need them at a later stage. You can even come back later and define new fields if you forget some. When you've finished defining your fields, you can move on to look at the layout. This process is quite similar to rearranging a layout from an existing template (see pages 52–53).

You start with the very basic default layout that FileMaker Pro provides, so this is where your planning on paper will come in handy. You can use the mouse to reposition fields and labels, as well as to add or delete elements such as text headings, to make your layout attractive and its content easier to understand.

FileMaker Pro field types

Choosing the right type of field for each piece of data is the most important task in database design.

IT'S POSSIBLE to design a database in which every field is a text field, such as in a simple database of first names, last names and dates of birth. But if you do this, you miss out on FileMaker Pro's extra capabilities for dealing with particular types of data. For instance, if date-of-birth information is entered into a text field, it can't be sorted into chronological order properly.

With databases where you want to perform manipulations or calculations, it's essential to look at the various fields that FileMaker Pro provides and choose the most appropriate of the eight different types available.

Define Fields for "My Jazz CD Collection.fp5"

0 field(s)   View by: custom order

Field Name	Type	Options

Field Name: Artist

Type:
- ⊙ Text
- ○ Number
- ○ Date
- ○ Time
- ○ Container
- ○ Calculation
- ○ Summary
- ○ Global

Create | Options...
Save | Duplicate
Delete | Done

Text
A field of this type can hold up to 64,000 letters, numbers and symbols used as text.

Number
A field of this type can hold numbers up to 255 digits long. You can perform calculations on data stored in a number field, multiplying a Price field by a Number Required field to get a total cost, for example.

Date
This type of field includes the day and month portion of the date. If you omit the year, FileMaker Pro enters the current year.

Time
A complement to the date field, the time field can store information in the form of hours, minutes and seconds.

Container
This is a special type of field that can be used to store graphics, sounds and other objects. With this type of field you can build up an illustrated database, such as a pictorial guide to plants, for example.

Calculation
This type of field holds the result of a calculation that uses values held in other fields, such as the total cost mentioned in the Number field description, for example.

Summary
In some databases it's useful to add a field that summarizes information from a number of records in the database, rather than just the current record.

Global
This type of field holds data that is the same for every record in the database. You might, for instance, put a company logo into a global field. Another use might be to hold a constant often used in calculations.

Defining a new database

It can take a while to define fields because you have to create them one at a time, but once you have them set up, they are ready to use. Here we show you how to create a simple database for a collection of jazz CDs.

1 With FileMaker Pro running, bring up the New Database dialog box by selecting New from the File menu. Select the Create a new empty file option and click on OK.

2 Type a suitable name for your new database file and select the folder where you want to save it. Then click on the Save button.

3 The Define Fields dialog box opens automatically. Type the name of the first field (Artist) in the Field Name text box. In the Type area, select the Text option and click on Create.

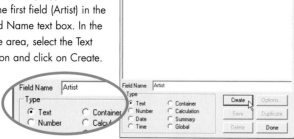

4 The field appears in the list at the top of the dialog box. Follow the procedure in Step 3 to add each of the extra text fields shown right.

5 Now add a number field to hold the duration of the first track. Type Duration 1 into the Field Name text box, choose the Number option and click on the Create button. Now repeat the process seven more times until you have number fields to hold the duration of each track.

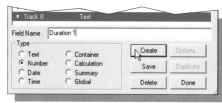

6 Create a date field and call it Recording Date. Select the Date field type and click on the Create button, as before. Now all the fields for our database are defined, so click on the Done button to finish.

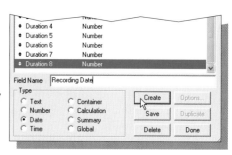

PC TIPS

Re-ordering fields

If you need to change the order of the fields you have added to your database, you can simply move them up and down the

list in the Define Fields dialog box. Click and hold down the mouse button over the small double-headed arrow next to the field name and then drag the field to the right position.

7 FileMaker Pro automatically creates an empty, basic layout for your database. You can now switch to Browse mode to start adding information (see pages 48–51), or tweak the design a little first (see opposite).

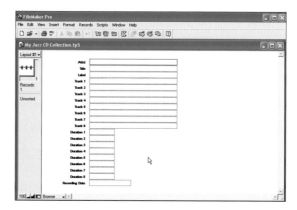

Changing your new database's layout

Now you have defined your database, it's time to improve its appearance.
Here we alter the layout of the jazz CD database, adding headings for clarity.

1 Follow the exercise on the previous page to get to the basic layout that FileMaker Pro provides. Switch to Layout mode by selecting Layout mode from the View menu.

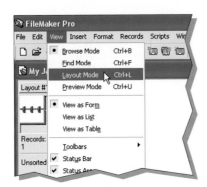

2 Use the mouse to drag and drop the fields and labels to new positions. Start with the Duration 1 field: click on it then drag it beside Track 1. FileMaker Pro shows you a dotted outline as you drag the mouse.

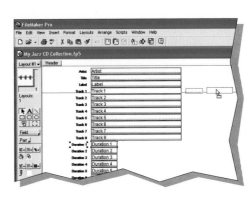

3 Continue to rearrange the fields and their labels to make the layout easier to understand. Here we've moved the duration fields alongside their corresponding track fields. We've also made room for some headings above each column and at the top of the layout.

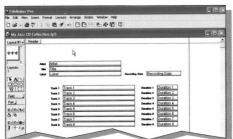

4 You can remove text labels from the layout without affecting the database itself. In this case, we don't need labels for each duration field. Click on each of the duration labels and press the [Del] key to remove it.

5 Click on the Text button on the status area to the left of the screen to add a heading above the list of tracks. Click just above the column of track fields and type a label, Track Names. Use the same method to add a Track Times label above the column of track durations.

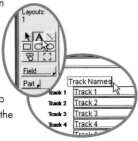

6 Add an overall heading, My Jazz CD Collection, at the top of the layout and right-click on it. Select the Text Format option from the pop-up menu that appears and use the Text Format dialog box to choose the font, size, style and colour you want. Click on OK when you've finished.

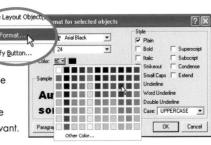

7 To make sure that the fields are clearly visible on the page when you come to enter information, you need to add a border to each. Right-click on the first field and select Field Borders from the menu that appears.

8 Tick the Top, Bottom, Left and Right boxes in the Field Borders dialog box and click on OK. Now repeat the process for all fields – you can select several fields at once by pressing the [Shift] key while you click.

9 Switch to Browse mode by selecting Browse from the pop-up menu on the Status Bar. You can now see the modified layout: it's already easier to find your way around. On pages 64–65, we'll show you how to enhance layouts even further.

FIELD ORDER

FileMaker Pro looks at the field positions on your database form to work out the order in which it will move from field to field when you enter data in Browse mode. Generally, it assumes that you want to enter data from top to bottom and from left to right, and so this is how you are requested to insert the data.

Adding more layouts

Layouts are flexible tools and they allow you to view the information in your FileMaker Pro database in many different ways. Here's how easy it is to add more layouts when you need them.

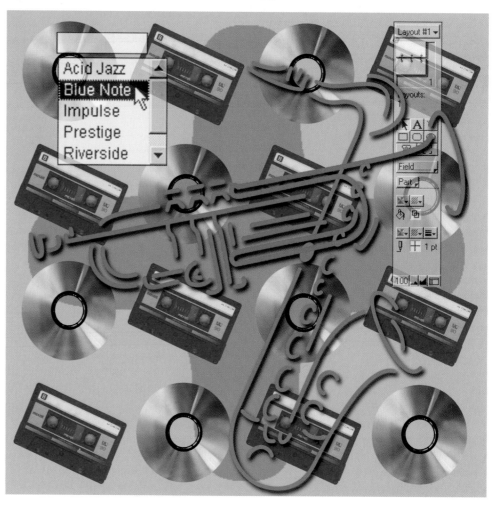

W e have seen that setting up a simple layout for data entry is part of the process of creating a new database file from scratch (see pages 54–57). However, there's much more to layouts than simply entering data: for example, you can use them to find information in your database and to set up mailing labels ready for printing.

The important thing to remember is that a layout itself does not store information – it simply provides a way of looking at it. The information is stored as the main part of the database file.

● More tools
You can have as many layouts associated with your database file as you like. For example, you might have set up an address book database that includes fields for name, address, postcode, telephone number and email address. The layout you use to browse these contact details might include all these fields, but the layout you use to print out envelopes will include only the name, address and postcode fields.

Adding a new layout to your database is almost as easy as modifying an existing one (see pages 52–53). Already included with FileMaker Pro are several pre-defined layouts that cover various common uses. These are the Standard layout (which is the one created automatically when you define a new

database), a columnar report, an extended columnar report, a single-page form, labels, envelopes and a completely blank layout. The single-page form and blank layouts are good for both browsing and data entry. With a blank layout you can create a customized browser or a data entry screen to suit your needs.

● Choose a name
FileMaker Pro will always ask you to choose a name for your layout. Pick a name that will remind you of the purpose of your layout: Envelopes and Labels, for instance. That way you'll be able to quickly find the layout you want when you come back to use your database again. Don't worry if you decide you want to change the name – FileMaker Pro allows you to rename, copy and delete layouts at any stage.

You can either create layouts to your own specifications, or use the ones that are provided in FileMaker Pro.

Starting afresh

If none of the pre-defined layouts suit your needs, it's best to start with a blank layout (see page 60). This allows you to position fields and other objects, such as text and graphics, exactly where you like. All the tools you need to add objects to your layout can be found in the status area at the left of the FileMaker Pro window (see The status area in Layout mode box, right).

Additional formatting tools are available either from the Format menu or simply by right-clicking on an object. You aren't limited to displaying fields as simple text boxes in your layouts. You can change their colour, size and text style, as well as adding borders. You can also use special commands, like Define Value Lists, while you are in Layout mode to make it easier and faster to enter information when you are in Browse mode. And, if your database includes a field that must always contain one of a small number of options, you can tell FileMaker Pro in advance which information is acceptable. When entering data, you need only select an option from the list instead of typing it (see page 61).

The status area in Layout mode

A FileMaker Pro layout presents the data contained in a database. To decide exactly how information is presented both on screen and in printouts, use Layout mode.

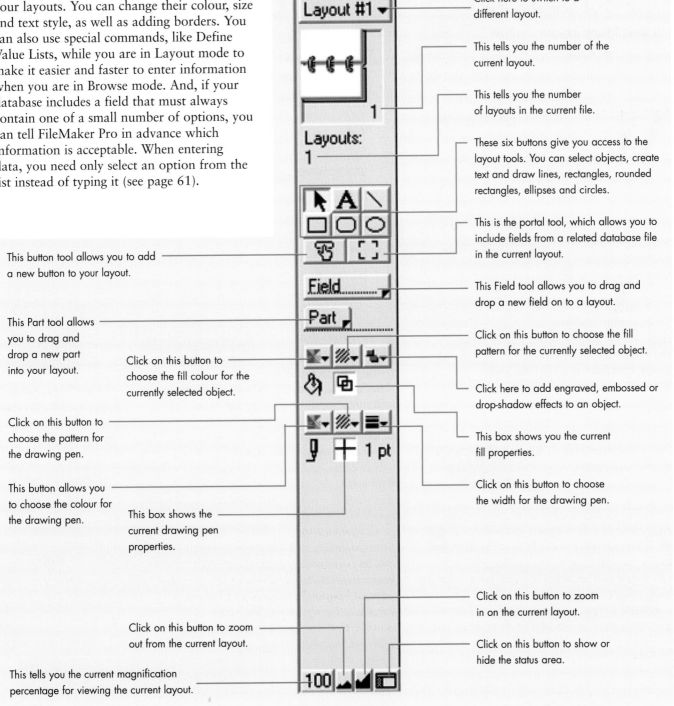

Click here to switch to a different layout.

This tells you the number of the current layout.

This tells you the number of layouts in the current file.

These six buttons give you access to the layout tools. You can select objects, create text and draw lines, rectangles, rounded rectangles, ellipses and circles.

This is the portal tool, which allows you to include fields from a related database file in the current layout.

This Field tool allows you to drag and drop a new field on to a layout.

Click on this button to choose the fill pattern for the currently selected object.

Click here to add engraved, embossed or drop-shadow effects to an object.

This box shows you the current fill properties.

Click on this button to choose the width for the drawing pen.

Click on this button to zoom in on the current layout.

Click on this button to show or hide the status area.

This button tool allows you to add a new button to your layout.

This Part tool allows you to drag and drop a new part into your layout.

Click on this button to choose the fill colour for the currently selected object.

Click on this button to choose the pattern for the drawing pen.

This button allows you to choose the colour for the drawing pen.

This box shows the current drawing pen properties.

Click on this button to zoom out from the current layout.

This tells you the current magnification percentage for viewing the current layout.

Adding a new layout

Here we show you how easy it is to create an additional layout for an existing database. We use the Blank layout option to create one completely from scratch.

1 When we created our new jazz CD database (pages 56–57), we also set up the initial layout. Luckily, you can have more than one layout per database file because we also need one for making cassette labels for those jazz recordings that are on tape. Let's start by choosing Layout mode from the View menu.

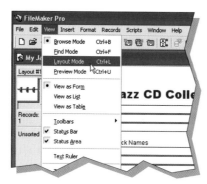

2 Now we're ready to begin building our cassette label layout. Choose New Layout/Report from the Layouts menu.

3 Type the name of your layout in the Layout Name box. We've chosen the descriptive name Cassette Label. Make sure that you select the Blank layout option from the list and then click on the Finish button to continue.

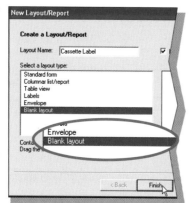

4 The screen will show a blank layout like the one below. This is the type to choose if you want to build a custom layout of your own.

PC TIPS

Alternative layouts

When working on a database with several alternative layouts, use the pop-up list of layouts located at the top of the status area to allow you to switch between them.

5 Now we can add the fields from our database that we want to include in the layout. Position the pointer on the Field button in the status area and drag the field to the position where you want it to appear.

6 Now FileMaker Pro will open the Specify Field dialog box for you to choose the field you want in this position. Select Artist in the list of fields and untick the Create field label box because we don't want text labels in this layout. Finish by clicking on the OK button.

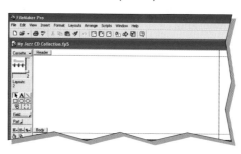

7 The Artist field appears in place on your layout.

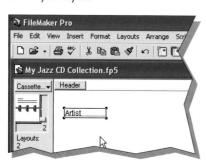

8 Here we've continued to use the same drag-and-drop technique to add ten more fields to our cassette label layout. We've placed them in roughly the right positions to start with but we can always come back later to move them, change their dimensions or apply formatting to them so that they print out neatly and fit on the cassette.

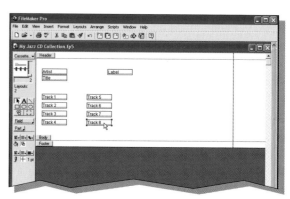

Formatting pop-up list fields

Make your new database layout easier to use by adding ready-made lists to enable speedier data entry in the future.

1 Here's the cassette label layout created on the previous page. At the moment, all the fields are plain text boxes but we want to modify the Label field to work like a pop-up list so that whoever enters information can choose a record label from the list instead of having to type it in.

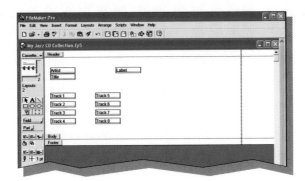

2 Start by clicking on the Label field to select it, then choose the Field Format option from the Format menu.

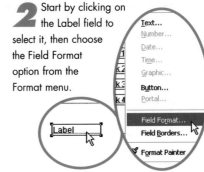

3 FileMaker Pro will now open a Field Format dialog box like this. Select the second option in the Style area and then select Pop-up list from the list box.

4 Now set up the choices for the Label field. To do this, click on the using value list box and select the Define Value Lists option.

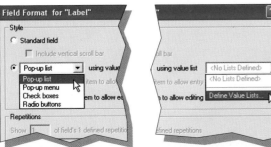

5 The Define Value Lists dialog box opens. Click on the New button at the bottom of the box. In the Edit Value List dialog box, type a name for your list in the Value List Name text box.

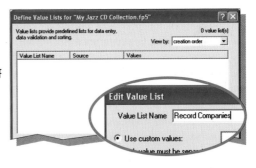

6 The large text box in the Edit Value List dialog box is now ready for your list of choices. Remember to press the [Enter] key after every entry so that each one is on a separate line. Click on the OK button to continue.

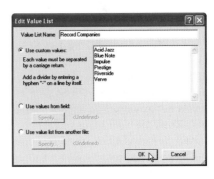

POP-UP LISTS IN FILEMAKER PRO

Most Windows programs use features called drop-down list boxes. These let you choose from a list of options. FileMaker Pro lets you add these list boxes to your database layouts. People entering data into your database can choose from a list of options rather than having to type the information into a text box each time.

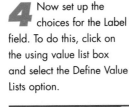

There's nothing to distinguish a pop-up list from a normal text box until you click on it. When you do this, the list of available options appears and you choose one in exactly the same way as you would if you were using a conventional drop-down list box.

7 Click on the Done button to close the Define Value Lists dialog box and return to the Field Format dialog box. Make sure there's a tick in both boxes of the Behavior area of this dialog box and then click on the OK button.

8 Switch to Browse mode to see how the finished pop-up list works on the Label field. All you have to do is click on the Label field and the list of choices will appear. Then you can select the one you want from the list.

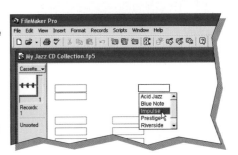

Finding and printing database information

A database file can hold lots of information, but you may well want to locate and print particular bits of this data. Here we show you how to print data from FileMaker Pro.

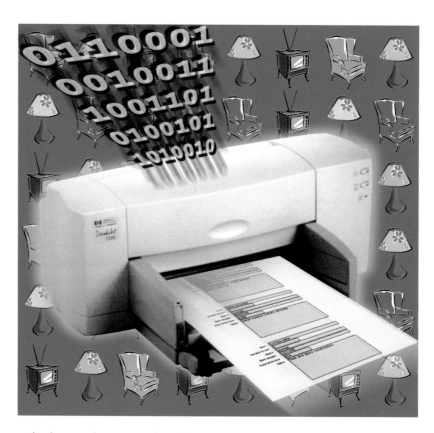

So far we've concentrated on setting up database files and organizing how the information can be laid out on screen. However, there are many occasions when you'll need to go in and find information within the database and also times when you will want to print out some of that information. For example, you might want to produce a set of mailing labels for a particular sub-set of people in an address book database.

As you'd expect, FileMaker Pro includes tools to enable you to find and print out information from your database. First, you use Find mode to tell FileMaker Pro which records you want and then you choose how you want the document to look by selecting a layout before clicking the Print command.

The printed layout follows the same style as the one you have created on the screen. If you haven't already got a suitable layout, you can always add a new one especially for printing (see pages 58–61).

● Finding records
Find mode lets you choose a sub-set of records to work on or print out. You are presented with a blank layout: type the information you want to find into the relevant fields and click on the Find button. FileMaker Pro then searches the database for records that match your entry.

For example, if you want to print an envelope for a specific person in your address book database, you could type 'Blake' into the surname field and 'Sarah' into the first name field. After the search, FileMaker Pro shows

only the matching records – almost certainly just one person. With this technique you can easily choose sub-sets of information: for example, choosing CDs from a particular record company in our jazz CD database (see pages 56–57). FileMaker Pro also lets you search for records with numerical and date information, such as all records in a home contents insurance database where the value is over, say, £200.

● Before printing
It's a good idea to check that all of the fields fit inside the page by viewing the position of the margins (see Final print check box, right). Another sensible precaution is to preview on the screen what your printout will look like before you actually commit it to paper. You can easily switch to the Preview mode by choosing this option from the View menu. This will ensure layouts fit to a printed page.

It's often handy to have a printed record of the data stored in your database for quick reference.

PC TIPS

Final print check
You can check whether all your text and fields will actually fit on the printed page by viewing the page margins. To do this, make sure that you're in Layout mode and select Page Margins from the View menu.

Printing specific records in a database

Here we show you how to print just those items of information that you want from a database, instead of printing the entire contents.

1 Here's a simple home contents database, containing basic text and numerical fields. We want to print only those records that cover items in the lounge. Select the Find mode command from the View menu.

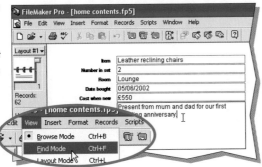

2 FileMaker Pro presents what looks like a blank record: type in the information you want to find. In this case, we've typed 'Lounge' into the Room field. Click on the Find button in the status area on the left-hand side of the screen.

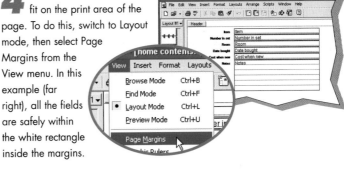

3 FileMaker Pro switches to Browse mode and shows the first matching record. To indicate that you have selected a sub-set of the 62 records in the database, the status area shows the number of records found – 17 in this case.

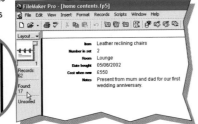

4 Now check how the fields fit on the print area of the page. To do this, switch to Layout mode, then select Page Margins from the View menu. In this example (far right), all the fields are safely within the white rectangle inside the margins.

5 It's also wise to see exactly how the records will print on the page. Click on the Mode button in the bar at the bottom of the FileMaker Pro window and choose Preview from the menu that appears.

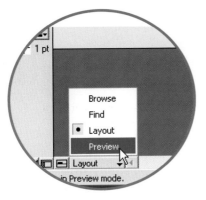

6 You can now see how the records matching the 'Lounge' search appear on the printed page. In this case, there are three records printed per page. If there's a problem, you can return to Layout mode and adjust the layout without wasting paper.

7 When everything's OK, choose Print from the File menu. The Print dialog box works much like those of Word and Excel. In most cases you'll want to print the records you're browsing – as shown here. Click on the OK button to print the pages.

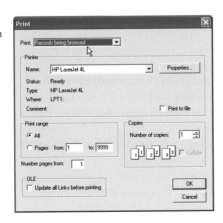

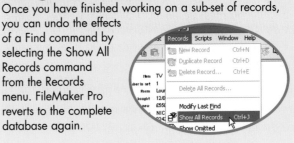

Adding graphics to database layouts

Graphics will brighten up your layouts and can make them easier to work with. Here are some tips for mastering FileMaker Pro's drawing tools.

Modifying layouts in FileMaker Pro is a simple job and on pages 54–57, we show how you can even create new layouts to suit your own purposes. You can also arrange and format the fields and text labels to make your layouts much easier to work with. However, you can create an even greater impact by adding graphics to your FileMaker Pro layouts.

If it's done properly, adding some graphical elements to your layouts will enhance them considerably. Graphics can actually make your layouts easier to understand, as well as improving their overall look.

Layout mode provides several drawing tools which are accessed by buttons in the grey status area on the left side of the FileMaker Pro window. These work much like the drawing tools found within Microsoft Paint (see Stage 1, pages 76–77) and also those in Word (see Stage 3, pages 46–49). You can draw straight lines, rectangles (including squares), ellipses (and circles) and rectangles with rounded corners. You can also control the properties of these items, for example, changing the colour and thickness of lines and outlines, as well as the type of shading used.

While these tools sound rather basic, when combined and used with different colours, they can help you to create really effective layouts.

● **The whole story**
Being able to create graphics is only half the story, though. FileMaker Pro includes several features that make it easy to manipulate graphics and position them accurately in a layout. All graphics objects can be modified

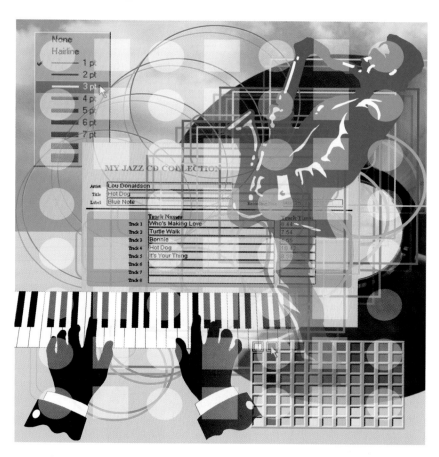

By using lines and simple shapes in combination you can quickly create effective layouts for your databases.

after they've been drawn, so you can change any of their properties, move them to a new position, or even resize them. You can also place them on top of or behind each other or other objects in the layout. This facility can be used to create backgrounds for your layouts, as shown in the example opposite. These backgrounds can make the database more eye-catching and easier to read.

It can be quite difficult to position graphics accurately just by eye, but help is available from FileMaker Pro. It provides useful tools such as rulers, positioning grids and guidelines to help you align items precisely. If these get in the way later, you can easily remove them from view (see Drawing guides box, page 65).

from view (see Drawing guides box, page 65).

PC TIPS

Grouping objects

Sometimes it's convenient to group several graphics objects together and treat them as one item. In Layout mode, hold down the [Shift] key and click on all the objects you want to group together. Finally, select the Group option from the Arrange menu.

Inserting graphics in a layout

Improve the look of an existing FileMaker Pro layout by adding a colourful background and some neat dividing lines.

1 Here's the jazz CD collection database we've already created (see pages 56–57). To make the layout more appealing and easier to use, we'll start by adding a line to divide it into sections.

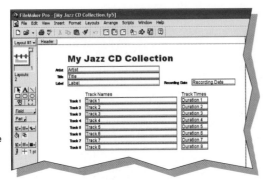

2 In Layout mode, click on the Pen Color button in the status area and choose the drawing colour you want from the palette. Then click on the Pen Width button and select the thickness of line you want.

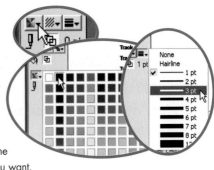

3 Select the Line tool (marked with a diagonal black line) and drag a horizontal line across the layout.

4 If you put the line in the wrong place, simply drag and drop it into the right position.

5 Next, set the Pen Width to None, click on the Fill Color button and choose another colour from the palette. Then click on the Fill Pattern button and choose the one you want. We've opted for a solid fill.

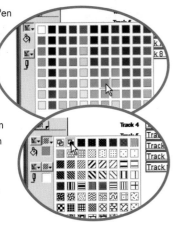

6 Click on the Rounded Rectangle tool and drag a large rectangle around the fields at the bottom of the layout.

PC TIPS

Drawing guides

You can use the View menu to switch on several aids that help you position objects accurately in a layout. Select Graphic Rulers to display rulers for measurement; choose Ruler Lines to make a positioning grid visible; or pick T-Squares to bring up horizontal and vertical moveable guidelines.

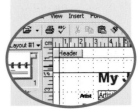

7 The rectangle obscures some of the fields in our layout. To fix this, select the rectangle and choose the Send to Back command from the Arrange menu.

8 Finish the layout by setting the fill colour for the fields to white. To do this, select all the fields and choose white from the Fill Color palette.

Working with records

The records in your databases are stored in the order they are entered, but they can be re-ordered so you can view them in any way you like.

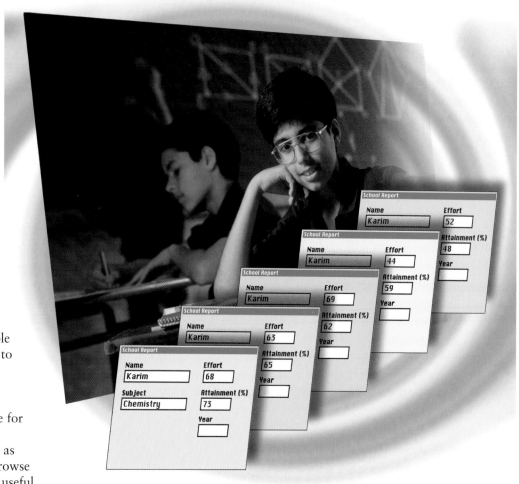

Creating databases, entering data and designing layouts to make them easy to use is only a small part of what FileMaker Pro is capable of achieving. When it comes to working with records, it is likely that you'll spend time performing such activities as looking through the database for specific records and deleting, duplicating and editing them as necessary. FileMaker Pro's Browse mode contains a selection of useful tools to make this type of work easy.

● Manipulating records

For example, a club membership database will need to be regularly updated to reflect the fact that some members might not want to renew their subscriptions. The person using the database might decide simply to delete the records of all members who do not renew. This would be a straightforward task of locating the records of lapsed members and choosing the Delete Record command from the Records menu.

Duplicating a record creates an exact replica of it. While exact duplicate records are rarely needed, this feature can be useful when you want to add a record which duplicates most of the information from an existing record. Select the Duplicate Record command and then edit the new record by clicking on the relevant fields and retyping the information. Don't

forget that any changes you make will be saved automatically – you don't have to save the file yourself. It is especially important to remember this when deleting records, as, unlike in Word or Excel, there's no going back a step if you change your mind.

● Databases with many records

Searching through a database to delete, duplicate and edit records is no problem when your database contains just a handful of records. However, most databases grow quickly – there can be hundreds or thousands of records, even in simple databases – and browsing through a big database looking for records can be an arduous task.

FileMaker Pro can do the work for you by looking for the records you want. By using the Find command (see pages 62–63), together

FileMaker Pro's facility for sorting records into any particular order is both quick and easy, and extremely useful.

OMITTING RECORDS

There might be times when you want to exclude a particular record from the set that you can see in Browse mode. You can do this by displaying the record you want to hide, then choosing Omit Record from the Records menu. You can use the Omit Multiple option in the Records menu to hide several consecutive records.

with the Sort command, you can quickly locate and concentrate on the relevant records. This is important, as it's not only business databases that grow to include large numbers of records. For example, if you list the contents of your home in an insurance inventory, it might stretch to well over 100 records. An avid stamp collector's database will quickly surpass even that.

● The Sort command

When looking through your databases in Browse mode, you will see the records in the order that they were entered. FileMaker Pro provides several ways for you to browse through these (see Quick ways to browse box, below). For information that needs to be presented chronologically – for example, in a club-membership database where it's necessary to see who has been a member of the club the longest – viewing entries in date order is fine. Imagine, however, that there are several categories of member – Standard, Premium and Associate – and that the database reflects this with a Category field for each record. By using the Sort command, you can view the records by any category you want, making your search easier.

● Sorting different types of data

FileMaker Pro can sort the database by almost any kind of field. Text information is simplest: by default you'll see an ascending alphabetical sort (A to Z) but you can choose descending order (Z to A) instead. You can also create a custom sort order if ascending and descending are inconvenient (see page 69).

Numerical fields can also be sorted, so re-sorting a customer-order database based on the value of the order is easy. Similarly, it is a simple process to sort data by date and time. There are some types of fields, such as Container and Global, that cannot be sorted although it's unlikely that you'd want to order records by such fields.

● Planning for a sort

You'll soon find the Sort command indispensable for browsing and manipulating records. With experience, you'll discover that predicting the types of sort you will require on a database helps you plan the fields needed. For example, if you use a single field to hold both first and last names in a database, it's complicated to sort them by last name. For this reason it's better to use two fields so that you can sort easily by last name or first name.

Quick ways to browse

IN BROWSE mode, the grey status area on the left side of the FileMaker Pro window gives you three ways to browse through records. Each method is useful for a particular purpose.

The first way is to use the two Rolodex-style index card icons at the top of the status area. Click on the bottom index card to move forward one record or click on the top index card to move backwards by one record. The number of the current record is shown below and to the right of the bottom index card. This method is useful if you want to move through a small number of records.

The next method is to use the small tab just to the right of the two index cards. You can use the mouse to drag this up and down – the number of the record you've scrolled to is shown in the same place as before. This method is useful if you want to browse between records that are a long way apart.

Finally, if you know the number of the record you want to see, you can click on the record number below the index cards and type the new number in. When you press the [Enter] key, FileMaker Pro will display the record you want to see.

Just click on the bottom index card to move forwards, or the top index card to move backwards, through the records.

You can use the tab at the side of the index cards to move quickly through a large number of records. To do this, click on it with the mouse pointer and drag it up or down.

It is also possible to click on the record number and then, in the box next to it, type in the number of the record you want to go straight to.

Sorting in a database

Here we start re-ordering records in a typical FileMaker Pro database. In this example, we've used a child's school reports.

1 Here's a simple database that stores information about children's school reports. Each record can hold information on one subject from a child's school report for each year. Let's see how we can sort the records in the database in order of highest marks attained.

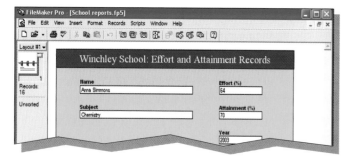

2 While working in Browse mode, go to the Records menu and select the Sort command.

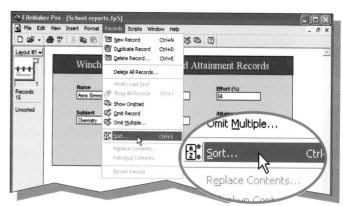

3 The Sort Records dialog box appears. Click on Attainment in the list box of fields on the lefthand side and then click on the Move button.

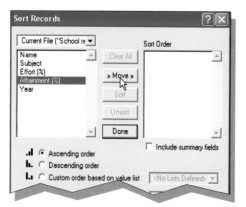

4 Attainment appears in the Sort Order panel on the right. Click on it to select it and then choose Descending order (inset) from the options at the bottom of the dialog box. Instruct FileMaker Pro to sort the records in the database by clicking on the Sort button.

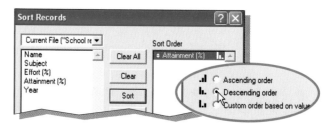

5 The indicator in the status area tells you that the records have been sorted. The first record is now the one with the highest attainment score. Click on the cards in the status area to browse through the database.

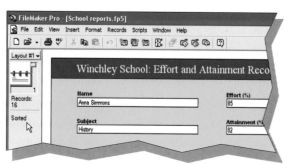

6 When you want to undo a sort to return to the complete database, simply re-open the Sort Records dialog box and click on Unsort.

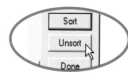

MULTI-FIELD SORTS

You can sort records by several fields by adding more than one field to the Sort Order panel (Steps 3 and 4). For a phone listing in an address database, for example, you can sort records by last name and then by first name.

7 Now the current record is number 2 out of 16. The message in the status area changes to remind you that the records are unsorted.

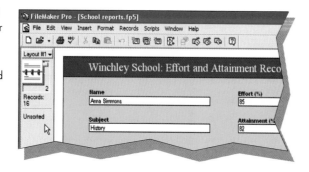

SHORTCUTS

FileMaker Pro includes many keyboard shortcuts to make working with databases much quicker. For example, to bring up the Sort Records dialog box, just press the [Ctrl]+[S] keys together.

FileMaker Pro

Sorting records into a custom order

Simple ascending or descending sorts aren't always the answer to your needs but by using FileMaker Pro's custom order lists, you can sort in any way you like.

1 In this database of people involved in an amateur dramatics production (right), we need to do a sort that shows the records in order of the importance of the roles played by everyone, from producer and director to actors and technical crew.

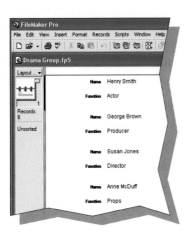

2 To begin, select Sort from the Records menu.

3 The Sort Records dialog box appears, with the two fields in this simple database listed: Name and Function. Select the Function field, then the Custom order based on value list option.

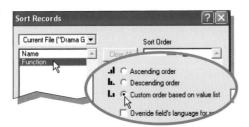

4 The next job is to tell FileMaker Pro the order in which to sort the records. Click on the list box at the bottom right of the Sort Records dialog box and choose Define Value Lists.

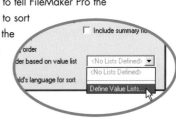

5 A new dialog box opens. Click on the New button and then type in a name for the value list in the Value List Name box (we've chosen Roles).

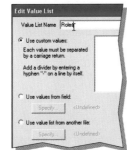

6 Now type the functions in the large text panel on the right, putting them in the order that you want the drama group members to appear. Press the [Enter] key after each entry so that each one is on a new line. Next, click on the OK button and then the Done button on the next screen.

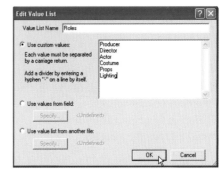

7 Once the Sort Records dialog box reappears, make sure that the Function field is still highlighted and press the Move button to add it to the Sort Order list on the right. Now you can tell FileMaker Pro to carry out your custom sort by clicking on the Sort button.

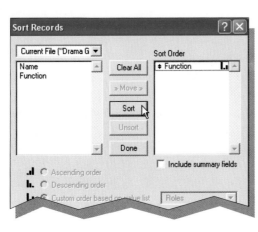

8 Your custom sort appears. The people involved have now been sorted into an order that reflects the importance of their roles in the production. The producer and director are at the top of the list.

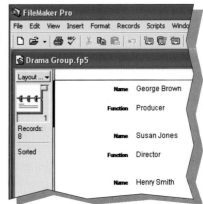

Saving space when printing

Learn how to use FileMaker Pro's special printing features and you can make your printouts look better, and save wastage by using paper more efficiently.

Printing from FileMaker Pro is simple (see pages 62–63). However, when you're printing several records, you'll often find that there's a large amount of wasted space – and paper – if some of the fields are blank.

For instance, perhaps your database has seven fields to handle long addresses, such as Suite 17, Unit 7, Madison Industrial Estate, Long Lane, Cricklewood, London NW2 9ZZ. If so, you'll find that records with much shorter addresses, such as 79 Acacia Avenue, London N3 2TW, will print with four lines of blank space within them. At best this creates ugly areas of white space, and at worst it wastes many sheets of paper.

A similar problem affects fields placed side by side on a layout. For example, it's common practice to use two fields for names: the first name and last name. If you place these fields side by side, those records with short first names will leave large gaps before the last name. You could shorten the first name field box and drag the last name field closer, but long first names will then be truncated. With a little preparation, however, you can avoid all these problems.

● Sliding fields

By using a technique called sliding, you can tell FileMaker Pro to conserve space when printing such layouts. The program checks for empty space (completely blank fields and/or fields with little data) and slides other fields to close the gaps.

Fields can slide horizontally (left) or vertically (up) or in both directions at once. Horizontal sliding is especially useful for closing up space between related fields, such as the first and last name, or between fields and the actual text of the letter. Vertical sliding means records with many blank fields take up less space down the page.

Fields aren't the only items you can slide on a layout – almost any object can be slid. When you slide a non-field object, it doesn't shrink but simply moves closer to the data contained in the field towards which it slides.

Try out some of FileMaker Pro's user-friendly commands to make your data printouts look more professional. Saving space on the printed page also means you'll waste less paper.

Client list					Client list
Name					Name
Mr	Jim	F.		Brown	Mr Jim F. Brown
Mr	Hector			Chrome	Mr Hector Chrome
Ms	Phylida	P.		Dunthorne	Ms Phylida P. Dunthorne
Dr	Sylvester	K.		McGee	Dr Sylvester K. McGee
Mrs	Catherine	B.		Plows	Mrs Catherine B. Plows
Mr	A.	V.		Swifton	Mr A. V. Swifton

The printout on the left is what you get if you print without sliding fields to occupy empty space. Sliding fields reduce the gaps between the names to fit them into the space provided (above right).

Sliding fields on layouts

Making fields slide to conserve space is a simple matter of ticking boxes in the appropriate dialog box. Here we show you how to slide fields both horizontally and vertically.

1 This FileMaker Pro file holds details of playgroup attendees. It has fields for Child name, Parent first name, parent surname, Address and Postcode. Select Preview from the button at the bottom of the screen.

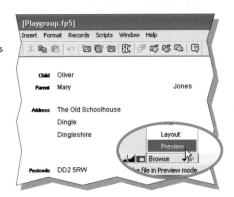

2 The Preview shows how the records will print on the page, unless instructed otherwise. In this example, there's a lot of wasted space between the Parent First name and Surname fields, and between the Address and Postcode fields.

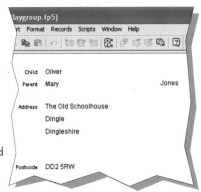

3 Switch to Layout mode and then click on the Surname field. Select Sliding/Printing from the Format menu. In the dialog box that appears, tick the Sliding left box and click on the OK button. Do the same for the Parent field.

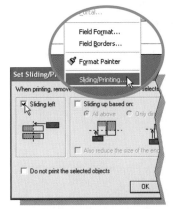

4 Sliding fields are indicated by small arrows on the field borders which show the slide direction. If you can't see them on your screen, click Show on the View menu and select Sliding Objects from the Show sub-menu.

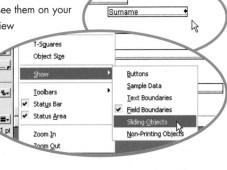

5 To minimize vertical white space, select the Address field, bring up the Set Sliding/Printing dialog box (see Step 3), then tick the Sliding up based on: box. Click on the OK button and repeat the exercise for the Postcode field.

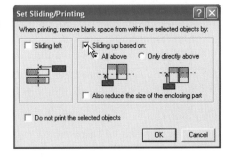

6 It's also important for field labels to slide with the field. In this example, we need to set up the Postcode label to slide. Select the label, and repeat the same process as for the Postcode field.

7 Now switch to Preview mode again. You can see how the gaps between the addresses and postcodes have closed up and also how the Parent First name and Surname fields are closer together.

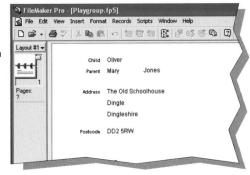

PC TIPS

Preventing objects from printing

You can save space and paper by setting some layout objects as non-printing. Click on the object and then bring up the Set Sliding/Printing dialog box (see Step 3). Tick the Do not print the selected objects box. The object will appear on screen, but not on the printed page.

Introducing fields for special purposes

Not all the information you want to store in a database will fit neatly in a text or number field. We show you how to solve this problem using FileMaker Pro field types.

Many databases are created from simple text and number fields. However, some data is neither text nor numbers. For example, you might need to store dates, images and values calculated from fields. For this sort of data, using the right field type is crucial.

Dates, for example, are one of the most common types of field. Using a proper date field instead of simply typing 25 November 2002 into a text field allows FileMaker to carry out searches and calculations based on simple chronological functions.

There are many other types of information that you might want to store in a database. Examples range from everyday items such as fixed figures and regular calculations, to more exciting elements, such as pictures, Windows sound recordings (see Stage 5, pages 20–23) and even video clips. For example, you could create a single database that stores photos, sounds and video clips of your children as they grow up. FileMaker Pro has been designed to deal with all types of material. And by choosing the right type of field you can create a more effective database.

● Container fields

As an example of non-numerical, non-text data, consider a register of every car owned by the members of a Lancia enthusiasts' club. This is likely to include names and addresses in text fields, date of joining in a date field, and details about the cars in more text fields. But what would really make the database useful is if it could hold a picture of each car.

This is a perfect use for Filemaker Pro's Container fields, which can be set up so that

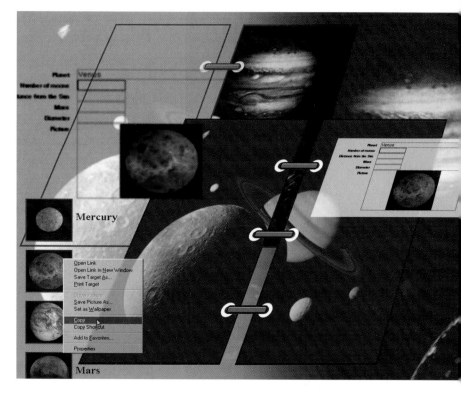

Databases of astronomical material can hold images, calculated orbits, dates and other types of data.

as you move from one member record to the next, the picture of the car changes accordingly. In fact, Container fields are designed to hold just about any type of object, so there is no excuse for limiting yourself to simple text.

● Global fields

There are also special fields to help you to handle other types of data. For example, a company creating a database for a price list might need to add VAT to each item. The database could be set up with a number field called VAT, but then someone would have to type the data (17.5%) into every record in the database. This also means that if the VAT rate changes, someone would have to go through the database changing the information in every record. There's also a risk of records being missed and some prices being wrong.

By using a Global field to store the VAT rate, the problem is solved in one go: a Global field ensures that the information is the same

PC TIPS

Account and phone numbers

Although phone numbers and account codes are obviously made up of numbers, they both often have text characters, such as hyphens, so it's better to treat these types of numbers as text rather than numerical data. If you use a number field for phone numbers, 0999895734 would be stored as 999895734 because the leading zero is dropped for numeric data.

for every record, so typing the information once adds it to every other record. If the VAT rate does change, typing the new figure into one record updates it for all of them.

Global fields aren't just limited to numbers. You can also use them to store text, date, time and even Container data. Of course, since all the fields contain the same information, you can't use a Global field for searching or sorting the records in a database.

● Calculating with a database

In the example above, it's very likely that the VAT for each item in the database needs to be worked out and added to the cost of the item to produce the overall figure that will appear in the price list. The Calculation field is designed for exactly such a purpose.

When you create a Calculation field, you tell FileMaker what calculation you want carried out. It will then put the result in the field. The VAT example is simple: the extra amount to charge is the price multiplied by the VAT rate (which is already stored in the Global field discussed above). By typing in a simple formula, similar to that used in an

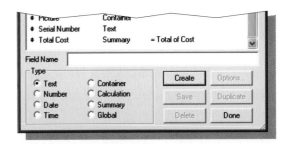

When you are creating a database, or modifying an existing one, you can insert any of these different types of fields by simply selecting the appropriate one from the Define Fields dialog box.

Excel spreadsheet, you can ensure that FileMaker does the calculation for every record in the database. This prevents repetitive data entry and helps avoid the possibility of mistakes being made.

● Versatile fields

Calculation fields are very versatile because they can deal with more than just numbers. For example, you can get FileMaker to work out the day of the week automatically from day, month and year information which is held in a date field.

Summary fields

Summary fields are a special type of field used to collate information from several records in the database file. Used properly, such fields can save lots of time and effort.

WHEN IT comes to getting accurate analyses or summaries of information contained in a database, Summary fields are ideal. For example, a home inventory might contain number fields to store the value of each item in the database, with one item per record.

As you buy and dispose of household items and update the database, it's important to keep track of the overall value of your home contents for insurance purposes.

As items change in a household inventory database, FileMaker can automatically maintain a total value.

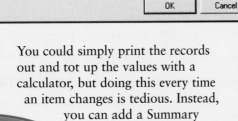

You could simply print the records out and tot up the values with a calculator, but doing this every time an item changes is tedious. Instead, you can add a Summary field to the database and tell FileMaker that you want to know the grand total of all the Cost fields in the database.

There are several different types of Summary field, including Total, Average and Maximum, and each is selected by a simple mouse click.

As soon as you make a change to the database, the Summary will automatically update to show the new figure.

● Flexible summaries

The total figure might be the most common type of Summary field used in a database, but FileMaker can provide others too, including an average value, a maximum or minimum figure, or a count of the number of fields. These can all be used in a variety of different ways when working with everyday data. More advanced options for the Summary field include Standard Deviation, which is useful for statisticians.

Putting pictures in Container fields

If you want to incorporate in a FileMaker Pro layout items other than text, such as pictures or even sound, you will have to use a Container field.

1 The Container field is ideal for holding unusual sorts of data, such as pictures. Here we'll create a bank of information about the planets in the Solar System. Start by creating an empty database and saving it as Solar System.

2 Use the Define Fields dialog box to add a text field for Planet, and number fields for each of the following: Number of moons, Distance from Sun, Mass and Diameter.

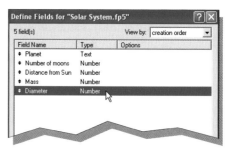

3 Now type Picture into the Field Name box, select the Container option from the Type area and click on the Create button. Then click on the Done button.

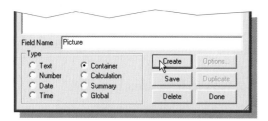

4 When the database layout appears, switch to Layout mode. Right-click on the Picture field and then select Graphic Format from the pop-up menu.

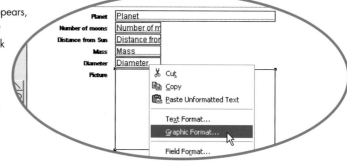

5 The Graphic Format dialog box opens to let you decide how pictures should appear in the field on the layout. Choose the Reduce or Enlarge option to make FileMaker adjust the picture to fit as much of the box as possible. Click on the OK button to continue.

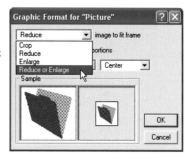

6 Now you need to find the pictures. You may want to look on the NASA Web site at http://photojournal.jpl.nasa.gov, which contains many excellent space images. Find a suitable picture (we've chosen Venus) and copy it to the Windows Clipboard by right-clicking on it and selecting Copy from the menu that appears.

7 Return to the database and switch to Browse mode to enter information. Right-click on the Picture field and select Paste from the pop-up menu (inset, top). Type text and number data about Venus into the other fields (inset, bottom).

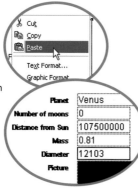

8 Here's the record for the planet Venus, complete with all its data and its picture in place. You can add pictures, numbers and text to the records for other planets in exactly the same way.

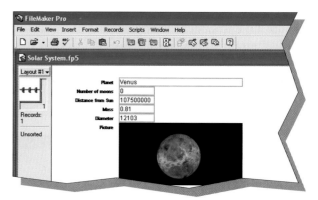

Using Global and Calculation fields

A great way of making the most of FileMaker's useful functions is to enter constant data only once and have calculations carried out for you automatically. Here's how to calculate the retail price mark-up on every item of a shop's stock.

1 Start FileMaker Pro and create a new empty database. When the Define Fields dialog box appears, add three simple fields: Item and Description as text fields, and Cost as a number field.

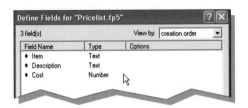

2 Add a new field called Markup and select the Global option from the Type area before clicking on the Create button.

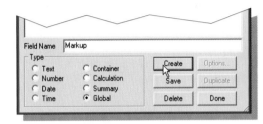

PC TIPS

Entering calculations

When setting up a calculation, you can save time and avoid field name mistakes if you double-click on the field names and then click on the calculation buttons in the top half of the dialog box instead of typing the entries by hand. The program also provides a set of in-built functions for more advanced calculations – we look at some of these on pages 76–77.

3 FileMaker Pro asks you what type of global field you want. Make sure the Number option is selected before clicking on OK.

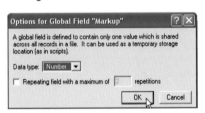

4 The Markup field appears in the top part of the dialog box as normal. Now add a Price field, selecting the Calculation field type before pressing the Create button.

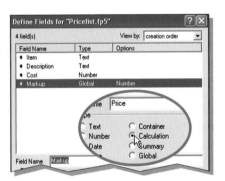

5 FileMaker needs to know what to calculate. In the Price = panel in the lower part of the dialog box, type: 'Cost*(100+Markup)/100' and click on the OK button. This adds a percentage profit margin (mark-up) to the cost of the item.

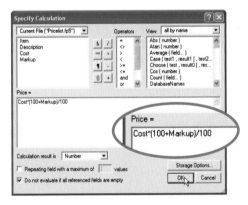

6 The Price field now appears in the Define Fields dialog box. Click on the Done button to create the database.

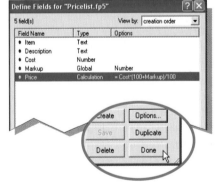

7 Now you can use the database (we've added some simple colour to make the database layout clear, as on pages 64–65). Start by entering some Item, Description and Cost information.

8 Type in a Markup percentage (we used 65%) and press the [Tab] key. FileMaker does the calculation for you and displays the result next to Price.

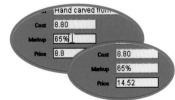

9 Press [Ctrl]+[N] to add another record. Notice how the Markup field, being Global, is already filled in. As soon as you type a Cost figure and move to the next field, FileMaker works out the price for this new item.

Calculations and functions

To make adding mathematical functions easy, FileMaker Pro provides calculation fields. These work with many types of data in a variety of documents – not just with simple sums, but also with a wide range of calculations involving numbers, text and other functions.

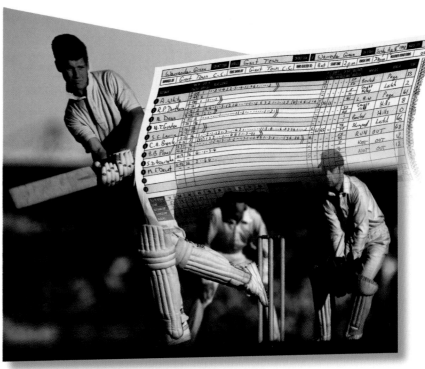

With Calculation fields you can easily create useful summaries of complex sets of figures. On the next page, we show you how to calculate batting averages.

The beauty of calculation fields is that they allow you to make calculations on data in all types of fields (see pages 72–75) – without the bother of keying all of it into a calculator.

To make them work, you need formulae that tell FileMaker Pro how to perform the calculation. You create these formulae by combining basic existing formulae called functions. Each of these functions performs a particular calculation to produce a single, specific value.

● Types of function

FileMaker Pro has 13 groups of functions: text, number, date, time, aggregate, summary, repeating, financial, trigonometric, logical, status, design and external.

Number functions are the most widely used of all. They are used, for example, to calculate quickly the square and square roots of any number, to round a decimal number to the nearest whole number, or to generate random numbers.

Surprisingly, perhaps, text functions are also widely used. These let you make calculations and manipulations with text fields. You might wonder what calculations you could possibly do on text, but text functions are remarkably useful. You might, for example, use text functions to split a text phrase into individual words (which is useful if you want to split a single name field into separate first and other names for sorting). You can even work out the number of characters or words in any text, and replace one section of text with another. You can also use text functions to convert text fields that hold numerical information to true numerical data, which you can then use in calculations.

● Time and date functions

Time and date functions, of course, give values based on times and dates. Using these, you can, for example, split dates into day, month and year or times by second, minute and hour. A time and date function might help you set up a database that automatically tells you when accounts are overdue, for example.

Aggregate functions produce results by performing calculations on several fields at once. For example, the Average function works out the average of several fields. Other aggregate functions can work out the highest and lowest values in a set of fields. Logical functions provide true/false information on relationships in data.

As with simple Calculation fields (see page 75), functions are added through the Specify Calculation dialog box. The functions are listed and you add them to formulae that you build with the field names.

OTHER FUNCTIONS

It's worth exploring other functions to see how they can help you design your databases.

Financial functions work like numerical functions, allowing you to work out values for interest payments, for example. For school work, trigonometric functions give you sines, cosines, tangents and so on.

Status and design functions provide information about the database itself, including its file size, the current size of the FileMaker window and its field names.

Using a function to calculate averages

One of the most commonly used functions calculates an average for a set of figures. In this example, we'll calculate average batting scores for cricketers in a five-way cricket tournament.

1 Start by choosing New Database from the File menu and use the Create New File dialog box to save the new file.

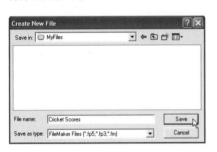

2 Create a text field for Name and then five number fields for Innings1 to Innings5 as shown here. These fields will store the individual scores from each game.

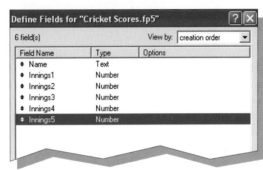

3 Add a calculation field called Average Score and click on the Create button to bring up the Specify Calculation dialog box.

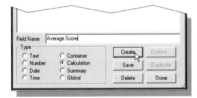

4 Scroll through the list of functions on the right of the dialog box to find Int [number]; this rounds a number to the nearest whole number. Double-click on it to add it to the formula being built in the Average Score = panel. The word 'number' is highlighted in the formula, so any other functions added will replace it.

5 Find the Average function and double-click on it to add it to the formula. The field text is highlighted ready for replacement.

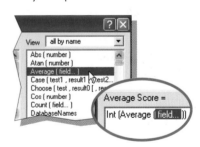

6 Double-click on Innings1 in the list of fields on the left of the dialog box and type a comma after the Innings1 field in the formula.

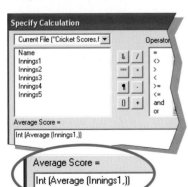

7 Repeat Step 6 for the Innings2, Innings3 and Innings4 fields. Add Innings5, but since this is the last in the list, don't add a comma after it. Click on the OK button and then click on the Done button in the Define Fields dialog box.

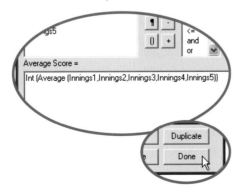

8 FileMaker Pro shows the database in Browse mode and you can start typing in the information for the first record. The Average Score field is then updated automatically as you type in the scores for each of the five innings.

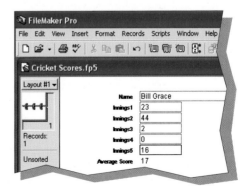

Introducing FrontPage

If you want to start making your own Web site, or just experiment with Web editing for fun, try Microsoft's Web editor: FrontPage.

Microsoft's FrontPage will guide you through the process of designing a Web site, from the concept stage to attractively realized pages that'll have visitors flocking to your site.

Many different types of program can be used to create Web pages, but it pays to be choosy. For example, the Notepad program supplied with Windows lets you save text files in the HTML format used for all Web pages (see Stage 3, pages 132–135). This is a great free program, but the downside of this approach is that you need to know the HTML language to be able to key in the HTML code before you start. And, although HTML is one of the easier programming languages to learn, creating Web pages by typing HTML is hard work.

● Why not use Word?
If you have Microsoft Word on your PC, you can use it as a simple Web editing program. You can create your page using Word's familiar commands and then save the page in HTML format (.htm) instead of the normal document format (.doc) used in Word.

However, while Word makes it easy to create a simple Web page, it lacks the more advanced commands that you need to create and manage multi-page Web sites. It's better to use a tool that is dedicated to this task.

● Choosing a Web editor
Not surprisingly, almost all professional and home-enthusiast Web authors use special Web-editing programs to create their HTML code.

These programs are designed to be easy to use, allowing you to create Web pages as easily as you'd create a leaflet in Microsoft Word. It's a simple matter of pointing and clicking to insert pictures, add colour to text, or link pages together. The Web editor automatically creates the necessary HTML code, leaving the Web author free to get on with the design.

These dedicated programs are packed with toolbar buttons and menu commands that are solely aimed at Web page design. One of the more user-friendly of these packages is Microsoft FrontPage. It's simple to use and has many features that help you create interesting, easy-to-use and visually appealing Web pages.

In addition to helping you to design Web pages with text and graphics, FrontPage can also assist in managing your Web site, with tools to perform

FRONTPAGE

FrontPage is available as both a standalone program and as a part of the Microsoft Office suite of programs. If your PC has both Word and Excel installed, it's possible that you also have FrontPage. To find out, click on the Start button and then look for the Microsoft FrontPage entry in the All Programs menu. If it's not there, you can add FrontPage to your PC by buying the standalone program for around £130.

routine maintenance tasks such as keeping track of all the links between pages and remembering to update the relevant pages when necessary. This is an important issue, because even a simple Web site can comprise several dozen individual files.

FRONTPAGE INSTALLATION AND FIRST TIME USE

You install FrontPage by inserting the CD and following the on-screen prompts. Note that FrontPage – like Windows itself – must eventually be activated by registering the program by telephone or Internet. You can start the program 50 times before activation is required, thereafter the program will not start until it's activated.

When you start it for the first time, you will see the workspace shown below. However, on some PCs, you may first be asked if you want FrontPage to be your default Web editing program.

Unless you are already using another Web editing program which you would prefer to remain the default, click on the Yes button to move on to the main screen.

> **FrontPage**
>
> Microsoft FrontPage is not currently your default Web page (HTML) editor. Would you like to make it your default editor?
>
> ☑ Always perform this check when starting FrontPage
>
> [Yes]   [No]

The FrontPage workspace

The FrontPage workspace looks much like a word-processor window, helping to make the task of creating Web pages as easy as typing a letter.

START FRONTPAGE by clicking on the Start menu, then All Programs, then the Microsoft FrontPage entry. In a few moments the window shown below will appear. It's a good idea to take time to explore FrontPage's menus and toolbars before you start to use it. The similarity with other Windows programs – Microsoft Word in particular – means that you probably already know many of the commands you will need when you use FrontPage for Web editing. You'll find you'll be creating Web pages within a few minutes.

Standard toolbar

The buttons on this toolbar give one-click access to file opening, printing and saving commands and also make it easy to add pictures and hypertext links to a Web page.

Title bar

Like all Windows software, this shows the program. The name of the current Web page is also displayed in this bar.

Menu bar

These 10 menus provide access to the full set of FrontPage commands, from options for opening and closing files to others for adding links to Web sites.

Formatting toolbar

This toolbar lets you use the most common formatting options for text items in your Web pages.

Views bar

The icons in this bar give you different views of your Web site. The usual view is the Page view, which is the display most commonly used in the exercises on the following pages.

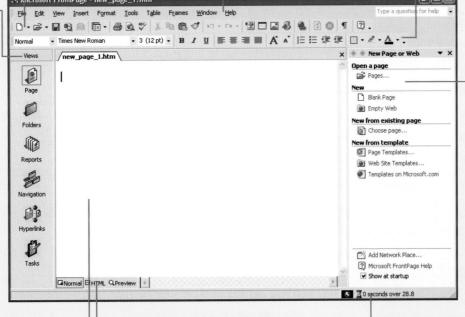

Task Pane

This panel has three pages, covering the creation of new pages and Web sites, Clipboard options and FrontPage's Search command.

Document window

This is the work space for your Web page. You can work on several pages at a time, copying material from one to another to save time, for example.

Page View buttons

These buttons let you switch between view modes. You'll usually work in the Normal Pane, but you can also use the HTML Pane to see the code used and a Preview Pane to display your page as seen through a Web browser.

Status bar

An estimate of the amount of time it would take other Internet users to download your page appears here, together with a progress indicator.

Creating a simple Web page

FrontPage's point-and-click approach means that you don't have to bother with the intricacies of the HTML language. Here's how to create a Web page in five minutes.

1 Start FrontPage and click on the Create a new normal page button. Type the text for your Web page into the document area. In this example, we're creating a simple **home page**. When you have typed your text, use the buttons on the Formatting toolbar to format it.

2 You can separate the different sections of a Web page by adding a thin line across the page. First position the text insertion point on a blank line and then select Horizontal Line from FrontPage's Insert menu.

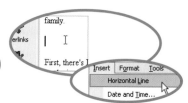

3 The line appears as a very thin horizontal rectangle extending almost all the way across the page. This is the default for the lines in HTML, so it's very common on Web pages.

4 You don't have to accept the line's default appearance, however. To fine-tune the line's look, right-click on it and select Horizontal Line Properties from the pop-up menu.

5 When the Horizontal Line Properties dialog box pops up, set the figure in the Width box to 80. This restricts the line to 80 per cent of the Web page's width. As the Center option is already selected, it'll be equally indented from both left and right sides of the page. Click on OK.

6 Finish editing your text and select Save from the File menu. First, you need to give this page a title; this will appear in the Title bar of the Web browser whenever the page is viewed. Click on the Change Title button to give the page your own title. Type the new title into Page title box and then click on OK.

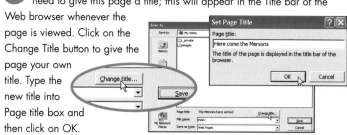

7 Now use the Save As dialog box to save this page. Always give your Web pages clear and simple names. For this exercise, it's best to accept both the folder that FrontPage suggests (My Webs) and the file name (index), to which FrontPage will add an .htm extension.

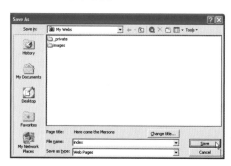

8 Once your file is saved, FrontPage displays a Folder List panel with your index.htm file listed at the bottom. To see what the document will look like when it is uploaded to the Web, click on the Preview button. It's always good practice to preview all of your Web pages before uploading them to the Internet so that you can correct any mistakes before making the files publicly available.

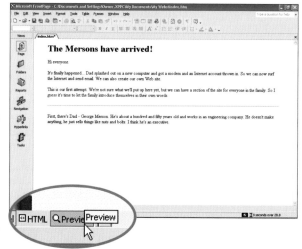

Add graphics to a Web page

Without graphics, the Web would be a dull place. Use pictures to liven up and illustrate your Web page.

1 Start FrontPage and open the index.htm Web page you created opposite. To add a background image, select Background from the Format menu. Tick the Background picture box when the Page Properties dialog box appears, and then click on the Browse button.

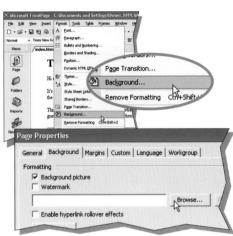

2 In the next window, locate and open a background image or texture for your page (see Finding Web graphics box, below). Click on the Open and OK buttons to return to your page.

3 The background image is repeated to fill the page. This one looks like the edge of an airmail letter against a wooden desk. However, the text on the page overlaps the coloured part of the image, making it hard to read.

4 You can fix this by indenting the text on your page. Select the text and then click on the Increase Indent button (you may have to do this twice, depending on your background image). This command indents text on both left and right sides to keep the text correctly positioned in the central area.

5 You can also insert pictures into the main part of the page. Move the text insertion point to where you'd like your picture and, from the Insert menu, select Picture and then From File. Use the Picture dialog box to locate the folder where you stored the picture.

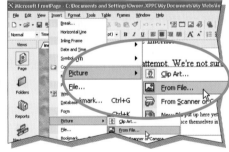

6 Select your image. It could be a scan, one taken with a digital camera or one downloaded from the Web. Click on Insert to return to the page.

7 Your picture appears in the document. You can centre it by selecting it and then clicking on the Center button on FrontPage's Formatting toolbar. When you are happy with your page, save the document. When you click on Save, you are also prompted to save embedded files – in this case, the images you inserted. Click on OK to save your files in the default location. To check the appearance of your Web page, click on the Preview button.

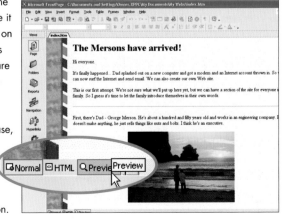

FINDING WEB GRAPHICS

You can create your own Web graphics with a graphics program such as CorelDRAW or even Windows' Paint program, or you can use photos captured by digital camera or a scanner. However, for many Web graphics, such as background images, textures, buttons and icons, it's worth searching the Internet. Use a search engine to look for royalty-free Web graphics (see Stage 7, pages 140–143). You will soon find that there are plenty of Web sites offering graphics and many provide a wide range, with thousands from which to choose.

Microsoft® FrontPage®

Uploading your Web pages

Make your Web pages visible to everyone with Internet access simply by copying the files you have created in FrontPage to the Web space your Internet Service Provider offers.

O nce you have finished creating your first Web pages with Microsoft's FrontPage, you're ready to upload them to your Web space. As soon as you have done that, anyone who types the address of your Web site into their Web browser will be able to see your Web page on their computer.

● Before you start
Uploading your Web pages isn't a difficult task – it should take only a few mouse clicks and a minute or two. However, you need to ensure that all the files needed are transferred. If you accidentally overlook a graphics file, for example, you might find that a background image or an important picture is missing when viewed by other Internet users.

Although there are many alternatives for uploading files, including FTP (see Stage 5, pages 134–137), FrontPage has built-in features that make it worth using for most Web authors. For example, it tracks exactly which files are used in your pages and automatically assembles them ready to upload.

Most Web authors update their Web pages frequently. Another advantage of FrontPage's Publish Web feature is that it tracks changes to Web pages and graphics, automatically uploading the latest versions to keep your Web site up to date (see PC Tips, right).

● ISPs and your Web address
The exact process for uploading your Web page files depends on your Internet service provider (ISP). Most ISPs have set up their Web server computers so that uploading is a

Before anyone can see your Web pages, you have to upload them to your Internet service provider (ISP). This might seem like a complex task, but FrontPage's Web Publish command makes it easy.

simple matter of copying the files to an area of the computer that includes the user name: members.firstmail.com/~fredsmith, for example.

Make sure that you know this address before you start. You'll need it, together with your user name and password, to start the copying process. This is the same user name and password you use to log on to your ISP and also to collect your email. Your user name and password data is required for security reasons, so that only you can upload files to your Web space.

Once you've finished copying your files, check the Web pages before telling everyone the Web site address. This helps to avoid embarrassing errors.

You can also register your site with the most popular search engines (see Stage 4, pages 134–137). These special Web sites help you to publicize your Web site and get more visitors.

PC TIPS

Stay up to date
Unlike FTP programs, which will happily upload files that you may have forgotten to save, FrontPage checks the status of files before it uploads them. If it spots one that has been modified but not saved, it asks you what you want to do before uploading it, and gives you the option of ignoring the changes or saving them before uploading.

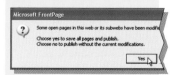

Uploading a Web site

Using FrontPage's built-in Web publishing feature, you can copy your files to your Web space so other Internet users can see them.

Microsoft® FrontPage®

1 Open FrontPage and then open the Web page you want to upload. Check that everything looks correct in the Preview Pane and then select Publish Web from the File menu.

2 FrontPage needs to know the exact address of your Web space. For most home computer users, this will be based upon your ISP's address – check your Internet account documentation to get this information. Type the address into the box in the Publish Destination dialog box and click on the OK button.

3 FrontPage prompts you to connect to the Internet if you aren't already connected. Follow your usual connection procedure and wait for the connection to be made.

4 If this is the first time you have copied Web pages to your Web space, FrontPage will ask if you want to create a Web at this location. Click on the OK button. You may also be asked to type in your User name and password again before you can proceed.

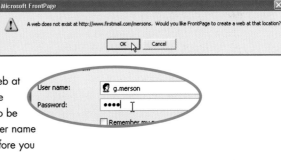

5 The Publish Web dialog box appears, listing the files used in your Web page in the main panel. These files are stored in the My Webs folder on your PC. The green ticks indicate the files that FrontPage will copy. Click on the Show button.

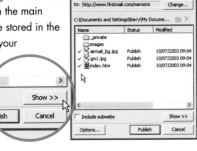

6 The Publish Web dialog box extends to reveal a panel that shows the files stored in your Web space. Initially, this panel is empty, except for two folders that FrontPage automatically creates. Click on the Publish command.

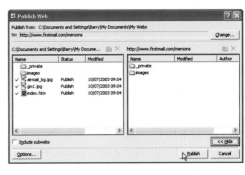

7 A dialog box pops up to show progress. Simple pages such as the one we have created on pages 80–81 take only a few moments to upload. When all the files have been copied to your Web space, another dialog box confirms that the uploading has been completed successfully and provides two links. Click on the first to open the Web page in your Web browser.

8 You can now see exactly what other people will see when they visit your Web page. Check that all is correct before letting friends and family know the Web site's address.

WEB SPACE

When you use the Publish Web command in future, note that the right panel in the Publish Web dialog box lists files you have uploaded before. It is blank for the first upload only. Use this panel to check the files already on your Web site, so you don't waste time uploading twice.

Link your Web pages

By linking Web pages together with hyperlinks, visitors to your site can jump directly to the topics that interest them. Such 'hot' links are the essence of the Internet.

While a simple page uploaded to your ISP's Web server is a good start, it is the creation and linking together of several interesting Web pages that produces a fully fledged Web site. A Web site may consist of anything from half a dozen to several hundred Web pages. Visitors to your site should be able to move easily and quickly from one page to another via hypertext links.

First, you need to create the new Web pages to link to and from. The number of pages you have to design will depend on the type and amount of material you plan to put on your Web site. One aimed at dog lovers, for example, might have one page devoted to each breed of dog, displaying information on size, temperament, grooming and so on. A commercial site aimed at promoting a self-employed person's business might have pages describing the services provided, a pricing structure, examples of past work, recommendations and contact details.

● Creating extra pages
Using FrontPage, it is just as simple to create these pages as it was to create the initial index.htm file (see page 81). All you do is add the appropriate text and pictures by using exactly the same commands.

As you create these Web pages, you also add links between them. These links provide the objects – text or pictures – that visitors click on to move to another page (or a different part of the same page). For example, a commercial Web site listing vehicles for sale would almost certainly have a set of links on the home page to connect to individual pages for cars, vans, motorbikes and so on. The page for cars might then include links to further pages – one for each manufacturer, then one for each model.

There is no limit to the number or format of links in your Web pages. Some Web sites just link pages sequentially, while others use pages that have links to every other page in the site. But while the choice is yours, you should spend time planning how your site will be organized to keep things manageable (see Site organization box, opposite).

Most sites are set up so that the home page acts as the hub of the Web site, which allows a visitor to find every page on the site by following the links that start there. To make sure your site works properly, you need to edit your home page – the index.htm file – to add links to new pages so visitors to your Web site can follow the clickable links from your home page to all the other pages on your Web site.

● Types of link
There are several different types of link. The most common are those that transfer visitors to another page on your site (see page 86).

Without links, a Web site is limited, but connections are easy to set up with FrontPage.

WHAT IT MEANS

HYPERTEXT

The HT in HTML stands for hypertext, which is the general term used for text documents where you click on hot spots in one document to see another document. The information you see when you look through many programs' Help files is also arranged as a series of hypertext documents.

Another type is the Anchor link, which looks just like a normal link but works slightly differently, taking visitors to a particular part of the same Web page instead of another page. Anchor links are particularly useful for helping visitors get around long Web pages. They are often used in long and detailed FAQs, the frequently asked question pages that you find on many Web sites.

● Exploring more links

When you gain more experience of using FrontPage, you can add other links to help make your Web pages more interactive. For example, you can add a mailto link that automatically starts up the visitor's email program so they can email you quickly and easily for feedback on your site, and you can also add links that allow people to download files from your Web site.

Site organization

Carefully planning at an early stage how the pages on your site link together could save you work later on.

TO MAKE the best of your presence on the Web, you should use several pages and add links to join them together with point-and-click connections. These links make your Web site efficient and easy for visitors to use.

Sites of just half a dozen or so pages are quite easy to organize in your head, but as your plans get more ambitious, it pays to do some preparation on paper first. If you don't plan well, you run the risk of creating a site that contains all the right information, but is very difficult for visitors to browse around.

Remember, if people can't find something of interest quickly, they're likely to move on to someone else's site. This is important for commercially orientated Web sites, but it also applies to personal-interest sites.

● Planning your Web site

Start by taking a sheet of paper and drawing a box in the centre to represent your home page. Now draw extra boxes, one each to represent the other pages you wish to add to your site. Starting with the home page, draw arrows between the boxes to indicate the links that will connect the pages together. As the pages and lines grow outward, the Web site's interlinking boxes start to resemble a spider's web, and you can see where the term 'Web' came from.

When all the connections have been made, try to look at the site from the visitors' point of view. First, they will see the home page, so ask yourself if it makes the content of the site perfectly clear. Are there too many intermediate pages before you reach the really interesting

ones? Can some closely related pages be combined into one? Is part of the site completely cut off from other parts, requiring visitors to back-track?

Some of these questions you'll be able to answer only after you have actually created the site. However, the idea of the exercise is to consider any potential problems first before going to the considerable effort of creating the Web pages themselves. While you can, if you want, start making your pages straight away without considering the links, remember that it's a lot easier to redraw a site on paper than it is to change dozens of Web pages once you've set them up.

Once you have added linked pages in FrontPage, you can see a graphical representation of these links in your Web by clicking on Hyperlinks in the Views bar. You can use this view to check that your links are as you planned.

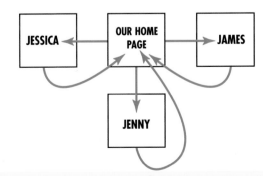

This is the plan for a very simple Web site, yet with just four pages there are already six links: three from the home page to each of the other pages, and three back.

Adding a link

You can set up hypertext links between the Web pages you create with FrontPage in seconds. Here's how to link pages on a family Web site.

1 Open FrontPage and create another page for your Web site. Use the formatting commands to style the text and the Insert menu to add pictures as before (see pages 80–81). Here, we've created a page for one of the family members.

2 Save this Web page, but do not close it. Give the page a descriptive title and then save it in the same folder as the index.htm home page you created on page 80. When you name the file, be careful not to use any spaces or special characters (see File names box, below).

3 To add a link from the index.htm page to the new page, you must edit the index.htm page. Open this file in FrontPage and move the flashing bar that indicates the text-insertion point to the position where you want this link to appear. Select Hyperlink from the Insert menu.

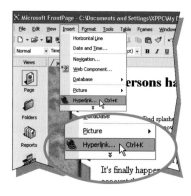

4 When the Insert Hyperlink dialog box appears, make sure the Current Folder is selected, click on the page you have just created and then type the text you want to use as your link in the Text to display box. Click on the OK button.

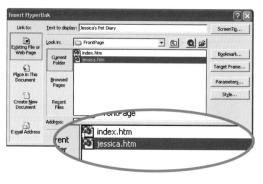

5 You can now see the hypertext link, underlined in blue, in the index.htm page. Notice that the link is a lot more user-friendly than a file name, because you can use spaces and special characters in a title.

Jessica's Pet Diary

FILE NAMES

Although titles can include spaces and special characters (see Steps 2 and 6), it's not a good idea to include either in the actual file name. Windows lets you use spaces and some special characters in file names but other Web server computers may not understand them. This can prevent links from working.

6 Now you can test this link. Save the changes and switch to the Preview Pane, then click on the link you have just created.

7 The Preview Pane now switches to the new page. You can use this technique to add links from your home page to other pages on your site.

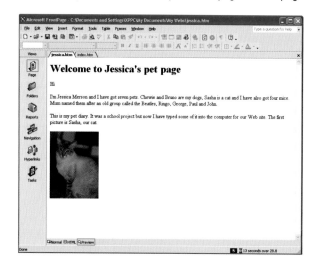

PC TIPS

Picture links

Most Web authors like to use picture links as well as the text links shown in Step 6. The process is the same, except that instead of moving the text-insertion point to where you want the link (see Step 3), just click on the picture. Once you have told FrontPage which Web page you wish to link to, it will make the picture a clickable link.

Adding an anchor

By using anchors you can make your links point to any part of a Web page, which is perfect for long Web pages.

1 Start by opening the Web page to which you want to add anchors. Usually this will be a page that is divided into several sections. In this case, a page is divided into types of photoposter. Anchor links will make it easy to move from one part of the page to the start of any other part.

2 Scroll down the document so that the text-insertion point is just in front of the first category. Select Bookmark on the Insert menu. Note that in FrontPage terminology, an anchor is called a bookmark.

Microsoft® FrontPage®

3 Type a name for this anchor into the Bookmark name box. Click on the OK button. FrontPage adds a tiny bookmark icon – underlined with a dotted line – at the position of the anchor. Don't worry – this won't be visible when the page is viewed with a Web browser. Repeat the process for all of the other anchors you want on the page, making sure to give each anchor a unique name.

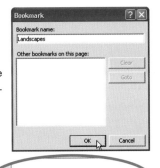

4 Once the anchors are in place, you need to add the links that will jump to them. At the end of the first section of the page, add a new line listing the categories for which you have added anchors. In this example, we've used a hyphen to separate each category of photograph so that it looks more like a list than a line of text.

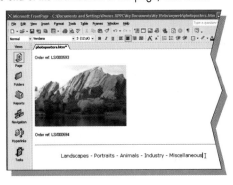

5 Highlight the first category in the line – the word 'Landscapes' – and click on the Hyperlink command on the Insert menu. In the Insert Hyperlink dialog box, ensure you select Place in This Document under Link to, then select the Landscapes anchor in the list of bookmarks before clicking on the OK button.

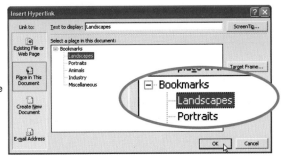

6 Once again, the hyperlink text is underlined in blue to indicate to your Web visitors that it is a link. Note that because you had first selected some text in the Web page (the word 'Landscapes'), it is this text that is hyperlinked instead of the title of the page.

Landscapes - Portraits -

7 Repeat the process for the other anchors in your Web page. To make your page as visitor-friendly as possible, use the Edit menu's Copy and Paste commands to repeat this line of hyperlinks after each section in the Web page.

Landscapes - Portraits - Animals - Indust

8 Now preview your Web page using the Preview Pane. You can test all your anchor links: each time you click on one, the Preview jumps to the invisible anchor.

PC TIPS

For long Web pages, it's worth adding a 'Back to the top of page' link at the bottom. A visitor who's browsed to the end of the page can return to the top with a single click – instead of having to use the scroll bars.

Formatting text

Just as formatting text in a word-processed letter helps to make its message clear, so formatting text on an Internet Web page makes information on your Web site easier to understand.

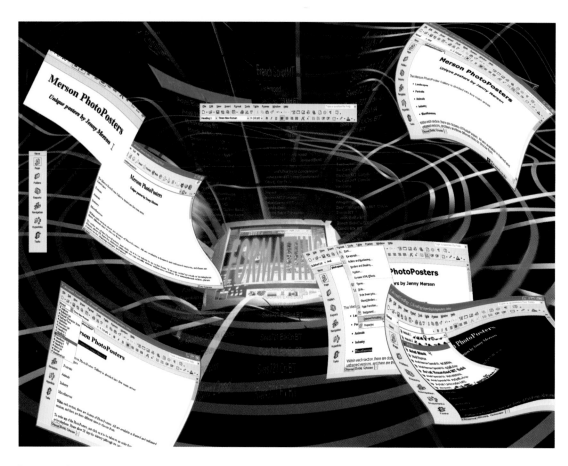

In the complex world of the Internet, your Web site will stand out if its words are clear and well laid out.

Thanks to FrontPage's 'what you see is what you get' (WYSIWYG) approach, if you can use a word processor then you can transfer the same skills to creating Web pages. Typing text and inserting pictures on a Web page, for example, use almost the same processes as Word. The same is true for formatting your text to make it clear and easy to read.

It helps that the FrontPage toolbars include buttons for many of the formatting options that can be found in a word processor. Open up FrontPage next to Microsoft Word on your screen and you'll see that some of the buttons are identical. Adding bold and italics, and making paragraphs of text line up on the left and right margins, are all easy. There are also buttons to add indents, make bullet lists and add colour to text (see page 90).

● Fonts and the Web

Despite the fact that some commands appear in both programs, there are differences in the way they work. The most important of these is the use of fonts.

Although you can use different fonts in your Web pages, just as you can in Word documents, you need to think through the effects. The pages that Web authors create with FrontPage will be displayed on hundreds of different computers: not just Windows PCs, but also Apple Macintosh machines or hand-held computers. The Web page creation and publishing process includes a tricky and easy-to-overlook problem. While the words and the formatting in your Web site will appear exactly as you see them in your Web browser, you cannot be sure that a visitor's computer has the same typefaces as yours. If

SHORT CUTS

FrontPage shares many of the quick and easy text formatting keyboard shortcut commands of other Windows programs. You can use [Ctrl]+[B] for bold; [Ctrl]+[I] for italics; and [Ctrl]+[U] for underline.

WHAT IT MEANS

SERIF AND SANS SERIF

Serif typefaces include tiny flourishes in the form of short lines at the end of, and at an angle to, the upper and lower strokes of a letter. The text in this box is in a serif typeface, called Sabon. Sans-serif typefaces – such as the bold text heading below – have no embellishments.

the typeface isn't present, and on some Web browsing devices such as Internet TV there are few fonts, another one will be substituted.

Sometimes these differences will be slight, with just a minor variation in line length for the main text on the page. But the more fonts you have used in your design, the more likely it is that the differences will make a fairly substantial alteration to the way the page looks. For instance, if you have used several typefaces to make different parts of your page visually distinct, any such distinctions may disappear altogether when viewed by a visitor.

● Popular typefaces

The safe option when choosing fonts is to stick to the handful of common typefaces. Mostly these fall into two categories: serif and sans serif. Good examples of these, which are

found on almost all PCs, are Times (serif) and Arial (sans serif). Verdana (also sans serif), was specifically designed for display on the Web and is therefore a good choice. Experienced Web designers often stick to these basic fonts because they can be assured of what people visiting their sites will see. Some experts even prefer to design Web sites without typeface commands so that they look fine for those few visitors who use old Web browsing programs that don't show multiple typefaces at all.

If you really must use an unusual font for a particular element of your design, such as a heading or logo, you could avoid the problem by creating a graphic of the text using a graphics program such as Paint Shop Pro. That way, you can ensure that no matter what fonts are available on visitors' computers, it will always appear as you intended.

Web page widths

It doesn't matter how narrow the FrontPage window is when creating your Web page because the visitor's Web browser controls the paragraph widths.

YOU MIGHT not notice it but there's one crucial difference between the FrontPage window and a word processor window: there is no ruler in FrontPage. This is because in a word processor you must ensure your text fits inside the printed page, while on a Web page an author cannot know how wide the page will be on visitors' screens.

A Web browser wraps text from one line to the next according to the width of the Web browser window. Open up one of your Web pages – or visit any Web site – and resize the window to make it narrower and then wider. You will see the text reflow, but the width of paragraphs almost always depends on the width of the Web browser window. If someone with a 21-inch monitor views a Web site that you've created on a 14-inch screen, what they see will look very different from your original creation. The most annoying problem is that they will see long lines of text that are actually quite hard to read from one line to the next.

You can estimate the effect that different widths of Web browser window will have on your Web page by changing the size

of the FrontPage window itself. If you are using a high resolution screen, for example, drag the right edge of the FrontPage window inwards to see how the text reflows. This will help you to spot potential problems, but it still can't solve them since the HTML that FrontPage produces is unaffected by dragging the window. Ideally, you should specify the precise width of your paragraphs.

Different Web browser window widths can make the same Web pages appear very different.

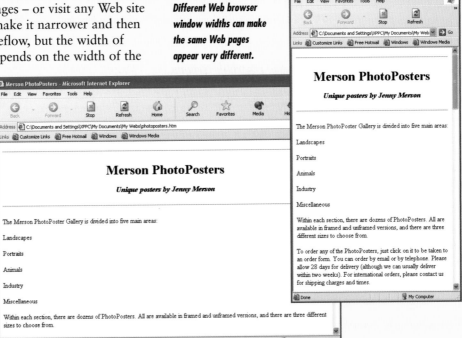

HTML heading styles

HTML includes a set of ready-made text styles. With a few clicks you can add several formatting effects at once to any text in your Web page.

1 Start FrontPage and open up one of your Web pages. In this example, we've opened an unformatted page that's looking a little too plain. While we could simply use the Formatting toolbar to change type size, emphasis and so on, using headings is quicker and maintains consistency.

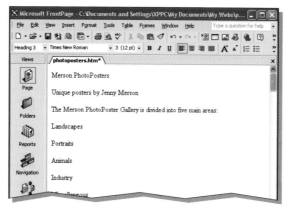

2 Start by selecting the major heading in the Web page. Now click on the arrow next to the Style box on the Formatting toolbar. FrontPage lists the ready-made set of related formats that are part of HTML. Click on the Heading 1 entry.

3 Your heading is now much bigger and in bold. Because this heading style is part of the HTML standard, you can be sure that the same effect will be visible to everyone using other Web browsers.

4 Now select a sub-heading and apply a different Heading from the Format menu. You might want to experiment with various headings until you get the right size and weight compared to other text sizes in your document (the smallest headings might even prove smaller than your main text).

Unique posters by Jenny Merson

5 You can also use some of the other text formatting commands in combination with the headings. Select the major heading and click on the Center button on the FrontPage Formatting toolbar. Note that while the Bold button has no effect – because the Heading styles already include bold emphasis – you can still add italics if you need them. We've done this for the sub-heading here.

Merson PhotoPosters

Unique posters by Jenny Merson

6 You can also use FrontPage's Font Color button (inset) to add suitable colours to your headings and sub-headings. Choose colours that give contrast against the background of the Web page, but don't make the colours too jarring, or the text will become difficult to read. If necessary, you can change the background (see Background colours box, below).

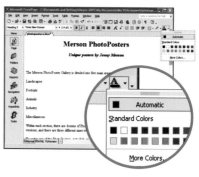

7 As usual, the real test is what the page looks like in a Web browser. Save your changes and then switch to the Preview Pane to see the effect.

PC TIPS

Background colours

For some lighter text colours, the default white page background makes text hard to read, but you can change it to a different colour. To do this, first click on the Background command in the Format menu. When the Page Properties dialog box appears, click on the drop-down box next to Background and choose a new colour. If you don't like any of the 16 colours named, select the More Colors option to see a wider choice and select the one you like.

Using fonts in your pages

A careful choice of fonts can help to make your Web page stand out from the rest while remaining easy to read.

1 Open up your Web page in FrontPage. In this example, we want to change the typeface used for most of the page from the default – Times New Roman – to something more modern. Start by selecting all the page contents: choose Select All from the Edit menu or press [Ctrl]+[A].

2 Now choose a different typeface from the Font list box. This lists all the fonts installed on your computer, but it's a good idea to avoid unusual and uncommon fonts (see pages 88–89). If you choose a font that's supplied with Windows, such as Arial, most Web visitors will have it.

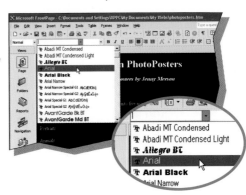

3 You can now see the effects of your font choice. Notice that the two headings keep the same emphasis settings that you selected when you chose Headings for them.

4 Just as with a word processor, choosing contrasting fonts for different parts of your Web page helps to make the page look more stylish – and, with careful font selection, easier to browse. We've changed the headings typeface to the Verdana font that's supplied with Windows. It's a modern sans serif typeface that has more impact than Arial.

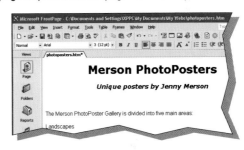

5 Changing the type size can also help to make the structure of your Web page easier to follow. Select the text and click on the Bold and the Increase Font Size and Decrease Font Size buttons to make these changes.

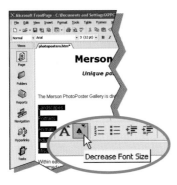

6 In this example, reducing the size of the five categories of poster and emboldening them has made the list stand out much better against the main part of the text.

7 To create even more impact, you can add bullet points to the list. Select the text and then click on the Bullets button found on the Formatting toolbar.

8 The bullets appear and the list is indented. These two effects really make the information stand out, and you can be sure that the combination of font sizes and formatting makes your page quick to understand and easy to follow for Web visitors.

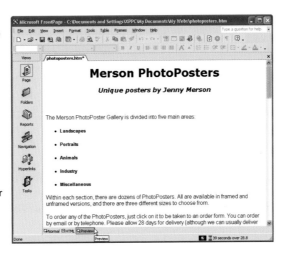

REMOVE FORMATS

If you find that you want to remove the formatting for some or all of your text, select the text you wish to alter and then click on the Remove Formatting command on the Format menu. This is particularly useful when you can't remember all of the text changes you have made; it instantly reverts to the default Times New Roman font. If you also want to remove the styles, select the text and choose Normal from the Style list box.

Backgrounds and colours

The Web would be a very dull place indeed if every site used the same colours and backgrounds. Employ the tricks and techniques of the Web design experts to make your site stand out from the crowd.

When you're planning your Web site, it's natural to spend a lot of time working out how to structure it, what text and graphics you're going to use, and how you're going to divide the site up into separate pages and then link them all together. However, it's also important to consider the look and feel of your Web site.

While there's nothing wrong with accepting FrontPage's default suggestions for colours of background, text and links, for example, it's likely that you can do better yourself. Moreover, there may be times when the default suggestions don't really suit your site. Unlike typefaces (see pages 88–91), where it is advisable to stick to the handful that can be found on almost all computers, colours and backgrounds are very diverse and offer almost unlimited choices.

● Planning ahead

If you want your site to stand out, it pays to spend some time considering the colour and background options open to you. By default, the Web pages that FrontPage creates are all black text on a white background. As we've already seen (see page 90), by choosing a different colour scheme, you can rapidly give your site a striking look.

It's also a quick and easy procedure to add a background picture or pattern to your Web pages (see page 81). FrontPage itself doesn't come with any sample background graphics, but there are thousands of royalty-free images

FrontPage provides you with a whole palette of colours to brighten up your Web pages and attract lots of visitors.

of all types available for free download from the Internet (see Stage 7, pages 140–143). You can drop these straight on to your page, or use a graphics program such as Corel PHOTO-PAINT (see Stage 3, pages 74–89) to edit them before using them in your Web pages.

● The importance of links

One area that needs special attention is the colour of the links on your Web pages. The standard approach is that when someone visits your Web site for the first time, text links appear in bright blue. If they click on the link to visit another page, then return to the original page, the link changes to a darker, bluish-purple colour. This allows people to see where they have been as they browse around an unfamiliar site.

Although it's a good idea to adopt the above practice, you don't have to keep to these particular colours. There might even be times when it's necessary to change it, for example, if you've chosen a background colour or picture that makes the blue and/or purple hard to read when viewed on the computer screen.

● Download issues

When adding this colourful polish to your Web site, you need to bear in mind the impact that your choices will have on the length of time it takes visitors to download your pages to their computers.

The good news is that the choice of colours for text, backgrounds and links makes absolutely no difference to download times. Each colour choice is stored as just six code characters (such as CCFF77, DE6A00 and so on) in the HTML that FrontPage generates, and since a 56K modem can download around 6000 characters per second, you'd have to make thousands of colour choices in a page to add more than a second or so to the download time.

Backgrounds require more thought, however. A background picture is just like every other picture you use in a Web page, in that it's a separate file that must be downloaded along with the Web page. Most background images used on the Web are about 2–10KB (the equivalent of around 2000–10,000 characters) and each one would add approximately a second or two to the download time. Pictures are also tiled on a Web page in much the same way that Windows tiles the Desktop background. This means that you should avoid patterns which have distracting, uneven joins – the ideal background is continuous and seamless.

COLOUR OR PICTURE?

If you choose a background picture for a Web page, it will overlay any background colour. The background colour will only be visible if visitors have turned off the display of images in their Web browser (which people with slow modems may do to speed up the download).

Colours and the Web

Find out how to extend the range of colours you can use on your pages with FrontPage.

WHEN YOU first start working with colours in FrontPage, you might be a little disappointed to find that there seems to be only a handful of colours available. These 16 colours, bearing names such as Fuchsia, Olive and Aqua, have been used since the earliest days of colour computing. When HTML was devised, these commonly available but rather basic colours were also specified.

In today's Web world, relying on just this limited palette of colours to make your Web site look good would be impossible. It doesn't help that the 16 colours themselves are either too dull or too bright and this means that text often looks garish against these backgrounds.

Fortunately, since the early days of HTML, extra facilities for specifying any of 16 million colours have become available for Web designers. Since most Web surfers now have computers that can display all these colours, it's well worth exploiting the full range when picking colours for your site. As this range is far wider than the human eye can distinguish, you are bound to find one that is suitable for your purposes.

Unfortunately, Microsoft's programmers still list only the 16 basic colours in FrontPage. If you want to use the full range, you must first specify the colour by using the More Colors entry at the bottom of the list. You can then choose from one of Windows' 134 colours, or select a completely different tone from the colour picker panel that appears when you click on the Custom button.

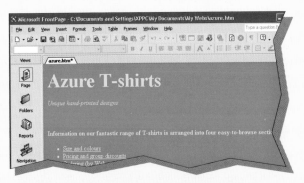

The set of 16 colours provided by FrontPage makes for dazzling, eye-watering colour combinations that aren't always visitor-friendly.

At first glance, FrontPage seems to offer just 16 colours for your text and background, but many others are available.

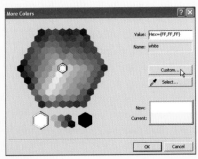

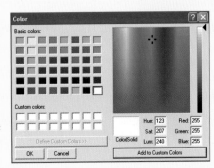

Once you have clicked on the More Colors option in the FrontPage list of colours, the More Colors dialog box appears. Click on the Custom button to display Windows' 48 colours and the colour picker panel. This allows you to create virtually any colour you want.

Customizing link colours

Here's how to change the default link colours of blue and purple so that they match or contrast with other colours on your site.

1 Here is a simple home page with links to several other pages. The links show up as blue in the FrontPage document window – the Web's default colour scheme. However, this can cause problems with certain Web page designs.

2 For example, try changing this Web page's background to a mid-blue. First, select Background from the Format menu. On the Background tab of the dialog box, there are several settings that let you select different colours for parts of your Web page. Click on the colour box next to the Background option to see the available colours. Although FrontPage lists only a handful of basic colours, many are too garish, so select the More Colors option.

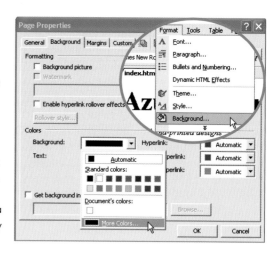

3 In the More Colors dialog box, click on the Custom button. At the right of the Color dialog box is a smoothly shaded spectrum of colours. Click the mouse in this box to choose your colour and then click on the Add to Custom Colors button. It then appears as a coloured rectangle in the Custom colors section at the bottom left of the dialog box. Select this rectangle and click on OK and then on OK in the More Colors dialog box.

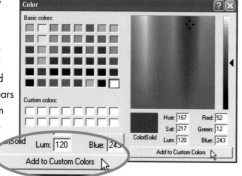

4 This colour looks great, but the text links have disappeared. The blue background is too close in colour to the default blue of the links.

5 To fix this problem, select Background from the Format menu once again. The Background tab of the dialog box also has settings for the text link colours. Change both the Hyperlink and Visited Hyperlink options, choosing two colours that are easy to tell apart and that contrast well with the blue Web page background. Click on OK when you've finished.

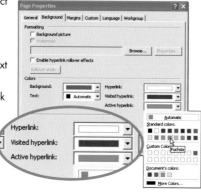

6 Save your Web page and open it up in your Web browser. When the page first loads, all the links will appear in the colour you chose for the Hyperlink setting – white in this case. Click on one of the links to visit another page.

7 Immediately click on the Back button on your browser to return to the previous page. Now you can see how well the colour you chose for the Visited Hyperlink works against the background, and check that the difference between the two link colours is easy for Web visitors to tell apart.

PC TIPS

Clearing browser history

Web browsers store a list of pages they have opened previously, so to check your Web pages properly (with 'unvisited' link colours) before uploading them, you need to use the browser command that clears the history of links you have visited. Look under your browser's Internet Options or Preferences command.

Customizing backgrounds

With thousands of background images available free on the Internet, there's plenty of material to help you design your Web pages. Images can also be edited in a graphics program.

1 Open a page in FrontPage. Here we've decided to change the solid blue background added in the exercise on page 94 to a more textured background. Choose Background from the Format menu.

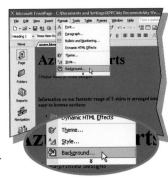

2 Under the Background tab of the Page Properties dialog box that appears, tick the Background picture box and click on the Browse button. When the Select Background Picture dialog box appears, locate and select an image. Click on the Open button and then on OK in the Page Properties dialog box.

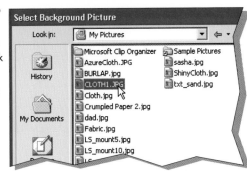

3 Your Web page background is now tiled with the image you chose. In this case, the effect of the creased cloth looks fine, but the page looks grey and rather lifeless.

4 To fix this, you can change the colour with a graphics program. We've used Corel PHOTOPAINT, but most image editing programs will be suitable. Use the program's colour adjustment commands to achieve a better result. Here, by increasing the amount of blue and decreasing the amount of red and green in the grey tile, the colour has completely changed.

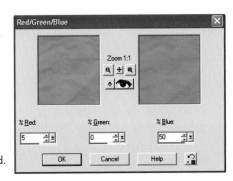

5 Once you have created an image with a more attractive colour, save the image, making sure to give it a different name. That way you can still use the original picture at a later date without having to undo your changes.

6 Now you need to choose your revised background image. Bring up the Select Background Picture dialog box again (see Steps 1–2), and locate and select your new graphic.

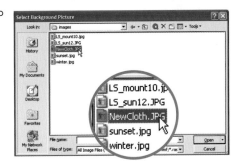

7 You can now see the effect of the change. The Web page looks a lot more appealing than it would with either a plain white background or a dull textured one. By using the colour controls in a graphics program, you can add to the number of background images available for use in your Web pages.

PC TIPS

Non-printing backgrounds

The printing of Web pages is often an overlooked part of the Web design process. Although Web authors may ignore it, they do so at their peril as many Web site visitors print out pages for reading offline. Although Web page backgrounds are great for setting the tone of your Web site, on many Web browsers, the background images themselves don't print out. Even those with Web browsers that can print background colours and images – such as Internet Explorer v6 – will see a blank background unless the Web visitor has made a point of turning on the ability to print backgrounds. Always do a text print-out of pages to make sure that the absence of the background doesn't adversely affect them.

Hardware

Exploring virtual reality

Virtual reality (VR) is much talked about as a way to escape into a world of fantasy and indulge your wildest dreams. So what can virtual reality offer for the home computer user?

Virtual reality (VR) captures the imagination in a way few other computer applications have before. Being able to wander around a make-believe world, encountering realistic objects and feeling as though you are manipulating them with your own hands, makes the world of 3D far more accessible and more fun than any other form of computer activity.

WHAT IT MEANS

HMD

This stands for Head Mounted Display – the technical name for a virtual reality helmet. These helmets track your responses as you view a computer-generated virtual world through tiny monitors encased in the front of the helmet. The shape of Head Mounted Displays varies from product to product, but they usually look like a cross between a bicycle helmet and an over-sized pair of sunglasses.

● A whole new world

The best definition of virtual reality is that it's an artificial world, created with computer hardware and software, presented to the user in such a way that it appears and feels like a real environment. For the past few years, the first thing that came to mind when VR was mentioned was the virtual reality helmet (or HMD, as the technology is also known). This is still the most familiar face of virtual reality, but there is now hardware available that can be connected to a home PC.

Although the hardware and software that give the best virtual reality experience still remain within the confines of military development, the technology is moving into the mainstream. High-street games arcades already feature virtual reality headsets and specially written 3D games. While they can be expensive, virtual reality hardware and software are becoming more readily available to home computer users. PC add-ons,

The virtual reality helmet – a headset equipped with motion sensors, stereo display screens and speakers – is the classic representation of VR. In fact, there is much more to the technology than just this.

such as joysticks that push back against your hand movements and lightweight helmets that reveal a convincing 3D world, are now much more affordable.

Over the next few years, the advances in this hardware and its associated software is going to make it possible for home computer users to enter virtual worlds that will astonish users with the vividness and intensity of their simulation.

● Game software experience

Even if you don't have access to VR hardware, you can still sample the experience on your existing PC by playing a state-of-the-art computer game, such as *Unreal Tournament 2003*. In a game such as this, the amazing 3D graphics really do give the illusion of entering and participating in a virtual world. In another field, Internet-based worlds called MUDs (multi-user dungeons) give a different kind of virtual experience that's less action-oriented, where your strategy builds upon the convincing 3D computer graphics.

● Greater involvement

But even the best of these games is still quite a long way from true VR. Looking at your monitor and hearing sound through your PC's speakers involves only two senses – sight and sound – so this gives something of an incomplete experience. The sights and sounds of the real world outside can also be a distraction.

Special hardware has therefore been developed which fulfills the need for a more complete sensory involvement with the artificial environment of VR. There have been some experiments with the sense of smell, but this and the sense of taste have been largely ignored by the VR pioneers. Instead, technologists have concentrated not

only on making the simulations of sight and sound more realistic but also on adding the sense of touch to the experience. VR hardware mostly aims to improve the 3D visual effect and add an element of touch that far surpasses what can be achieved via the mouse and keyboard.

The items described here are usually dedicated to stimulating one particular sense as vividly as possible. Although some of this equipment is currently so expensive as to be beyond the reach of the home user, it's almost certain that prices will steadily fall. After all, it was only 20 years ago that a computer with the power of today's average home PC would have cost many years' salary and therefore been out of reach of most ordinary people.

● Home computers and VR

Until very recently, most virtual reality helmets have been far too expensive for home computer users. Those that have been more reasonably priced (although still costing a few hundred pounds) have tended to be of such poor quality as to be ineffective. But recent advances in miniaturization have started to make it possible for some affordable, high-resolution headsets to become available.

VR technology is bound to become more important in the near future. But an HMD isn't the only hardware that is available for your virtual excursions, and here we shall be taking a look at other current equipment, from affordable games controllers to sophisticated tools.

● Force feedback devices

Starting with the most basic, force feedback devices, such as the Microsoft *SideWinder Force*

Virtual reality accessories, such as the VR helmet, help to enhance the feeling of actually being part of the game that you're playing. Such technology, which was once extremely expensive, is now rapidly coming within the price range of the average home computer user.

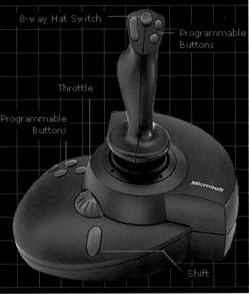

The force feedback joystick (above) is the affordable face of virtual reality. When playing games such as the MechWarrior series (top), this will provide tactile feedback based on your actions.

Feedback 2, are down-to-earth and affordable inventions (at around £60). This technology is becoming ever more popular as a component in ordinary joysticks and other games input devices, such as steering wheels and throttle controls.

All force feedback devices work via hardware and software standards established by Microsoft. Their exact function varies from product to

WHERE TO GET VR HARDWARE

Force feedback joysticks and simple VR devices can be bought from computer stores, but most other VR equipment can be rather tricky to find, especially anything other than the cheapest HMDs. Cybermind UK Ltd specializes in such objects and can be contacted on 01509 643 407 or via their Web site at www.cyberminduk.com/.

product, but basically they allow you to interact with the controller (such as the throttle) to provide a realistic experience of what's going on in the game or VR world you are in. For example, if you are playing a racing game and drive the car over some gravel, the controller might start vibrating to simulate a bumpy ride. Then, if the car gets damaged and you try to perform a change of direction, it might offer some resistance to your movement. This makes the game-playing experience a lot more realistic, and support for force feedback is now being added to an increasing number of games titles.

Cybermind's top-of-the-range hi-Res 900 model costs £3695 and includes a motion tracker. VR helmets such as this are light and don't restrict the user's movements. Heavy helmets tend both to hinder your enjoyment and to disorient you, leading to feelings of dizziness.

● HMD – the options

An HMD is the core component of any virtual reality hardware setup and most designs are already in regular use in industry and the military. However, making an affordable home version has been difficult, as cutting corners usually results in a less than satisfactory virtual device. Perhaps the most successful home HMD is Cybermind's hi-Res series. Sadly, such systems are still extremely expensive: the basic hi-Res 900 model costs £1790. This headset runs along the same principles as most other HMD devices. It fits around your head so that it completely covers your eyes, and inside it are two small monitors, one for each eye, and speakers for stereo sound. What makes the experience interactive is the HMD's motion-tracking device. This works by monitoring your head movements, so that when you look up, for example, the headset calculates the degree of movement to ensure that

your view in the 'virtual world' will move up by exactly the same amount. The result is that you are able to move your head quite naturally and to use these normal responses as a way to navigate the virtual world. Wearing the headset for too long can lead to disorientation, but the monitors are specially designed to prevent eye strain and dizziness.

● System compatibility

Futuristic hardware isn't much use, however, if you do not have the software needed to run it properly. Owing to the current expense of the hardware and the lack of a clear market leader, most of the Multimedia software companies don't, in fact, offer support for any type of true VR hardware.

However, Cybermind has ensured that its particular make of headset doesn't need any extra patches or software at all. By simply selecting the mouse option within an existing game, the Cybermind headset will interpret the movement of your head in exactly the same way that the PC will interpret a movement of the mouse in a normal game.

● Software simulations

This method of hardware support is called 'dumb', because it doesn't know whether the movements it is conveying actually mean anything useful. As a result, it doesn't make

much sense for you to buy a headset for use with a strategy game, where the purpose of the mouse is only to move a cursor.

However, for action games that you play with a first-person view, the simulation works extremely well. A good example is the *Quake* series of first-person perspective battle-style games. In *Quake* you already view the action as if from the eyes of the lead character, so adding a VR headset makes very little difference to the gameplay but it does immerse you thoroughly in the action. Expect to see this type of VR-style involvement in more PC games in the near future.

● Virtual reality gloves

The second most common piece of VR equipment is the glove. But for the average home computer user, its extremely high price (thousands of pounds) is likely to ensure that it remains of academic interest only for some time to come.

Worn on the writing hand, a VR glove is dotted with motion sensors on each of the fingers and around the wrist. These sensors measure the position and movement of your hand and relay information about these

ADDING VR HARDWARE

Installing VR hardware devices on your computer isn't as hard as you might think. Cybermind's headset, for example, simply plugs straight into the monitor and joystick ports, with no further hardware connections necessary. Other VR hardware might appear to be more complicated, but the installation is still via a simple plug-in connection at the back of the PC.

measurements to your computer. This information is then used to create a virtual hand in the 3D world.

The virtual hand is usually displayed on screen, and you interact with it in much the same way as the headset, as it relays movements from the real world to the virtual scene and allows you to pick up 3D objects as if they were real. This piece of

Feel your way around the world of virtual reality with Immersion Corp's CyberGlove, shown above.

hardware isn't as central to the VR experience as the helmet, but it does go a long way towards helping to create a convincing and interactive virtual world.

● 3D manipulators

A VR glove might be extremely good at giving you a chance to manipulate virtual objects, but neither this nor the HMD are particularly useful as navigational devices. Although they can provide an incredibly realistic visual and sensory experience, you are still limited to the traditional keyboard or joystick as a means of

moving around (although a VR glove can often be used like a mouse, enabling you to point at a spot and then press an internal button to move).

A 3D manipulator, however, is a more affordable device, and one that gives you a much more intuitive method of navigating in three dimensions. The most simple are usually the cheapest and such devices look like joysticks without a base – you simply tilt them to move in the required direction. More sophisticated manipulators are shaped like balls and can be held in your hand. The ball allows for movement in any direction. A number of buttons around the handle of the device give you access to specific features, such as zooming or shifting your viewpoint. Devices like this cost hundreds of pounds, but look set to become much cheaper in the future.

● Touch-simulation interfaces

For the virtual reality fan who wants everything, a haptic interface is a must. These devices are hugely expensive, but they do enable the ultimate experience in simulation of the sense of touch.

The easiest way to describe how a haptic device works is to imagine inserting each of your fingers into a thimble and using these as a way of

The SpaceBall 5000 from 3Dconnexion (www.3dconnexion.com) is one of several hi-tech controllers currently available to help you navigate your way through the world of virtual reality.

interacting with the computer and 3D world. The 'thimbles' contain tiny pressure points that simulate the texture of the virtual object that you are 'touching' by moving against the skin on your fingers. The more expensive systems, which can cost several thousands of pounds, work with all five fingers and measure the position and rotation of your hand, combining the capabilities of the VR glove with the haptic interface, to create a realistic sensation when you touch virtual items.

Although these high-end virtual reality add-ons are too expensive for most home computer users, the companies that develop them are slowly bringing prices down. Before long, you may be able to actually feel folders and files as you move them around a virtual 3D desktop.

CHEAP VR ON A CONSOLE

A cheap alternative to VR on your computer is a home games console, such as the Dreamcast or Sony PlayStation. These are specifically created for playing games and for featuring state-of-the-art graphics. Although when first released they tended to beat the PC on graphics power, they can't be upgraded and so will not be able to keep up as new technology appears for your home computer.

At present, they are still widely used and titles such as *Enter the Matrix* and *Gran Turismo* are some of the best examples of current 3D graphics and gameplay. Most of these consoles include basic force feedback controllers, which tremble in your hand as you fire a shot or drive over rough terrain.

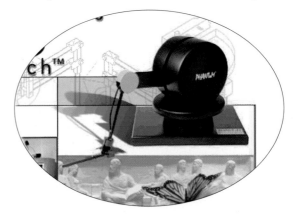

The bizarre device shown above is a haptic interface. It's designed to recreate the texture and feel of an object appearing on your computer screen or in a VR environment.

Seeing your PC on TV

A large percentage of the purchase price of your computer is taken up by the monitor. But there is an alternative to paying for a PC screen, provided you have a TV.

Y ou might have wondered why it is that you pay a hefty sum for a standard-sized PC monitor – and much more for anything larger – when you've probably got a perfectly good TV screen taking pride of place in your sitting room. This is an important point, especially as it's generally the monitor that takes up so much desktop space and makes the computer a relatively fixed item. Your desktop system unit is probably quite portable and not at all hard to move from one room to another, but the surprisingly heavy monitor makes moving it around a chore.

● PC to TV

You'll be pleased to know that numerous firms now offer a solution in the shape of devices that allow you to display your PC image on a television screen, and this practice is likely to become more common. To do this, you can add a VGA-to-TV adaptor, which converts the signal from your PC into one that can be displayed by your TV. Some of these devices are designed specifically for

laptops and are marketed as business presentation devices, allowing you to plug a laptop into an on-site television and play presentations on it. These plug into a PC Card (also known as PCMCIA) slot in the laptop, but others are suited for home use with a full-size desktop PC.

● PC displays on TV

The RealVision Technology uTV-2000 is a personal-stereo sized device that plugs into your PC's USB port and lets you view PC screens at resolutions from 640x480 to 1600x1200 pixels. Thanks to USB's plug-and-play feature, connection is easier than with alternative devices, where you need to unplug the monitor from the PC to plug a cable into the graphics card output. There is also a PCMCIA version that you can use with notebook PCs that lack USB ports.

It can be very useful to be able to output your computer signal to a large television screen for serious business presentations, or just for fun.

CAPTURE CARDS

A small number of PCs may already be able to display their monitor image on a TV. This is more likely if you have added a video capture card to your PC. Some of these cards come with video out connectors – check the documentation that came with your PC or video capture card for details. Consult the manual or user guide for your TV, too. Many mid-range and high-end TVs come with sockets for extra audio-video sources. Depending on your model of TV, you may find that you can connect the card directly to your TV with a pair of phono-to-phono cables. You can buy these for under £10 from an electronics shop.

TV SCREEN VERSUS PC MONITOR

Although these two devices are based on the same cathode-ray tube technology and look similar, the computer monitor has a far higher specification than the average television. It's designed primarily for close-up viewing, such as writing letters and editing photos. In these situations, you need to see a lot of fine detail and high contrast between black text and the white page. You also need a very steady display that is kind to your eyes – you're sitting so close to the screen that any minute image fluctuations can cause fatigue and headaches.

In contrast, the TV screen and its image are designed to be viewed from several feet away. It also displays moving images. This combination of factors is less demanding for the manufacturers and the TV designers can make compromises that provide bigger screens at lower costs. In particular, the fact that you sit so far away means that any minor image fluctuations are far less noticeable than on a computer monitor.

For these reasons, when you display certain computer images on a TV screen – a static image of word processor text, for example – fine detail may appear blurred and more difficult to read than on your monitor. However, where VGA-to-TV adaptors really come into their own is in the field of DVD movies and games. Both have constant movement and there's no need to read detailed information, so the compromises don't affect the image quality.

Within a few minutes of plugging the USB cable into the PC and connecting the uTV-2000's video output to your TV's video output, you can be watching DVD movies on your TV or enjoying an action game on your wide-screen TV. It also comes with a credit-card sized remote control that lets you position the Windows Desktop on the TV screen and then adjust the colour and brightness settings. You can even zoom in on different areas of the screen.

● No wires
To avoid trailing wires around your home, you can combine a VGA-to-TV adaptor with a wireless system using a device such as the Wireless pc2TV from US company AITech (www.aitech.com). The AITech Wireless pc2TV provides a wireless connection between the VGA-to-TV adaptor and the TV. It can even relay the signal up to 60m through walls, depending on their density, so you can operate the PC in one room, while other people are watching the picture on a television in another.

You can also monitor the computer picture from the other room – this can be handy if you want to control what your children are viewing on the computer, for example. You can even buy additional receivers that will enable you to relay your PC signal to several televisions at the same time. There are other manufacturers who produce similar devices that work in the home on a wireless basis – most are sold through high-street electronics shops.

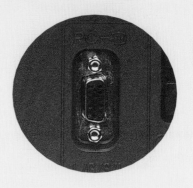
● Getting a good picture
There are drawbacks to using a TV as a monitor, of course. Regardless of the manufacturers' claims, be aware that you won't get as good a picture on a TV as on a PC monitor (see TV screen versus PC monitor box, above), although it can still be impressive and, of course, bigger. The picture will certainly be much better and a lot cheaper than the technology of a few years ago.

On the positive side, such devices will allow you to video your PC output, which could be handy for business presentations. If your PC has a DVD drive (see Stage 4, pages 100–101), you can also watch DVD movies on your TV, without having to buy a separate DVD player.

The uTV-2000 system allows simple connection of your PC to any size or type of television.

Adding a TV tuner

If you plug a TV tuner into your PC, you can view your favourite television programmes on your computer instead of on your TV.

Installing a TV tuner (either as a card or as a USB peripheral) enables you to watch TV on your PC. Depending on the device you buy, you can also access TV text services, such as Teletext, and radio as well. They can all be controlled by on-screen software.

While many extra computer devices can be added without opening up the computer, some useful add-ons need to be fitted inside the case. Adding extra memory is usually the reason why most computer users open the casing on their computers (see Stage 3, pages 94–95) but fitting a TV tuner card can be another reason for doing this. If you've never opened up your PC before, it's best to opt for a USB model like the one shown opposite.

● How expansion cards work

Expansion cards, such as the TV tuner card, have a connector which fits into a slot on the computer's motherboard. Once fitted and set up correctly, the expansion card works as

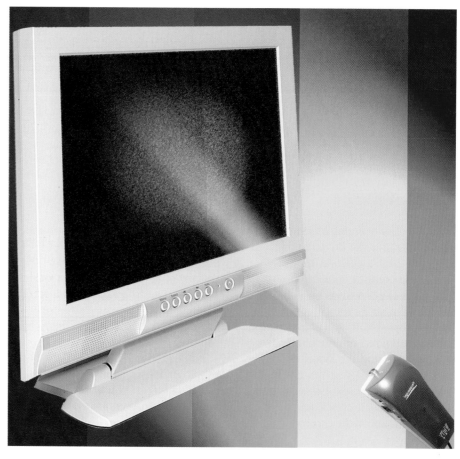

The easiest way to add a TV tuner to your PC is to buy a model that connects to one of your PC's USB sockets – it can be ready in the time it takes for a commercial break.

if it were a part of the motherboard, sending signals to and fro. With a TV tuner card, these signals include the television picture in digital form.

● Fitting an expansion card

When fitting an expansion card, you first have to ensure that your PC has a slot that can accept it. There are two

types of slot in a modern PC: Peripheral Component Interconnect (PCI) and Accelerated Graphics Port (AGP). PCI slots are general-purpose slots designed to accommodate most types of add-ons, from modems to network cards. An AGP slot is a special form of PCI slot intended for the fastest 3D graphics cards.

A typical PC has between three and five PCI slots and one AGP slot. The AGP slot is almost always occupied with the PC's graphics card, but you should find that some PCI slots are vacant. However, it pays to check that there's an empty PCI slot before buying a PCI TV tuner. Consult your PC's manual for information on its expansion slots.

TV TUNER OPTIONS

When choosing an add-on for watching TV on your PC, you have several options. The lowest-cost option is a simple TV tuner card, such as Pinnacle's PCTV, which takes the form of an expansion card that plugs into the PC's internal PCI bus (see Stage 6, pages 104–105). These cards can cost as little as £30 and even the most basic allows you to record TV programmes to your PC's hard disk to watch later.

USB models, like the Hauppauge WinTV USB shown opposite, are far easier to install, but work in much the same way. Basic models concentrate on providing TV tuner and recorder features, but others add extras. For example, the Hauppauge WinTV Nova-t (around £100) receives and displays free-to-air digital terrestrial channels. Visit www.hauppauge.co.uk and www.pinnaclesys.com for details.

Installing a TV tuner

It is quick and easy to add TV watching to your PC's repertoire if you opt for a TV tuner that connects via USB. We've chosen the Hauppauge WinTV USB model, but the process is almost identical for other makes and models.

1 Switch your PC on and make sure all programs are closed. Then plug the WinTV USB's USB plug into an empty USB socket on your PC.

2 Windows XP detects the hardware and pops up a dialog box. Click on the Next button and follow the on-screen instruction to start installing the TV tuner's driver software from the supplied CD-ROM.

3 When the process of copying files to your PC's hard disk is complete, the final installation page appears. Click on the Finish button and Windows will confirm that the hardware is now installed in a small bubble at the bottom right of the screen.

4 Next, you must install the program that actually tunes into the TV signal and displays the image on your PC. With some TV tuners, this may start automatically. It's best to accept the default options and click on the Install button to install the software. Click on the Finish button when the process is complete.

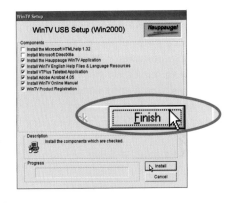

5 Connect the TV aerial to the input of the TV tuner. Some models may have different connectors to suit cable or digital satellite set-top boxes. Follow the manual's instructions on which socket to use.

6 Now you can start the software, either by selecting it from the Start menu or double-clicking on its Desktop icon. The first time this TV tuner software starts, it asks whether you want to scan the TV signal for channels. Click on the Yes button.

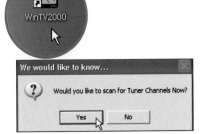

7 The software now communicates with the TV tuner to tune into all of the TV channels being picked up by your aerial. Each is listed in the Channel Configuration dialog box. Click on the OK button when the Scanning process is complete.

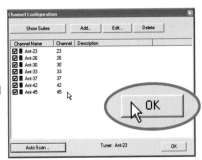

8 The TV software shows the first TV channel in your list, and the soundtrack plays through your PC speakers. The controls on the left let you switch from channel to channel, adjust colour and sound, and also let you alter the size of the TV viewing panel.

Adding a second hard disk drive

Although upgrading the hard disk is a complicated process best left to the experts, a grasp of the factors involved will help you buy the right hard disk and understand the changes to Windows that follow.

If your computer has been bought in the past six months or so, it's likely to have a large hard disk – anywhere between 20 and 60 Gigabytes (GB). That's more than 4000 times as much as the first business PCs sold in the early 1980s!

With each new software program you install and with each new document you create, you fill up the available space. For older PCs, with hard disks of 5GB or less, space might already be tight, but the problem can affect every computer user eventually. Even a 20GB hard disk will eventually fill up as software becomes more advanced and consumes ever-increasing amounts of hard disk space.

● Solving the space problem
Although Windows XP has a disk compression feature, it slows the PC down and rarely yields much extra space, so a better solution is to add more hard disk space.

Hard disks are relatively inexpensive. You can either replace your existing hard disk or add a second one. As replacing the existing disk involves

Adding a hard disk is a complicated job and therefore one that is best left to your local computer store.

reinstalling every program, folder and file from the old hard disk to the new one, most people leave the original in place and simply add another.

However, there are complicating factors. Some new add-ons are easier to install than others. There's no denying the fact that adding a second

hard disk is one of the most difficult hardware upgrades you can make. While adding a TV tuner (see pages 104–105) is easy, even for a PC novice, adding a second hard disk is not to be undertaken lightly.

To start with, it's important to choose the right type of hard disk to work alongside your existing one. Most home computers use a hard disk standard called EIDE (or sometimes Ultra ATA). Buying a second EIDE hard disk means that you won't require any extra hardware to add it to your existing PC. The alternative, called SCSI, is only popular on high-end business computers and needs a special card to work with most PCs.

Although you can mix the two hard disk types inside a single computer, you may find that an extra controller

Choosing a new hard disk

WHEN IT comes to size, larger hard drives tend to be much better value. Always buy a reliable brand of hard disk and get as much capacity as you can afford.

Spin speed indicates how fast the hard disk rotates – usually 5400–15,000rpm. The higher the figure the better, since a high spin speed means that data can be read from and written to the disk surface faster, giving better performance.

Seek and access times refer to how quickly the read/write head in the hard disk can locate data on the disk's surface. Typical figures are 5–10 milliseconds (thousandths of a second). The lower this figure is, the faster the time.

Throughput measures the maximum rate at which data can be transferred from the hard disk surface in a second. A rate of 100MB per second is typical.

card is required. It is much easier to choose the same type of hard disk as the one you already have.

● Physical considerations

Adding a hard disk is also a physically complicated procedure. Unlike the TV tuner card, it doesn't simply slip into an empty expansion slot. There are two cables that need connecting inside the computer. Once that's done, the technical issues are more involved, too. To prepare a hard disk for use, you will need to use the PC's BIOS screens (normally hidden) to tell the PC how to access the hard disk and there are no wizards to help you. The utilities involve wiping all computer data from the new hard disk. This introduces a risk of accidentally deleting the information stored on your original hard disk.

● To DIY or not to DIY

For these reasons, most home computer users should seriously consider finding a professional to do the job. Due to the large number of variables involved, it's not possible to create a step-by-step guide that works for all computers. The guide below provides pointers, rather than explicit instructions for installing a second hard disk. All but the most advanced users should seek expert help. The best option is to buy the second hard disk locally. If possible, check the model you intend to purchase in operation, as the fastest hard disk drives can be quite noisy for home use. Then get your local computer shop to install the new disk.

Technical issues when adding a hard disk

Adding a second hard disk to a computer is a multi-stage process. The following guide is intended to give you an insight into the complex process that your computer shop will go through to complete it successfully.

Checking inside the PC:
1 Shut down your PC, switch off the power supply at the mains socket and open up the case.
2 Is there a spare bay for the drive to fit into? Is it the right size for your hard disk? Most hard disks fit 3.5in drive bays.
3 Is there a spare connector on the EIDE cable that connects to the motherboard? If so, does it reach to the drive bay where the new hard disk will go?
4 Is there a spare power supply lead for the new hard disk?

Fitting and connecting the new drive:
1 Check the drive documentation for any necessary special adjustments to the drive before fitting.
2 Check the EIDE socket on the new hard disk to find which end has the number 1 pin.
3 Fit the hard disk, fixing it into place with the screws supplied.
4 Connect the EIDE cable to the hard disk, making sure that the side of the cable closest to the number 1 pin also leads to the number 1 pin on the EIDE socket on the motherboard.
5 Connect the power supply lead to the new drive.

After the new drive is fitted in place:
1 Start up the PC and listen for any beeps which indicate that the drive is incorrectly installed.
2 If the PC doesn't start correctly, recheck all the previous steps.

If the original hard disk starts correctly:
1 Go into your computer's BIOS setup screen (your computer manual will tell you how).
2 Find the part of the BIOS setup screen that handles hard disks. The first disk covers your original hard disk; to add the new disk, use the Auto-detect command on the second disk.
3 Save these changes and exit the BIOS setup screen. Your PC will restart.

After Windows has started:
1 Windows detects the new hard disk and a small bubble panel appears at the bottom right of the Desktop.

2 Open the My Computer window. You will see a new hard disk icon, labelled D:, next to the C: drive.
3 Spend some time getting used to this new assignment of drive letters to minimize the risk of misplacing files and programs.

Note: You may find that some CD-ROM software installed before you added the second hard disk (i.e. when the CD-ROM was assigned the drive letter D:) may no longer work. This is because the CD-ROM drive is now assigned the letter E. Windows can easily lose track of such software. If this happens, you will probably need to reinstall the software.

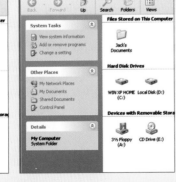

After a second hard drive has been added (right), your My Computer window will have an extra icon and the CD-ROM drive will also have a different name.

Uninterruptible power supplies

The electricity supply to your house does sometimes fail, so an uninterruptible power supply for your PC protects it from loss of data in the event of an emergency.

Y ou're calmly working away at your PC, putting the finishing touches to that long, complicated and vital business presentation in Microsoft Word. You've got the final version of your Excel figures open with quite a few substantial additions. In the background, you've nearly finished a 45-minute download of the graphics you need to create the final impressive effect. And you haven't yet saved any of this afternoon's intensive work. Then there's a power cut, your PC crashes and all your hard work is lost. There's nothing for it but to shout, shrug it off and then work through the night trying to repeat everything you did in the day. This is, of course, a worst-case scenario, but it could – and does – happen.

● Be prepared for the worst

If you had an uninterruptible power supply (UPS), a power cut wouldn't matter at all; the UPS would keep your PC going long enough for you to save to disk all your valuable data in RAM. Basically, a UPS is simply a power supply with a battery that runs your PC for a short time in the event of any problem with the mains power supply. There are several varieties of UPS suited to different potential problems and levels of security and, naturally, they vary in price.

● Types of UPS

There are two main types of UPS: simple devices designed to protect a single PC and the more sophisticated boxes which can cope with major crises in large PC installations.

An off-line, or stand-by, UPS is the simplest, offering protection for a single PC. The device contains a

Home computers can cope with ordinary domestic power fluctuations but not a total failure, or surges caused by lightning. That's when a UPS comes into its own.

battery and power-conversion circuit, together with a switch that detects power cuts. When the off-line UPS senses that the mains power supply is low enough to be considered a power cut, it supplies the PC's power from the UPS's battery-powered 'inverter' instead. This gives you the time to save any data in RAM and to power down the PC in the correct, and safe, manner.

Off-line UPSs are cheap, with prices starting at £50 or so, use little power and don't take up much desk space. But switching to battery power when a voltage problem is detected can take several milliseconds, during which time your PC is not receiving any power. It's still possible that this brief

UPS SUPPLIERS

It's not all that easy to find an uninterruptible power supply (UPS) in the average high street shop, although specialist computer stores should stock some. A good place to browse is in the catalogues of PC peripheral suppliers, such as Misco (www.misco.co.uk) and Inmac (www.inmac.co.uk). For more information on power supply problems, you can also visit UPS manufacturer sites, such as www.apc.com.

interruption could damage the PC or endanger data that has not been saved. So where absolute security is required, an off-line UPS is definitely not recommended.

The line-interactive UPS is an enhanced variant of the off-line UPS. In this case, the UPS has a battery and inverter that come into action immediately a power cut is sensed.

Online UPS

For the highest level of protection, you need an online UPS. As the name suggests, this type of UPS is in constant operation – even when the mains supply is functioning normally – and the battery charger, battery and inverter are always online. The AC mains supply is converted to DC and then back to AC again before it reaches the computer. This means that any disturbance in the power supply – caused, for instance, by the operation of large machinery or even a stroke of lightning – is ironed out before it reaches the computer.

Because an online UPS is constantly in use, it guarantees the supply of 'clean power'. For this kind of peace of mind you pay more; online UPSs start at around £80–£100, and the price increases with the number of computers you need to protect. UPS protection for a network of, say, 10 PCs could cost in excess of £1000.

Power problems and your PC

If you've never experienced a major power cut while working on your computer, you may wonder why

Liebert's Powersure Line Interactive is geared towards supporting groups of PCs. Sealed, maintenance-free batteries are a feature of the models in this range.

anyone would need a UPS at all. The answer is that even if power cuts are rare (at least, in the developed world), the mains power supply can be unstable enough to pose a threat to your PC. There are many ways in which the power supply can damage your PC, from spikes and brownouts to sags and surges (see Power problems box, below). If your PC is engaged in 'mission-critical' work, such as carrying out

transactions on the Internet or managing your office network and telephone systems, then even that small threat can be worrying enough to make installing a UPS essential.

Do you need a UPS?

Whether you need a UPS depends on how 'mission-critical' your work on the PC is. If you are in the habit of saving early and saving often; saving work to the hard disk; setting your applications to save frequently; and keeping regular back-ups of important work, you shouldn't need to worry about this type of problem.

Big businesses, however, cannot afford the risk of a crucial network server going down, even if that risk is quite small, so £50,000 or more spent on protecting computer and telecommunications equipment is good value if it guarantees power and prevents work loss.

The peace of mind that a UPS provides needn't cost much – this Belkin Regulator Pro Silver Series costs under £100.

APC's Back-UPS protects your PC from lightning strikes conducted through your phone line and modem in addition to safeguarding your power supply.

POWER PROBLEMS

Some people claim that as much as 80 per cent of all computer and electronic malfunctions are caused by disturbances in the power supply. These disturbances come in a variety of guises, complete with their own rich vocabulary. The main types you will hear about are explained here.
- 'Spikes' are short bursts of high voltage in the mains supply, sometimes caused by lightning, which can fuse circuits in a PC.
- 'Sags' and 'surges' are, respectively, under- and over-voltage fluctuations in the supply, caused by other electricity-hungry equipment in or near your home.

- 'Brownouts' are reductions in mains voltage caused by increased demand. These usually occur at peak times (such as half-time in the televised showing of the World Cup Final when everyone puts the kettle on) and could cause your PC to crash if the power supply falls to a very low level.
- 'Power failure' is a term that speaks for itself – the power supply is cut off completely. This is the worst case and the damage this causes can be considerable, such as lost or corrupted data and/or damage to the system itself.

Memory card readers

Many digital devices, including MP3 players and digital cameras, use removable memory cards to store data. If you add an inexpensive card reader, you can also open files stored on the cards and save data onto them using your desktop PC.

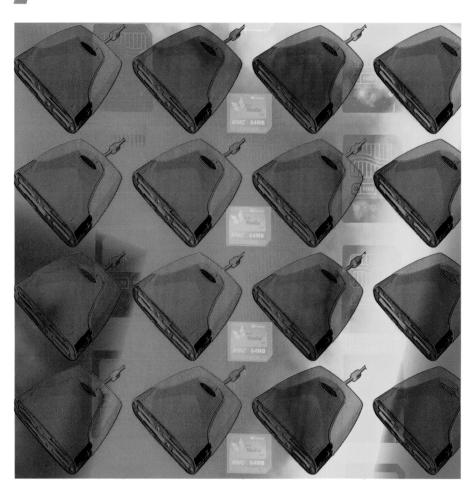

A memory card reader is quickly and easily fitted to your PC and can save you time, provide extra storage, and lets you transfer data to and from many digital devices.

A s digital technology becomes smaller and finds its way into more portable electronics gadgets, storage devices have to shrink too. Portable MP3 players use memory cards to store music and digital cameras use similar cards for the snapshots you take. These cards are a fraction of the size of the PC's hard disk – typically about the size of a large postage stamp and just a millimetre or so thick. Few have any moving parts, which makes them robust enough for life inside a portable gadget.

● Data transfer

If you add a memory card reader to your PC you get some useful benefits. For example, you can take a digital camera's memory card out and read the images directly on your PC. This saves you having to connect the digital camera via a USB cable to transfer your photos, so you don't have to switch the camera on and use up any of its battery power just to copy your photos to your PC.

Even if you don't have any of these digital devices, a memory card reader can be useful. When you insert a memory card into a reader, it works exactly like another hard disk, and you can use it to store any of your PC

documents. For example, if your documents take up less than 128MB of space, you can back them up to a 128MB memory card in a fraction of the time it takes to back up to a zip disk or CD writer.

● Choosing a card reader

Some card readers fit inside the PC, but due to the extra time required to install one – and the increased risk of damage – most home PC users are advised to opt for an external model, which you can fit in seconds (see opposite). Memory card readers cost from £15–£30, depending on how many types of card it can accept (see Types of memory card box, right).

(see opposite)

TYPES OF MEMORY CARD

There are several competing memory card formats. Check the documentation that came with your digital camera (or other digital device) to see which of these formats it uses:

Compact Flash: mainly used in high-end digital cameras (includes IBM/Hitachi Microdrives).

Memory Stick: Sony's own format for its MP3 players and digital cameras.

SmartMedia: a common format for mid-range digital cameras and MP3 players.

MultiMedia Card: another format popular for mid-range devices.

Secure Digital: these look identical to MultiMedia Cards but use slightly different electronics.

xD-Picture Card: a very compact card from Fuji and Olympus.

Installing a card reader

If you opt for an external memory card reader with a USB plug, you can start reading from and writing to removable memory cards without any complicated installation procedure.

1 In this example, we've opted for Sitecom's Multi-Memory Reader-Writer, but most memory card readers work in the same way. Start by positioning the card reader on your desk so that its cable can reach to your PC.

2 As a safety precaution, close all programs and documents. Then plug the card reader's USB plug into a spare USB socket and wait a few moments for Windows to detect and set up the necessary driver. Windows XP already includes a driver for the Sitecom reader, but check your card reader's documentation to see if you need to install software from a CD-ROM.

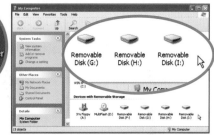

3 When the setup process is complete, double-click on the My Computer icon. The card reader's slots appear as one or more extra drives in the Devices with Removable Storage section, next to the floppy disk and CD-ROM drives. This reader has four slots so four extra drives appear.

4 Now insert your memory card into the appropriate slot in the card reader. Within a second or so, the drive icon for the slot is updated. Double-click on this icon.

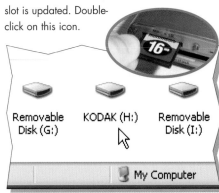

5 The window now shows the contents of this memory card – in this example there are two folders. Double-click your way through these folders just as you would for folders on your hard disk. In our example, which is a memory card from a digital camera, Windows displays thumbnail images of our snapshots.

6 You can copy these files – whether they are photos, MP3s or any other type of data – to your PC's hard disk. Open the folder you want to copy them to and drag the icons from the memory card window into the hard disk folder window.

7 Because the memory cards work like extra disk drives attached to your PC, you can use your programs to open files stored on the memory card. Here we are opening an MP3 file directly from a memory card by using the Windows Media Player's Open dialog box. The data will be copied to the PC's memory and replayed through its speakers.

PC TIPS

Some card readers are designed to accept only one type of memory card, but these can be a false economy. If you opt for a model with slots for all of the common memory card formats, you have more options in the future. For example, if you later buy a device that uses a different format, you can use the same card reader instead of having to buy another.

The limits of PC power

Most computer buyers will have noticed that PCs are not only becoming more and more powerful, they are getting cheaper all the time. It may surprise you to know that the computer industry has come up with a theory to explain this phenomenon – the so-called 'Moore's Law'.

Intel's very first microprocessor, the 4004, was introduced in 1971 and featured a mere 2300 transistors. The 1997 Intel Pentium II had 7.5 million of them; the Pentium III, which powers most modern PCs, had 28 million; and the latest version of the Pentium 4, released in 2002, has a staggering 55 million – an increase of almost 24,000 in 31 years.

You might think that such an astonishing increase in power would have taken everyone, including the experts, by surprise. Yet as early as 1965 (six years before Intel had even built a marketable microprocessor) one man had predicted the pace of change with an accuracy that still holds true today. His prediction has long been enshrined in the law that bears his name – Moore's Law.

Intel's Pentium 4 processor, shown here with the chipset, has an amazing 55 million transistors – a triumphant example of Moore's law in action (see box, below left).

● Discovering Moore's Law

In 1965, Gordon Moore, a co-founder of Intel and now the company's chairman emeritus, was preparing a speech for a gathering of the computer industry. He began to plot a graph showing the growth in chip performance (see Moore's Law graph box, left), and in doing so noticed a striking trend. Each new chip appeared within 18–24 months of the previous one and although each contained roughly twice the processing power of its predecessor, it sold at the same price. Hence, Moore observed, computing power doubles every 18–24 months, but costs the same.

Moore's observation predicted a continuing growth in computing power that many experts found very hard to swallow at the time. Yet Moore's Law proved to be remarkably accurate, pinpointing a trend that has continued for more than 35 years. During this time, the Law has become

MOORE'S LAW GRAPH

This graph from chip manufacturer Intel clearly illustrates how Moore's Law has held over the years. The scale on the left shows the number of transistors per chip, while the scale running from left to right shows time in five year periods. By 1985, the Intel 80386 chip had more than 100,000 transistors while the 80486 exceeded one million before 1990. Today's Pentium 4 has more than 55 million transistors on a single chip.

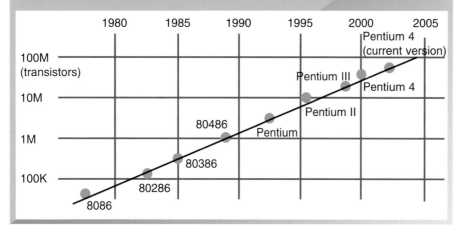

a core computer industry belief, on which chip and computer makers, as well as bulk-buyers of computer equipment, base their plans and forecasts. Soon, however, Moore's Law might need to be revised as it comes into conflict with the more powerful laws of nature.

● Size matters

The trend over the past 35 years has been for more and more transistors to be crammed into less and less chip space. This allows designers to add new features, while overall speed also increases because there is less distance for data to travel between transistors. But in a speech in September 1997, Moore voiced his concern that designers might come up against limitations set by the size of atomic particles. According to some studies, this point could be reached by 2017.

Chips are made by an optical lithography process, effectively a very sophisticated form of printing that builds up microscopically thin layers of components (see Stage 6, pages 100–101). Most current chip manufacture uses so-called '0.13 micron' technology – a measure of component size. In the coming months, many chip makers are moving to a 90 nanometre (or 0.09 micron) production process, allowing them to incorporate other circuits, such as more memory. But it has been suggested that the process might reach its limits within ten

years or so, while the insulators currently used – only four or five atoms thick – simply cannot get much smaller.

There's a power problem, too. Moore compared a 200MHz chip made with a 0.35 micron process to a notional 1GHz chip made with the 0.18 process. He estimated that the effect would be to double the physical size of the chip and to increase power consumption to 40 watts – at which point the chip would be producing dangerous heat.

In reducing the size to 90 nanometre and beyond, chip manufacturers can control heat dissipation. Despite this, and the noisy cooling fans used in today's PCs, more needs to be done. Supercomputers can use expensive Freon-based cooling systems, but for desktop and notebook PCs, chip makers must constantly find new ways of minimizing heat generation.

● An end to progress?

Intel and other microprocessor makers, such as AMD, face another massive difficulty – the huge investment needed to develop chips and build the

manufacturing plants. As chips get more complex and production processes shrink to a smaller micron count, the cost of building a plant increases exponentially.

Intel's success has allowed it to build up enormous cash resources, but other manufacturers are far less wealthy. Even when a chip has been developed, it still costs between $2 billion and $4 billion to build a manufacturing plant. That's money that even Intel, the most dominant company in the industry, has to think very hard about spending.

So, for the next decade, it seems that Moore's Law is likely to hold true. As chips become more powerful, they will also get cheaper in relative terms. That's good news for the consumer, although it does bring into play another 'law', which is that the PC you buy today is always likely to be 50 per cent cheaper if you wait a few months.

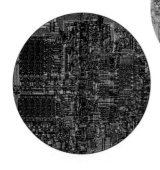

Microprocessors (above, left to right) have rapidly gone through many stages of development, from the first Intel microprocessor to the modern Pentium 4, with 24,000 times as many components packed onto the chip. But modern manufacturing technology (right) may be fast approaching an absolute limit.

Home Learning & Leisure

Airline ticketing systems

When you buy an airline ticket, you're not just buying a ticket to fly, you're buying a piece of information in a massive worldwide data network.

It has been estimated that the travel business worldwide has an annual expenditure on information technology of around $20 billion. It's a business that has always striven to be at the forefront of technological and commercial developments, as individual companies have tried to get an edge on their competitors by offering customers faster and more efficient service. And nowhere is this more true than in the air-travel sector.

Even though the Internet is changing the travel industry in some radical ways (see opposite), most people still buy their tickets from travel agents. And pretty much every travel agent in the developed world is linked to one of the big global reservation and ticketing systems. These systems, such as Galileo, SABRE and Amadeus, are among the largest and most heavily used data networks in the world. Typically, they are partly owned by consortia made up of the airlines themselves, but managed as independent companies.

There's much more to flying than meets the eye. For instance, behind the apparently simple process of being issued with a ticket and handing over your money, lies the very latest in superfast, reliable, high-tech computer systems.

● Information online

The core business of these ticketing companies is to maintain an accurate database of flight details and ticket availability, and to make that information available to participating travel agents and airlines, 24 hours a day, 365 days a year. With access to this information, sales staff can sell you a ticket and confirm your seat on the spot. This business requires some of the most sophisticated networking hardware and fail-safe computer systems around.

From the traveller's point of view, however, all that is seen is likely to be a standard PC on a travel agent's desk. These PC systems are normally supplied by the ticketing company, often free of charge if the agency does a sufficient volume of business. The PCs are fairly standard desktop machines – except that they might be linked by leased telephone lines to the ticketing company's central database. The software they run (apart from the standard set of word processor and other everyday applications) is the proprietary 'front-end' to the exclusive data held by Galileo, SABRE or Amadeus.

● Windows interface

The user interface for the travel agent has become increasingly graphical, with 'point and click' functions replacing older text-based systems. Although each company uses a different version, Windows forms the basis of them all. Using the software, the travel agent can call up information on flight times, seat availability and just about anything else in the world of air traffic. Much of the huge investment in technology is spent on ensuring that this happens quickly and accurately.

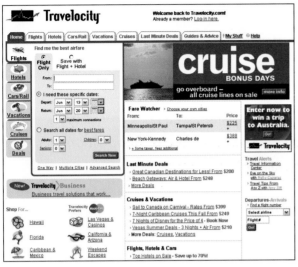

SABRE's Travelocity online booking system can be licensed by individual travel agents as a cross-branded Web site for direct customer holiday bookings.

Each company has its own huge centralized data centre. Galileo International, for example, has its main installation near Denver, Colorado. It links 46,000 travel agents worldwide, using over 170,000 terminals and supplying tickets from over 680 airlines. It also deals with many hotels and car rental companies. The amount of data flowing back and forth is astonishing: the Galileo data centre processes 255 million requests for information every day and over 92 billion transactions are being made each year.

● Hardware and networks
You need a solid hardware and network infrastructure to run such a system, and some reliable backup systems in case anything goes wrong.

Such data centres typically run their information systems on large mainframe computers with massive amounts of storage space and extremely fast parallel processors. Galileo and its parallel Apollo system run on 21 such mainframes, housed in a massive building with a floor space equivalent to 84 tennis courts, equipped with all sorts of sprinkler and alarm systems, and backed up by large emergency power supplies. Connections to locations throughout the world are maintained by a hugely complex combination of communications and networking technologies. You can now walk into a travel agent and, in a matter of minutes, book a seat on an aircraft to your desired destination.

● The e-commerce revolution
Some 40 years ago, air travel was the province of the rich, while today many can afford it. With much larger numbers of people travelling by air, it has become increasingly important that airlines and agents have instant access to reliable information on flights and seat availability.

Now travel agents and the airlines are faced with another revolution involving the public – the Internet. Much of the information that was

until recently hidden from public view is now widely available on Web sites, many of which are the airlines' own sites. It's a quick and safe business to buy airline tickets on the Internet, and in the coming years more and more people will do just that.

That's fine for the airlines, but it leaves the travel agents without their commission payments. So they too are joining the e-commerce revolution, using Web portals to get quick access to all sorts of extra opportunities, such as hotels and car hire, that they can sell on to their airline ticket customers. Galileo, SABRE and Amadeus have all backed this move by letting travel agents incorporate their booking systems into the agents' own Web sites. Whether booking direct with a real person or through a Web site, customers have never before enjoyed so much choice.

Having booked your British Airways e-ticket online, you can check in over the Web and even choose your seat on the plane up to one hour before it's due to take off.

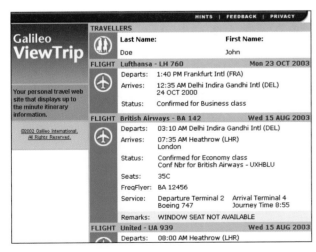

A development of Viewpoint from Galileo allows travel agents to check full itinerary details for every booking using the Web-based ViewTrip portal.

CUTTING OUT THE TICKET

Airlines are now moving towards ticketless travel. There are good reasons for this: lower costs, increased efficiency and greater customer satisfaction. Electronic ticketing is now used by most major airlines and all the major ticketing systems mentioned in this article. There's no single accepted standard, but the principles are very much the same, no matter who is issuing the ticket. In an electronic ticketing system what you do, in effect, is cut out the middleman – the paper ticket – by going straight from payment to boarding pass. You buy a 'ticket' (either at a travel agent, on the Internet, or from a self-service kiosk) and are given a unique code, which you then use to get your boarding pass at the airport, either from a member of staff or from an automatic kiosk. The airlines and travel agents save time and money in administrative, paper and delivery costs, while the passenger saves time and stress with the reduced need for queues.

Digital TV

There's been a huge amount of publicity surrounding the launch of digital TV in the UK. What's it all about, and will it make your TV more like a PC?

The promise of digital TV is that it can deliver more programs using less 'bandwidth' and with a higher picture quality than previous TV delivery systems. In addition, digital TV has also made it possible to deliver interactive services, such as home shopping, travel reservations and email, to homes that don't have personal computers.

Previously, TV transmissions in the UK were encoded in analog format using the PAL (Phase-Alternation-Line) system. PAL has been around since the black-and-white TV age, but it was struggling under the strain of the many additions that had been made to it since then, such as colour, teletext and NICAM stereo.

● Lack of radio spectrum space

PAL also, however, takes up a lot of space to transmit relatively little data. This is significant because the radio spectrum is becoming an increasingly overcrowded place, the astonishing growth in mobile phone use over the past decade being the main problem.

The broadcasters, of course, want to transmit ever more variety, in the form of increasing numbers of TV channels and interactive services. With PAL, there hasn't been enough room for them. There is also the added problem that analog TV

The ever-developing world of television has taken a huge leap into the future by going digital. This will present many new opportunities for purchasers, broadcasters and, of course, the viewing public.

transmission remains vulnerable to interference, and so might sometimes deliver a poor picture quality.

● How digital TV works

Digital TV uses digital compression techniques to cram pictures into approximately one-tenth of the space used in the PAL system (see How digital compression works box, opposite). Once the data has been compressed, it is then combined with sound, subtitles and any other necessary information. The whole mix is then encrypted and sent on ultra high frequency (UHF) channels to the home, where it is received by your TV aerial or satellite dish. Alternatively, you may receive the feed by cable through a local operator.

Either way, these digital signals have been encrypted not because they contain top-secret information, but because the TV companies can make you pay for receiving the services (although some digital services are free, see Free to view box, left). You can't decrypt the programmes without

signing up for the service, which in the United Kingdom means approaching your local cable operator such as NTL or Telewest, or Sky Digital for satellite reception. In all cases you need a set-top box which decrypts the signal and then decompresses the pictures to send the output to your television set.

● New digital TVs

The TV set does not have to be a new one; older TVs can cope with digital signals perfectly well. However, the new 'digital' TVs are specifically designed for digital use and contain all the necessary electronics inside them, although you will still need a satellite dish as well as a set-top box to receive Sky Digital.

Digital television sets are nearly all manufactured in the 'widescreen' format, which enables them to display pictures as on a cinema screen. A small but increasing number of TV programmes are produced in this format but it's mainly useful for watching movies designed for cinema.

FREE TO VIEW

If you buy a digital TV set or own a satellite dish with a receiver box, you can receive a number of channels without subscription. These are known as the 'free to view' channels. They include the standard 'terrestrial' stations – BBC1, BBC2, ITV1, Channel 4 and Channel 5 – plus well over 20 other TV and digital radio channels. Among them are additional BBC and ITV services, travel and shopping channels, and Sky News. For more details, see www.freeview.co.uk.

● What's on television?

For the first couple of years, digital TV channels offered pretty much the same content that you could find on any subscription channel. But gradually more use has been made of the possibilities of digital TV, such as information overlays (where a box may appear to show details of the channel and programme, for example), picture-in-picture modes (where another channel can appear in a thumbnail box in the corner of the screen) and the kind of fast and interactive text services that make the old-fashioned teletext seem like it belongs in the Stone Age.

Examples include the Sky News Active service which lets you switch between eight concurrent video news feeds while browsing the headlines at the same time. Sports programming has also taken advantage of the technology, not only letting you watch the action itself, but also giving access to statistics, team information and updates on other games being played. And you may even be given the opportunity to take part in quizzes.

● Interactive services

Using your phone line and an additional keyboard, you can turn your digital TV into a gateway to a

Sky News Active is just one example of the new wave of interactive services which take full advantage of digital TV technology. These let you switch between multiple simultaneous video feeds, read the news headlines and take part in viewer polls.

Digital technologies have begun changing our viewing patterns too, thanks to new computer-style video recorders. First introduced to home viewers with the TiVo service, but since rebranded under various names including Sky+, these video recorders incorporate hard disks instead of video tape. The big difference is that they are able to record and play simultaneously, so if you receive a phone call during your favourite programme you can pause it, then as soon as you put the phone down, continue watching from that point: there's no need to wait until the end of the programme.

You can emulate this kind of service by connecting your digital TV or set-top box to your PC if it has a TV-in port or TV tuner card. You can then use software such as *WinDVD Recorder* from InterVideo to record straight to hard disk, or even to a DVD video disc if your computer has a DVD-R drive, for immediate playback. Go to www.intervideo.com for details.

TiVo (right) video recorders store TV programmes on a PC-like hard disk so that you can watch them later. Software such as WinDVD Recorder (below) lets you do much the same thing on your own PC without subscription charges, as long as your PC has a TV tuner card or TV-in port.

● The future of TV

The benefits of digital TV are such that many satellite broadcasters, including Sky, have abandoned their old analog channels already. In the UK, all public analog TV services will be phased out from 2010.

Digital TVs have widescreen cinema-type dimensions, superb picture clarity and great sound, all of which provide a better-than-ever viewing experience.

variety of interactive services. Full Internet access from your TV isn't quite possible yet, but you can send and receive email, play online games and shop from your own home with a limited selection of well-known high street retailers.

HOW DIGITAL COMPRESSION WORKS

Digital TV compression is a process where only movement or detail in a digitized picture is used for transmission. A picture frame, when digitized, will be made up of 6.72 Megabits; at a rate of 25 frames per second, this equals 168 Megabits per second. After the compression, the same picture frame can be reduced to as little as 4–5 Megabits per second. As a result, more than one programme service can be transmitted on one UHF channel. The compression technique used – MPEG-2 – is also used by DVD.

School computers

Classrooms in primary schools used to be technology-free zones. But now they're likely to have an IT system that's as sophisticated as those found in most offices.

It is the aim of the British government to make the whole country PC-literate, harnessing IT and the Internet to increase skills and competitiveness in the global e-marketplace. The reason, of course, is that we are now at the beginning of a 'new knowledge economy', where IT skills will be essential to any job. Education, across the board, is key to this project.

In the world of education, it's not a simple matter of IT, but of ICT – information and communications technology. The government has made an undertaking to give all 5- to 16-year-olds training in this area, and it seems to be a commitment that is working out well in practice. School Web sites of all kinds abound, while there is no shortage of material for research and lesson planning.

● **Hardware in the classroom**

What individual primary schools actually have in terms of hardware and infrastructure can vary substantially, depending on budgets and the decisions of the head teacher.

Some teachers believe that computers are best used in dedicated 'ICT suites', with children timetabled to use them for a set number of hours per week. Another theory is that the computers are better used by being located in classrooms and becoming part of the everyday teaching apparatus whenever appropriate. In this way they can be 'embedded in the learning process', just as IT is in nearly all aspects of everyday life. Ideally, teachers would like the best of

both worlds, with a combination of suites and classroom computers, but budgets rarely stretch that far.

The base machine in primary schools is the PC, but the age and performance of these machines can vary widely. Many schools are using PCs that are several years old and have slow processor speeds, which is fine for simple software and basic tasks, but not so great when it comes to the Multimedia fireworks that really engage and captivate younger children.

When a school does have a significant budget, it is likely to buy PCs with a very similar specification to those used in the home or office: Intel Celeron or AMD Athlon processors of 1GHz or so for use as standard workstations; Intel Pentium 4 or AMD Athlon processors with 2GHz and

Computing in schools is moving on, but the early, slower computers still have a role to play in many classrooms.

more for work such as sound editing, which requires extra processing power; and large monitors and hard disks. The large PC companies such as Dell all supply schools, but the leading UK educational computer supplier is RM (Research Machines),

As schools acquire PCs, they are able to make use of the huge range of Multimedia titles available, as well as standard Microsoft applications.

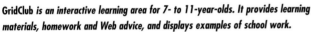

GridClub is an interactive learning area for 7- to 11-year-olds. It provides learning materials, homework and Web advice, and displays examples of school work.

Learning through play is a well-known concept but it is made even more enjoyable when lessons are conducted via a computer terminal and a mouse.

which provides a wide range of own-brand PCs, laptops and servers. Stand-alone PCs are not ideal for primary schools. Many have installed substantial networks, either as ICT suites or as school-wide teaching and administrative systems. Increasingly, primary schools are looking at using wireless networks to connect the whole building; they can be cheaper and less disruptive to install than fixed-wire systems and offer easier upgrading and expansion (see Stage 5, pages 96–97). Laptops, when schools can afford them, are also growing in popularity, largely because of the flexibility they offer.

● School software

Just as the hardware in primary schools will be familiar, so will much of the software employed; children

The BBC Micro's famous turtle was used to teach pupils how to program an object to move around the floor.

are taught to use the popular word-processing packages and Internet browsers. But they might well be ahead of many parents in their use of other business software. The presentation program PowerPoint, for example, is growing in popularity as a means for children as young as six or seven to structure their work and present it to a teacher or a whole class. Typically, they will have done much of the research on the Internet.

There is also plenty of specific learning software devoted to a given topic or Key Stage. Schools usually buy site licences so they can use multiple copies; the price per user falls the more licences are bought.

● Learning on the Web

Teachers in all educational sectors have welcomed the Internet as a liberating and exciting learning tool, but they also acknowledge that the sheer volume of material is daunting, and that some sort of filtering process has to take place.

Fortunately, there is a host of Web sites dedicated to the learning needs of different groups of children. Research Machines produce a highly regarded site called Learning Alive (www.learningalive.co.uk), which is packed with resources for specific projects, as well as giving plenty of tips on how to search the Web more effectively. It also includes news sections and advice on available teaching tools for teachers.

The government's own portal for education, the National Grid for Learning (www.ngfl.gov.uk), is a good starting point for all kinds of content. It will take children to the *GridClub* (www.gridclub.com), where 7- to 11-year-olds will find plenty of fun, interactive learning content, as well as a library and the opportunity to post their own stories and poems. There's also a link to TeacherNet (www.teachernet.gov.uk), where staff can find out the latest news and initiatives in ICT learning. The National Grid for Learning site also offers helpful advice for parents who are more perplexed than their children by 'new technology'. As children outstrip their parents in IT skills, many schools are now starting after-school IT training so adults can keep up with the younger generation.

THE BBC MICRO

The Multimedia PC is a relatively recent arrival in the primary school. Through the 1980s and early 1990s, the BBC Micro was the dominant machine in primary schools that had any kind of IT equipment. It was cheap, sturdy, easy to use and rapidly spawned a wide range of excellent educational software. It was often supplied with a 'turtle' (see left), a small robot that could be programmed by children to move around in specific directions by using the simple LOGO language.

Computers in music

Technological advances have meant that computer-generated music has become increasingly sophisticated and it is now possible to achieve impressive results on a home PC.

Computers are commonly used in the music business – and have been since the days of the Atari personal computer in the mid-1980s. For example, the mostly widely used professional mixing application, Cubase, started life on the Atari. Apple Macs subsequently became popular for making music and now the home PC has got in on the act.

For the purposes of music, a PC must either have a sound card or have audio hardware built onto the motherboard. Either way, this hardware is capable of two fundamental tasks. Firstly, it handles sounds, for example, for mixing, sequencing or digital recording. Secondly, it *generates* sounds thanks to a synthesizer chip. Together these two functions let you not just record and play back music on a PC, but actually perform it too.

● Combining waves
Early PC sound cards were based on frequency modulation (FM) technology. This synthesizer sound was created by combining two simple sound waves (called carrier and modulator) to produce a complex third sound – that which comes out of the speakers. By controlling the two different waves, a wide range of sounds could be created.

However, although FM can sound more than adequate for many types of electronic music, it isn't very impressive when required to produce acoustic sounds, such as guitar or

Before music is turned into air-borne analog sound waves that we can hear, it very often takes the form of digital signals. Increasingly, computer technology is being used both to create and to manipulate these digital signals.

piano. Only by adding a wavetable chip to the sound card circuits could these sounds be made.

● Sampling sounds
Instead of being restricted to carrier and modulator sound waves, these wavetable cards use digital representations of the sound itself to create synthesized sound, which might well represent a real musical instrument.

The quality of this sound depends on four factors. Firstly, the quality of the original recording. Secondly, the frequency of the sample. This is typically 44.1kHz stereo, which is the same rate at which CDs are recorded – hence the boast of 'CD-quality'

audio. Thirdly, the compression method used to store the sound: given the fact that much of the data required to create these sounds is stored in the hardware, compression is important. Fourthly, the number of samples that make up each instrument. This last factor represents the way in which sound changes in various different ways, for example, when you attempt to play a real instrument 'enthusiastically', rather than just getting louder.

● Quality and accuracy
An accurate representation of the subtleties of playing an instrument in different ways requires a great deal of sampling. For example, to accurately

The Dance series of music-mixing software from eJay (left) lets you play and record samples, edit them together in real time and play back the impressive results.

recreate the full range of sounds created by a piano would require hundreds of megabytes of data. As you can see, the quality of music a sound card (or indeed any synthesizer) can produce depends as much on the quality of its samples as it does on the hardware itself. This is why most music studios will have a mixture of different sound devices: a couple of keyboard synthesizers, a Multimedia PC and sound modules.

Apart from the different functions of these devices, such as having a keyboard, the variety is necessary to get an interesting range of sounds beyond those available with a regular sound card – at a price, naturally.

● MIDI system

This is where MIDI (Musical Instrument Digital Interface) fits in. We've gone into MIDI in some depth earlier in the series (see Stage 3, pages 108–111). MIDI is not actually a sound recording format, but rather one that tells an electronic instrument how to play. It contains various elements of information, including the note number and a velocity value – the details of how hard a key is struck. A MIDI file would contain the

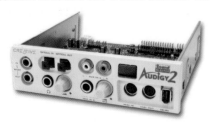

Serious PC audio enthusiasts can invest in advanced hardware, such as Creative's Audigy range, some of which include a multi-port front panel (above) for their computers.

same data on any system, and thanks to the General MIDI standard, it plays the right synthesized sound (trumpet, piano, etc) on any General MIDI system. However, the quality of that sound might vary enormously, depending upon the sophistication of the sound card and its on-board synthesizer.

The clever part of MIDI, then, is that you can use anything to create the music, then choose which instrument sounds will play it back later. You could strum a MIDI-compatible guitar and hear grand piano chords coming out of the speakers, or tickle the keys on your PC keyboard and hear the percussive sounds of a drum kit.

● Continuous controllers

MIDI is just a set of instructions so it doesn't involve much data. This makes it an ideal format in modern computerized recording studios. A MIDI sequencer 'records' information from every input device, then the information is layered into different concurrent channels, rather than being mixed down to tape. This, in turn, lets you adjust the digital tracks with continuous controllers, so you can change the nature of the sound, its frequency and so on, to make interesting effects.

MIDI and electronics don't cover everything, though. Musicians will want to mix some genuine acoustic sounds in with the electronic ones, such as a real guitar and vocal tracks. At one time this demanded specialist software to handle the digital and analog tracks side by side, plus an extremely high powered PC and a dedicated mixing desk.

Given that CD-quality recordings demand a lot of digital recording space –

When recording sound onto the computer's hard disk, the quality of the sound card circuitry greatly affects the final result. Low-cost sound cards often have basic analog-to-digital converters (ADC) that may result in lots of noise. Professionals upgrade their PCs with cards with very high-quality ADCs so that noise is all but banished. You can add these cards to a home PC – they usually cost from £100 to £400, depending on their features.

over 100MB per 10 minutes is typical – you also needed a combination of complex high performance hard disk arrays and multiple tape systems.

● Recording to disk

Thankfully, all this has changed in recent years. PC processors have progressed, memory is cheap and today's average hard disk capacity is more than 40GB, a volume previously unheard of. It's now possible to record straight to hard disk, mix tracks in real time and play them back immediately.

This is the basis for serious music software now used in professional recording studios, and also that of fun packages such as eJay's *Dance* series, designed for teens and music hobbyists alike.

Now everyone can set up their own recording studio on a home PC. Once you have laid down the tracks and mixed them to your satisfaction, you can copy your music straight to a CD-R for distribution or duplicating, or alternatively upload it as a series of MP3 files to the Internet and wait for your fame to spread!

Ocean yachting

It might seem an unlikely place to find the latest in high technology, but the modern ocean yacht is crammed with electronics and computer wizardry.

Until very recently, any improvements in designing, building and sailing a yacht were added piecemeal to centuries of accumulated wisdom. Drawings were done by hand, prototypes modelled and the yacht itself built by craftsmen using tried-and-tested techniques. Once the yacht was seaborne, its crew navigated using the traditional methods of dead-reckoning. But the advent of modern electronics and digital computers – and in particular the PC – has changed very nearly every aspect of traditional yachting.

Underneath the classic billowing sails and deck planking, the latest computerized equipment helps modern seafarers keep their ocean yachts on course with the minimum of effort, giving accurate information on navigation and the weather.

● Changes in navigation

The most revolutionary of these changes is in the navigation, steering and tracking of the vessels themselves. Thirty years ago, mariners used the techniques of dead-reckoning to find their way about the world's vast and featureless oceans. The tools of the trade were the compass, the sextant (to determine latitude and longitude from a reading of the stars), the paper chart and the chronometer. Using these, in conjunction with average speed and distance travelled, the navigator fixed a position for the vessel and plotted a course.

Dead-reckoning was always an uncertain science, however. Any number of factors, including inclement weather, radio failure, being distant from well-used shipping lanes, incorrect calculations or equipment problems, could quite easily lead to navigational error. For instance, a chronometer which is inaccurate by just a small amount could mean that a navigator would miscalculate longitude by hundreds of nautical miles.

● Precise positioning with GPS

Nowadays, the sailor knows exactly, to within approximately 10 metres, where he or she is anywhere on the seas, thanks to the Global Positioning by Satellite (GPS) systems. The on-board GPS receiver is updated every second or so from the system's network of 24 satellites, so knowing your exact location need never be a problem for sailors any more.

The GPS system can do even more for the sailor, however. By keying in the co-ordinates of a destination, it can even plot your course for you. The benefits for both the leisure and the professional sailor, in terms of safety and time savings, cannot be underestimated.

On most ocean-going yachts, and on many smaller ones, too, the GPS will be connected to an on-board PC.

INMARSAT

The global satellite system that keeps sailors in touch on their mobile satellite phones is managed by the Inmarsat consortium, to which many of the world's leading telecommunication companies belong. Inmarsat was founded in 1979 to develop satellite communications and distress and safety applications for the shipping industry. It has since expanded to provide mobile communications for remote locations where terrestrial communications are not reliable. Its main focus, though, remains on maritime communications.

In theory, at least, the computer used could be an ordinary PC, just the same as your desktop machine or portable; in practice, it's more likely to be a 'marinized' machine (perhaps even a fully waterproof portable) designed to withstand the buffeting of the yacht and being lashed by the most unforgiving elements.

Once the PC is linked to the GPS data and to various other instruments on the yacht that measure variables such as wind direction, tides and boat speed, the navigator can almost sit back and wait to be told the optimum course to take.

To do this, of course, you need a chart – the sailor's equivalent of a map. Before the electronic age, you would have needed to buy bulky and costly paper charts of all the regions in which you were intending to sail. Nowadays, many of these charts have been digitized and are available to the sailor on CD-ROM. The chart can then be loaded into the PC and used together with GPS to plot routes. Some of the PC software that manages all this will even give you a constant display of your ship's position on the PC monitor.

The Furuno GP80 series GPS Navigator is a compact and waterproof device with a 6-inch backlit LCD display that presents the yachting highway in 3D. The data can be fed to an autopilot, or to a PC or chart plotter for printing.

The FAX207 is a programmable 'weather fax' machine which receives high-resolution weather updates and satellite images, and prints them out directly.

● Weathering the storm

Knowing where you are and where you are going are vital when at sea. But it's just as important to have accurate meteorological information; after all, there's not much point in plotting a course if it's going to take you into the middle of a hurricane. This is where suppliers such as PC Maritime are useful.

Their software takes data from meteorological satellites and allows the sailor to view the weather charts and satellite pictures on screen, save them and then plot the development of weather systems on and near the desired route; if the planned route becomes treacherous the navigator can plot an alternative course.

● Keeping in touch

The development of satellite phones means that seafarers are able to keep in touch wherever they are – and, of course, this gives them another distress signal option in addition to the traditional 'mayday'. These telephones use the Inmarsat satellite system (see Inmarsat box, opposite). Originally, satellite phones were bulky items, but they have become much more compact and, on some models, both the main unit and antenna weigh less than 5kg each. Just like terrestrial mobile phones, these sea-going models are increasingly used to

connect to PCs and fax machines. The mobile office on the high seas is already a reality, but fully featured satellite phones are not cheap; you can expect to pay over £1000, with usage costing around £1 per minute.

● Safe sailing

As the price of digital equipment generally continues to fall, however, the leisure sailor can expect to see much of the equipment that was previously the exclusive province of the supertanker appearing in his small yacht. This should considerably improve the safety of sailing.

SITES TO VISIT

PC Maritime
www.pcmaritime.co.uk
The UK's main supplier of maritime software, including charts and weather analysis systems.

Furuno
www.furuno.com
Manufacturers of all kinds of maritime electronics, including navigation and communications equipment.

Nera
www.nera.no
Specialists in a number of satellite communications devices, including compact satellite phones.

Doctor at a distance

Sophisticated medical diagnosis and even treatment from a distance are now both possible, thanks to the marvel of telecommunications technology.

Although they might not know it, the medical profession have long been using what is called 'telemedicine'. At its most basic level of technological complexity, this field includes simple medical diagnosis and treatment of complaints over the phone. For example, if your child has a temperature and a rash, you call the doctor, describe what the rash looks like, and the doctor may instruct you to give the child some junior paracetamol and call again if it doesn't clear within a couple of days.

Now, with the range of computer and telecommunications systems made available within the last few decades, telemedicine – medicine carried out at a distance with the use of telecommunications technology – is a growth industry. It covers a range of techniques, from the simple everyday case described above to surgery carried out by robots under the command of a skilled doctor located thousands of miles away.

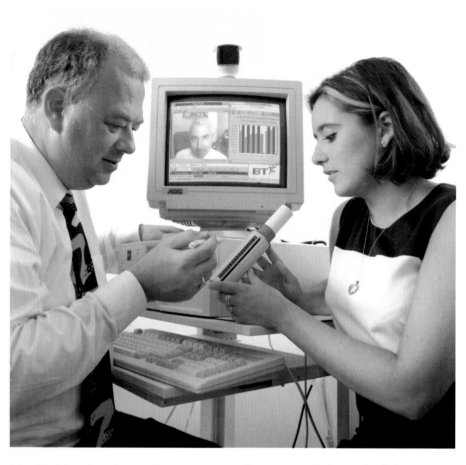

Telemedicine helps a doctor diagnose and treat a patient many miles away. To provide this type of medical video conference, the doctor and his colleague both need a PC, a Webcam and a high-bandwidth telephone connection.

● NASA beginnings
It's only in the past four or five years that the buzzword 'telemedicine' has become frequently heard, but it's something that's been around in quite a sophisticated form for a lot longer. A great deal of the early serious experimental work was, as with so much in the fields of computers and telecommunications, carried out by NASA as part of the US Space Program. In the 1960s NASA was, understandably, keen to keep an eye on the well-being of its astronauts and therefore devised telemetry methods

and systems for monitoring both the astronauts and their spacecraft. These early steps led to a number of experimental US programs in which NASA was involved.

● Rural medicine
One of the earliest experiments, on the Papago Indian Reservation in Arizona, highlights a major area of application for telemedicine: the remote, rural community. In such places, highly trained medical personnel are scarce, as is modern and expensive diagnostic hardware, such as scanners.

In the Papago project, two paramedics toured the area in a van fitted out with medical equipment, including an X-ray machine and an electrocardiograph. The van

transmitted the test results to a hospital, where they were analysed and the appropriate action was then recommended.

● Remote analysis
Today, this sort of setup is still representative of much telemedicine in remote areas, from Norway's frozen north to Australia's Gulf of Carpentaria. Indeed, a few of the latest telemedicine projects in some of the most advanced countries deliberately employ low-tech systems, so ensuring the widest possible public access.

In the UK, for example, the NHS Direct scheme uses just a telephone; callers speak to a nurse, who then directs them to the appropriate form of care. Alternatively, you can go to the Web site at www.nhsdirect.nhs.uk

EDUCATION

One of the biggest growth areas for telemedicine is in education, not just as a means of teaching large groups of students, but as a way of encouraging the ongoing education of healthcare professionals and specialists. Specialist instruments – such as the telemedicine stethoscope – help teachers reach a wider group of students. But it is streaming video on the Internet that is the key to the most powerful educational applications of telemedicine. A single lecture or surgical demonstration can be viewed by many people on their own PCs. Experiencing such a lecture remotely can be more fruitful than attendance, as the images and explanation can be saved, replayed and studied in detail.

for self-help guidance, a health encyclopedia, and an online enquiry form. This scheme has resulted in big savings in terms of time and money.

● Teleradiology

Defined as the remote analysis of X-rays and scans, teleradiology uses a digital camera or other device to capture and store the images, which are then forwarded to another location anywhere in the world, to enable expert analysis and diagnosis to take place.

With the advent of the Internet and other communications networks, this other location need not be physically close; you could send scans taken in Sydney to the world's top specialist in, say, San Francisco, and have an expert opinion back within hours.

● Web cam consultations

In theory, a doctor could show his consultation with a patient to another doctor located anywhere in the world, as long as both had a desktop computer, a simple Web cam and a reasonably fast Internet connection. In practice, a host of specialized equipment is available, produced by dozens of companies, mainly in the US. It's quite difficult, for example, to share the results of a simple stethoscope examination (auscultation). But, if you have a special telemedicine stethoscope fitted with a transducer and amplifier, you can share examination results with a number of local listeners or transmit them to specialists at remote locations.

● Telemedicine in the home

For the next few years, most of us will see the benefits of telemedicine in terms of increased efficiency in using scarce resources, largely through the use of the telephone or even email as the first step in a diagnosis. In remote areas, healthcare consumers will save time and get quicker specialist help with the use of some of the techniques described above.

In the future, however, it seems likely that telemedicine will reach right into the home in the form of some kind of medical module that will carry out a variety of health checks – on the heart, blood pressure and so on – and then transmit the results elsewhere for analysis.

A consultant analyses a baby's ultrasound image, which is being transmitted live over a network. The camera on top of the monitor is used to relay the doctor's voice and the image to the scanner and consultant at the remote site.

PROJECT MISSION

NASA were involved at the start of telemedicine and are still instrumental in its development. One of their latest projects is an attempt to use satellite networks for the transmission of medical data. This is because many truly remote areas are not sufficiently 'wired' to receive data-intensive information, such as 3D images or streaming video. Project Mission uses NASA satellites for the test, together with supercomputers at the Ohio Supercomputing Center. Researchers hope to move over to commercial networks when these have the required speed of transmission.

Garden design software

A fragrant rose and a home computer might not seem to go well together, but there's a wealth of impressive software available to help you design and enhance your garden.

Whether you've just bought a new home and want to design a landscaped garden from scratch, or are simply looking for a hardy perennial to provide a splash of colour, there is software available to suit your needs.

Novices and experts alike can benefit from the visualizing options that garden design software offers. Gardeners of any level will find the encyclopedias and plant finders included in these packages of enormous help, with their vast illustrated plant databases and their ability to find the type of plant you're looking for in seconds. Of course, such software can also be immense fun to browse through and play with.

● Geoff Hamilton's legacy

At one time voted 'Gardener of the Millennium', the late Geoff Hamilton was Britain's favourite celebrity garden expert, long before the current trend for lawn make-overs. Although not a computer whizz-kid himself, he was heavily involved in the creation of the original *Garden Designer* CD-ROM which, now in version 3,

Geoff Hamilton's 3D Garden Designer 3 includes a multi-tabbed Plant Encyclopedia for comprehensive planting information. You can even add your own notes in the specially provided areas.

still bears his name. The software is intended for the everyday gardener rather than landscape professional.

You begin by laying out your house and garden limits, and then you can add landscape features such as

rockeries and decks before thinking about planting. A number of ready-made garden layouts are provided to get you started. These are put together quickly from a bird's eye viewpoint. At any time, you can view a 3D display to see how the layout might look in real life. You can then 'walk' through this virtual garden, even previewing what it might look like in different seasons and how things will change after a few years.

As the software is aimed at the ordinary gardener, it also provides comprehensive advice on choosing your greenery, planting and long-term maintenance. A special multi-tabbed Plant Encyclopedia keeps all this detail together in one place, even providing areas for you to add custom information on your own progress.

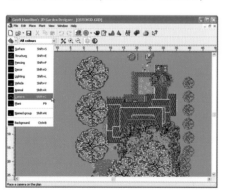
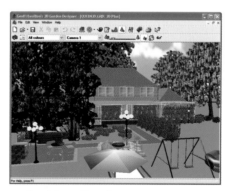

Having built a landscape layout from an easy top-down viewpoint (above left), Geoff Hamilton's 3D Garden Designer 3 lets you preview the effect of shadows, seasonal changes and annual growth. At any time, you can call up a 3D view (above right), either walking through it interactively or switching between multiple fixed cameras.

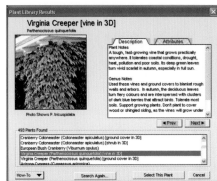

3D Landscape 2 Deluxe generates fast 3D models of your plans, which you can then 'walk' through. For practical gardening maintenance advice, call up the Plant Library.

● Serious gardening business

Those who treat gardening as a serious business as much as a leisure pursuit might want to take a look at *3D Landscape Deluxe 5*. It ties in nicely with Broderbund's other Home Design products, even importing house structures from *3D Home Architect* into your landscape.

Like other garden design software, *3D Landscape Deluxe 5* helps you choose the plants and shrubs for your plot, and offers detailed information on how to look after them. But one of its specialist features includes the ability to re-landscape the terrain in dramatic ways, adding slopes and hills as well as ponds and beds, in advance of professional excavation.

Another leading feature in this package is the very high quality of its 3D models. A technology called

3DTrueView produces near photo-realistic renderings of your home and garden designs. This will greatly aid visualization of the final result, and is a valuable presentation aid if you are planning the landscape redesign on behalf of someone else.

Not least, the program builds you a shopping list based on your virtual garden. This way, you know exactly what and how much to buy when visiting your local garden centre.

● Growth over time

Similarly named but aimed squarely at the green-fingered enthusiast rather than professional landscape gardener is *3D Landscape 2 Deluxe* from Focus Multimedia. In general approach and style, this CD-ROM has much in common with *Geoff Hamilton's 3D Garden Designer 3*.

You begin by adding plants and garden furniture from ready-made object libraries to your plot, seen from above, then re-arrange them as you see fit. A 3D mode enables you to walk through the virtual garden to view your changes and the program also has a feature that lets you change the seasons, including mid-seasons, and see the effect on your trees, bushes and flowers immediately. It's even possible to preview growth over time, and predict where shadows will fall during the day and throughout the year using the Shadow Caster.

Additionally, *3D Landscape 2 Deluxe* provides a Plant Library with photographs, descriptions and gardening advice for over 2200 plants. Especially valuable is the How To Guide with its tips, principles and techniques for achieving and maintaining a perfect garden.

CONTACT POINTS

**Geoff Hamilton's
3D Garden Designer 3**
Price: £19.99*
GSP
Fax: 01480 480 206

3D Landscape Deluxe 5
Price: £30*
Mindscape
Tel: 01293 651 300
www.mindscape.co.uk

3D Landscape 2 Deluxe
Price: £9.99*
Focus Multimedia
Tel: 01889 570 156
www.focusmm.co.uk

*UK prices

Part of Broderbund's Home Design range, 3D Landscape Deluxe 5 can import buildings created in 3D Home Architect, and offers superior 3D photo-realism, backed up with a large illustrated library of plants, shrubs and garden features.

Wine guides

Take your enjoyment of wine to the next level and create your own master cellar with the help of these Multimedia guides.

The perception of wine expertise as the province of the well-heeled and pretentious faded away a long time ago. But choosing what to buy can still be a haphazard and expensive business for the average wine buyer. The ideal solution would be to have an expert on tap to help you choose between the many thousands of wines available from around the world, and teach you something of wine production too.

Wine guides on CD-ROM go beyond mere words and pictures by allowing you to investigate the world of wine interactively, in some cases with animated demonstrations and videos. Accessing all this information from a PC means that you can compare and contrast different wines with each other and find out about their compatibility with specific foods, all with a few mouse clicks.

● Epicurial delight

For the ultimate in factual knowledge on just about every wine in existence, GSP's *Wine Encyclopedia* CD-ROM is easily as extensive in scope as an entire shelf of books on the subject. The software is essentially a database of 28,000 different wines but with an attractive and intuitive interface which encourages browsing and exploration. Each card in the database provides descriptive data on

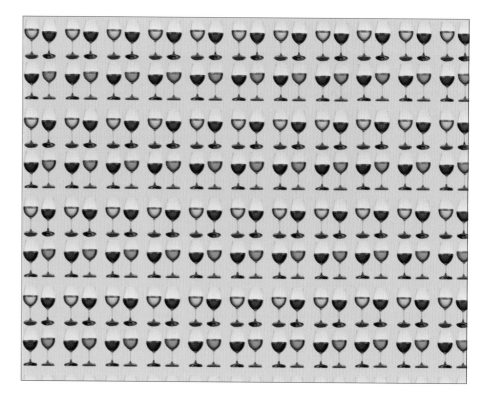

The sometimes daunting task of choosing an appropriate wine from the vast selection on offer becomes a pleasure with the help of an interactive wine guide.

the wine in question, 3000 of which include representations of the bottle labels to help you recognize the wine described when it is offered for sale. The wine cards also include handy cross-references to a database of wine producers, available via a single click of the mouse and complete with addresses, phone numbers and location maps.

The Wine Cellar Manager is a useful feature of *Wine Encyclopedia* that lets you add wines from the main database to your own list. You can use this facility to keep track of your own expanding cellar collection, so you always have up-to-date and accurate information on what's actually in there at your fingertips.

Unique to the program is its recipe section. Not only does this section suggest which wine would best accompany particular foods, *Wine Encyclopedia* offers a collection of 400 detailed recipes with cooking instructions and mouth-watering photos to match.

● Oz Clarke in person

Wine expert and TV personality Oz Clarke has lent his name to the successful and regularly updated Wine Guide series, published on CD-ROM by Focus Multimedia. Although the software incorporates an encyclopedia

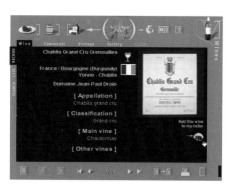

Search or scroll through the list of 28,000 wines in Wine Encyclopedia, *pick out your favourites and learn to recognise their distinctive labels.*

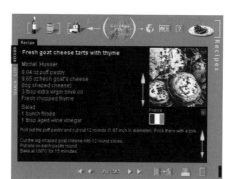

Wine Encyclopedia *goes beyond merely matching wines to certain foods by being the only guide to include actual recipes with cooking instructions and photos.*

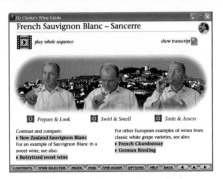

Oz Clarke himself introduces his Wine Guide when you click on the video button, and pops up again in scores of direct explanatory videos throughout the CD-ROM.

Watch and learn as Oz Clarke's Wine Guide shows you how to taste many popular wines, then compare them with recommended alternatives.

Oz Clarke's Wine Guide introduces the wine enthusiast to all the basics of wine tasting, from visual recognition to advanced tasting techniques.

of wines, producers and their regions, *Oz Clarke's Wine Guide* is more of an all-round Multimedia title for wine-lovers. Throughout the entire CD, the personable Oz pops up in integrated video clips to entertain and explain just about every aspect of evaluating and enjoying wine.

Among these is a section on wine-tasting in which Oz himself tipples and expresses his opinion on a number of popular choices. The Wine Selector is well-detailed too, providing basic domain profiles together with tasting notes and 'best years', and including custom fields for you to fill out yourself. Maturity charts help you spot the right time to buy and drink certain classic wines, while connoisseurs can refresh their knowledge of the vintage charts.

Also included is comprehensive advice on spotting styles, reading bottle labels and planning your own cellar. Those new to the world of viticulture can also explore the history of wine and its production.

● World video tour

Another TV celebrity wine expert, Jancis Robinson hosts a Multimedia guide on DVD-Video. *Wine – Jancis Robinson* is more than a simple VHS-to-DVD conversion though; it is a genuine multifaceted title to rival the CD-ROM approach.

The five hours of video on the single disc are split into snippets which can be viewed on their own or as part of longer presentations on wider topics. So you can simply sit back and watch the videos in

conventional half-hour programmes, or choose to navigate the DVD menus and watch short sections on various themes, from the correct way to open a bottle of champagne to understanding tannin.

Additionally, the DVD menus provide links to related information such as the meaning of the wine terms 'body', 'balance' and 'length'. You can follow Jancis on her video travels around the globe, clicking on the globe icon which appears from time to time in order to call up a map of each location. And when you think you have learnt it all, you can try the interactive quiz, accompanied by popping corks or slurping sound effects, depending on whether you get the answers right or wrong.

Of course, a CD-ROM or DVD is not going to replace a real glass of wine, but for the true wine devotee, there's no quicker or more convenient way of learning about wines and embellishing your cellar.

Jancis Robinson takes you on a wine tour of the world, from her own kitchen to the vineyards of Australia in her DVD-Video based title.

From look and taste to using the right type of glass, Wine – Jancis Robinson explains step by step how to undertake wine tasting in an expert fashion.

In Wine – Jancis Robinson, each location in the world tour is accompanied by a globe icon: click on it to display a map of the relevant wine-producing area.

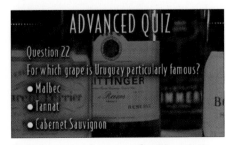

Having learnt as much as you can from Wine – Jancis Robinson, test yourself with a fast, interactive quiz, with different levels of expertise from beginner to advanced.

CONTACT POINTS

Wine Encyclopedia
Price: £9.99*
GSP
www.gsp.cc

Oz Clarke's Wine Guide 2002
Price: £19.99*
Focus Multimedia
Tel: 01889 570156
www.focusmm.co.uk

Wine – Jancis Robinson
Price: £17.99*
ILC
Tel: 020 7723 9606
www.jancisrobinson.com

*UK prices

The Internet

Audio-visual add-ons

The World Wide Web is full of Multimedia of all kinds. To take advantage of it, it's best to download and install a few useful audio-visual plug-ins and programs.

In its early days, the Web was a fairly static, one-dimensional experience. Sites were very much like online magazines. When you went to a Web address a single page loaded into your browser. Clicking on a link loaded another page, just as if you were flicking through pages in a magazine. There were pictures, but no animation, sound and interactivity.

Today, though, Multimedia interactivity is part of almost every professional site and a large number of amateur ones. Sound and moving objects are the rule rather than the exception. As the top browsers – Internet Explorer and Netscape Navigator – have developed they have become more adept at loading this type of material. But to get the most out of the Web, you may find it worthwhile to install some extra audio-visual software.

● Instant sound

Some audio-visual plug-ins are vital if you want to hear the full range of music and atmospheric sounds that many sites now use. These effects have to be delivered instantly when you interact with the features of a site, for example, when you move your mouse over a portrait photo and it says 'Hi, I'm Dave'; nobody wants to wait for a simple jingle or sound effect to download. But sound, and especially music, is not easy to deliver instantly. File size is a crucial issue. While MP3 files provide very high quality, they are also quite large and

take a considerable amount of time to download. This is why other file formats – such as MIDI (see page 123 and Stage 3, pages 108–109) and a variety of proprietary formats, depending on the plug-in – are preferred because they provide instant sound. Site designers may also use software such as Real Audio or Crescendo to add sounds – but the user then needs the relevant plug-in to experience these.

● Animation

If you want your Web site to be able to display eye-catching animations and interactive games, and if you want to view a range of sites that do this, then there are really only two choices of plug-in these days:

Adding sound and animation to a Web page makes it instantly more noticeable.

Macromedia's Shockwave and Flash players. Both of these allow Web designers to add small but effective interactive objects to their Web pages. Macromedia is the market leader in the field of Multimedia plug-ins, with over 500 million downloads of its players.

So many sites now use Shockwave and Flash that you'll be missing out on a lot of interesting action if you don't have them. Flash is the simpler of the two systems, while Shockwave offers more options to the Web designer, and so gives the user a richer experience with more Multimedia content and interactivity.

● Streaming media

In an ideal world, audio or video material is downloaded and played in real time, with little or no pause as the data is loaded onto your PC – a process known as 'streaming'. That's the theory, at least; with a 56K modem the practice lags far behind. However, as broadband Internet connection becomes more widely available (see Stage 7, pages 112–113) true streaming is a real possibility, letting you watch and listen to 'Webcast' events worldwide. To make the most of the video files and MP3 music files you will encounter, you need a more sophisticated plug-in.

This comes in the form of a breed of software known as the 'media player'. Media players allow you to play streaming media live from the Web, and act as off-line players for sound and video files stored on your hard disk, letting you play your collection of MP3 music. Also, they come with pre-selected Web sites where you can find media of all types for all tastes.

In the Windows world there are two main competitors vying for dominance: Microsoft, with Windows Media Player, and RealOne Player. There is also the QuickTime system from Apple, which is available for use with Windows as well.

BUFFERING

Streaming audio and video sites use a technique known as 'buffering' to give you the illusion of a seamless media experience. Data sent from the site is stored in an area of memory known as a buffer, and is retrieved from there when it is needed by your browser or plug-in. This way, the data can be displayed long before the whole file has been transmitted. With a 56K connection you are likely to get lots of jerky motion or stuttering sounds as there will be gaps in the delivery of different segments of the file. However, with a broadband Internet connection, the streaming should become seamless.

Sites for plug-ins

Here we take a look at the sites for those special plug-ins that allow you to experience rich Multimedia content on the Internet.

iPIX

www.ipix.com/

Web browsers are designed to display certain images – animated GIF banners and JPG photos, for example – without any extra software, but to view specially created 360-degree images you'll need an iPIX plug-in. These images are often used on Web sites where the designers want to show you the inside of a building or other location. For example, you might find an iPIX image that shows a car's interior on a car manufacturer's Web site. You use your mouse to navigate around the image, viewing it from several different angles.

The effect is seamless, and it provides you with a far better impression of the car's interior space than a series of static images.

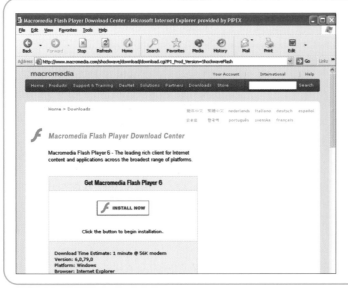

Flash and Shockwave

www.macromedia.com/

If you don't have these plug-ins, then get them right away. Without them, you just won't be able to take advantage of the creativity and interactivity on display on the Web. Any interesting interactive site is likely to be using one or both of these. Although they are two separate plug-ins, Flash and Shockwave work well together. The former produces relatively simple animations, while the latter brings you interactive Multimedia presentations and learning activities. You can download them separately, but it is better to download Shockwave, which also includes the Flash plug-in. Sites using Shockwave are often described as being 'shocked' and present users with a 'shocked' or 'non-shocked' option on an introductory page.

Liquid Audio

www.liquidaudio.com/

Liquid Player 6 is a very popular streaming and MP3 player. It covers the main file formats and also has its own proprietary Liquid Tracks format, so you'll need the plug-in for sites that use this format.

If you download MP3 files, Liquid Player 6 gives you powerful organizing features, as well as allowing you to save files onto, or 'burn', your own CDs. You can also use it to turn your own CD tracks into MP3 files, which can then be downloaded on to a portable MP3 player, for example. Liquid Player works with Windows XP's own Media Player, so that any portable MP3 player that you have already set up with Media Player will work with Liquid Player automatically. Liquid Audio also runs www.liquid.com, a Web site that lets you preview clips of commercial music releases so you can decide whether or not to buy them.

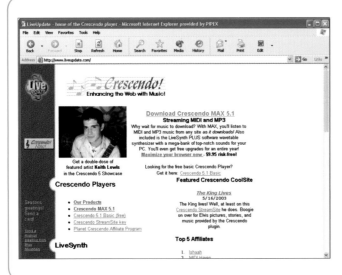

Crescendo

www.liveupdate.com/

Crescendo 5.1 Basic can stream MIDI files in addition to MP3 files. As such, it is worth obtaining, since it covers a lot of audio options. The Basic player is free, but for $9.95 (around £6) you can download Crescendo MAX 5.1, which also includes a high-quality software synthesizer for listening to MIDI files. This is a useful combination, as it incorporates many of the most popular music formats.

There are links to sites where Crescendo is demonstrated, so once you've installed the software, you can have a look at how effectively it can be used to generate musical accompaniment for Web pages. If you have taken advantage of Crescendo in making your own Web pages, you can submit your site for possible inclusion in the Crescendo 'Showcase'.

NookNak/NoiseNak

www.nakware.com

Not everyone wants music, or at least not all the time. When you have a CD blaring away and the phone rings it would be preferable not to have to fiddle around with Windows' volume control settings first. The NoiseNak and NookNak plug-ins from New Zealand give you a wide range of easy controls over the sound on your PC.

NoiseNak offers such features as automatically setting volume limits for times of the day or week and reducing the volume after a set period in which the PC is not used. NookNak allows you to alter various settings of your PC simply by moving your mouse over a corner of the screen. You can instantly mute the PC, for example, by moving the mouse to the bottom right corner of the screen; it's a lot quicker than using the volume control settings.

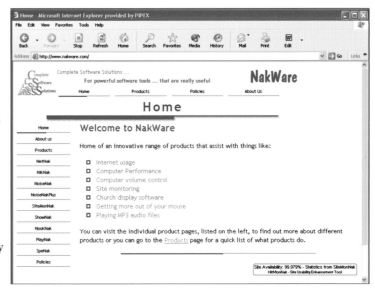

Media players

If you really want to have access to all the streaming media on the Web, make sure you have all three of the programs covered here.

RealOne Player

www.real.com/

The longest-standing name in this field is RealOne Player, which you can download from www.real.com. At one time this had a monopoly and quickly established a dominant position in the market. The player is a single program that uses RealAudio 8 and RealVideo 9 streaming formats. Many streaming sites use the Real formats for audio and video, so if you only download one extra media player, this is the one you should choose. RealOne Player offers all sorts of extras, including many 'channels' for streaming content, a list of Internet radio stations, and the ability to organize and play your MP3 collection.

Windows Media Player

www.microsoft.com/windows/windowsmedia

Microsoft underestimated the potential of Multimedia on the Internet, with the result that Real's plug-ins and player programs got a head start. Microsoft's answer was to turn the basic Media Player included with Windows 98 into the all-singing, all-dancing Windows Media Player available with Windows XP.

It's worth keeping your copy of Media Player updated. Visit this site for extra skins and visualizations (see Stage 4, page 25) to jazz up your Multimedia experience. You can also find plug-ins that add some useful extra features, such as DVD movie decoders.

QuickTime

www.apple.com/quicktime

You should have both of the above media players, but another useful program is QuickTime, Apple's technology for delivering Multimedia sound and video. This is built into the Macintosh operating system, but you can download a driver from www.apple.com/quicktime to run QuickTime files on a PC. In fact, there's a good chance you may already have a version on your system, since many Multimedia CDs use QuickTime and install it on your system with the program itself. Examine the Programs menu to check. QuickTime is widely used in the Mac world, in which many Multimedia designers work, so there's a lot of good material. But you won't be able to run QuickTime files in other media players since it uses its own file format.

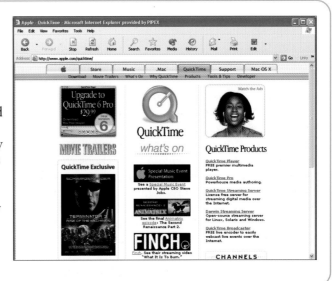

Encryption explained

If the privacy of the information you send across the Internet is important to you, encryption is the answer. One thing you might want to do, for instance, is encode your email messages so that they can be read only by people to whom you have given your own special code.

Please charge £150 to my credit card, number 5555 1236 5678 9876.

LNGKIJBrniTmAFr
YMgGgzk7EDzCHVj
Wfx7qgmcL1vw8Zvj72
R/HtwpxiHEw

Encryption – the encoding of computer information so that it can be read only by people who have a special code – may sound as if it belongs to the realm of spy fiction, but it is in fact an increasingly important part of Internet computing.

You might already be using encryption without realizing it. When you use a secure server for ordering goods from a Web site, for example, your credit card information is sent in an encoded form so anyone who intercepts it can't read it and use it fraudulently. Once it is received at the Web server, it's decoded so the company selling you the goods can debit your account as with a normal transaction.

● Inside encryption

Encryption is one of the most complex areas in computing. The companies that devise encryption routines use advanced mathematics to make sure that the encoded information is almost impossible to crack. The very best codes produced by encryption techniques are, quite literally, uncrackable.

However, encryption is also a highly controversial issue, provoking much pro- and anti-encryption debate, as it raises concerns about free speech and anti-terrorist measures. It is also an area where international government legislation and shadowy intelligence agencies are closely involved. In fact, the whole issue of encryption affects just about every area of the Internet, from the companies using the Web to make money, to the lunatic fringe.

● Arguments against encryption

The anti-encryption argument says that if you want to code your email, then you must have something to hide: you're a terrorist, a drugs dealer, or some other kind of dangerous criminal. Clearly, government agencies are concerned about being unable to intercept communications sent between suspected criminals or disreputable organizations.

The pro-encryption argument insists that everyone has a right to privacy, that the anti-encryption argument is merely paranoid and that your personal email messages should be just as sacrosanct as your personal letters or your diary. This lobby believes that everyone should be able to encode personal information.

DID YOU KNOW?

If you aren't already using encryption, every email you send can be read by anyone with the desire to do so and the necessary technical knowledge. Such a person could be a mischievous hacker doing it for idle fun, much like the people who scan mobile phone conversations; it could be someone who has targeted your email specifically for commercial espionage; or it could be a government agency trawling for potentially suspect communications. In any event, you should be aware that non-encrypted email is not secure and that confidential information should be sent encrypted or by another method.

● The Clipper chip

Probably the most significant development to bring this encryption argument to a head was the uproar surrounding the US government's Clipper chip initiative.

The Clipper chip is a sophisticated device the US government wanted to have installed within any equipment that might use encryption: computers, modems, digital TVs and so on. The Clipper chip uses a complex mathematical encryption procedure that's designed to be impossible to crack. However, there would be an important exception: the US government and its agencies would keep a record of everyone's encryption key in order to be able to decode anyone's encrypted information, should they decide this was necessary.

Although it seemed to take the US government by surprise, this proposal naturally led to a public outcry and three successive Clipper proposals have been abandoned.

● Other benefits

Encryption can have other benefits in addition to giving complete privacy. For example, it confirms the identity of the sender. This is important, as it's very easy for unscrupulous users with a little technical knowledge in this area to fake an email, making it appear to have been sent from someone else, which can cause chaos on bulletin boards and email lists on the Internet. If you receive an encrypted email and then decode it using the sender's key, you can be assured that it was sent by them.

Encryption also protects messages from being corrupted or tampered with during transmission, ensuring that a message is received precisely as it was originally sent. As part of the encoding, extra data is added that can be checked on decoding to ensure nothing has changed.

WHAT IT MEANS

KEY

When information is encrypted, a special code is used to turn the normal legible text into what looks like gibberish. This code is called the key. Many encryption schemes use two keys – a private and a public key – so that only the sender and intended recipient can read the message.

Easy-to-use encryption

Despite the complexity of the encryption process, using PGP (Pretty Good Privacy) – one of the most popular programs – is straightforward.

PGP IS based on public key cryptography. This works through two keys, a private key which you keep entirely to yourself and a public key which you let everyone know.

When you want to send an encrypted message to someone, you use the recipient's public key. This scrambles the information so that it can be read only by someone who knows the corresponding private key, ie the recipient. You can also use your own private key to 'sign' an email. The recipient can verify this digital signature through your public key, ensuring that it was sent by you and the contents haven't been altered.

The PGP software

The PGP program leads you through this complex process. The vital task of creating the keys is carried out by a slick Wizard-style process. After that, most functions can be controlled from within your email software, to which the necessary plug-ins are added during the installation. PGP includes plug-ins for

Eudora, Microsoft Outlook and Outlook Express. If you have a different email program, you can use the Windows Clipboard to encrypt and decrypt messages. The software includes online help and you can download the 246-page manual in Adobe Acrobat format from the PGP Web site (www.pgpi.org). Download and read it before you use encrypted messages.

Using your keys

Once you have generated your key pair, you must pass on your public key to whoever needs it. The key is just a block of text, so you can use normal email to send it. You can also post it on a Web site for downloading – there are dedicated key servers for this and the PGP software will handle the upload.

If you are emailed a key, or if you retrieve one from a public key server, check that it is genuine. The safest way is to ask the sender to read their unique 'fingerprint' over the phone, or to post or fax it to you. To see the fingerprint code, click on the key in the PGPkeys window and select Key Properties from the Keys menu.

Although a typical fingerprint (above) is a complicated piece of code, you'll find clear explanations of how to use this encryption technology in the comprehensive downloadable manual (below).

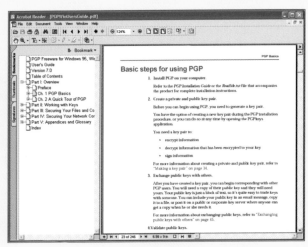

Go-faster Internet

The Internet was once an exciting development for a few scientists. But now there are over a billion users and Internet traffic is increasing phenomenally. How will the Net cope? And how will your connection improve?

For most users, the Internet appeared like a virtual Big Bang. First there was nothing, then, suddenly, there was a huge and ever-expanding universe. The Internet appeared everywhere: magazines, radio, TV and on business cards and letterheads.

The huge burst of interest and use has caused a correspondingly huge explosion in the amount of data that the Internet is being asked to transfer from site to site – and it can barely cope. As anyone who has tried to download files during US daylight hours knows, sometimes the Internet simply gets bogged down. Even fast broadband links that can download 50,000 characters per second are affected by other Internet traffic – reducing download speeds to a fraction of their true potential. At times, it's more of an information gridlock than a highway.

● Internet beginnings

The Internet began life in the late 1960s with the development of packet-switching networks. Information on these networks didn't go straight from computer A to computer B; it often took a circuitous route, such as from A to P to L to D to Q to B. Furthermore, not all packets travelled the same way. A little like a technical pass-the-parcel game, every computer along the line simply concerned itself with passing the packet on to the next, until it

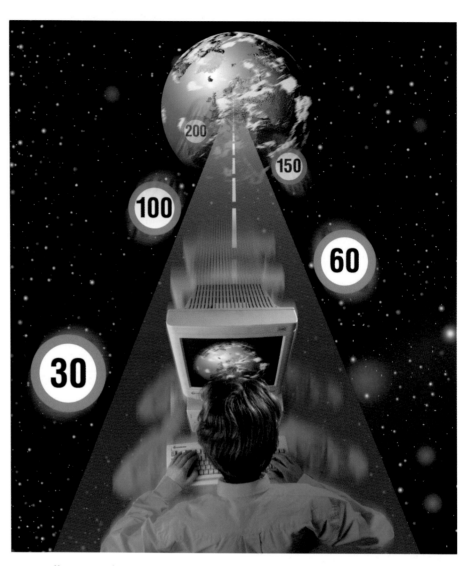

eventually got to the computer it was intended for. The speed at which the packets could be transmitted along the links that connected Internet computers was extremely sluggish compared with the modems of today.

The Internet first emerged in something like today's form when in 1985 the US National Science Foundation (NSF) linked together their five national supercomputer centres across the country via a 56Kbps national network. This was the original backbone of the Internet. As more and more people realized that the network was a great way of not just accessing the supercomputers for research but also for transmitting

With increasing Web traffic, it's not surprising that jams occur. Developers are preparing for the future to ensure your browsing stays quick and trouble-free.

WHAT IT MEANS

PACKET

All data files sent over the Internet are split up into much smaller chunks, called packets, that are sent individually along a chain of computers, from the source to the destination. The packets all include an address, which lets the network know where it should direct them to. When a packet finally reaches the destination computer, it is reassembled into the original file.

BANDWIDTH LEAPS

Bandwidth refers to the amount of data that can be transmitted in a given amount of time. Usually, this is expressed in bits per second. A typical modem connecting a home computer to a telephone line, for example, could handle 56,000 bits per second (bps). However, even an ADSL connection at 512Kbps is slow, compared to the flood of asynchronous transfer mode networks which run into gigabits (one billion bits) per second. Fibre optic networks improve the performance even more, achieving up to 3200 gigabits per second.

email, files and newsgroup messages, traffic soon exceeded the network's limits. Consequently, the backbone was upgraded in 1988, this time connecting 13 sites with a newer, faster 1.544Mbps line and the old one was closed. But the increase in traffic continued and during 1989–1991 the backbone was upgraded and extended once again. Other networks were developed independently, each one hitching onto this main backbone and by 1991 there were nearly 4000 of these 'hitch-hikers'.

In 1995, realizing that the network was under strain, the NSF transferred responsibility for the development and implementation of the Internet from the government to more commercial parties. It was decided that, rather

than a long, strung-out backbone, along which other networks could connect, there would be four connection points through which the global Internet traffic would operate. These Network Access Points (NAPs) are located in San Francisco, Washington DC, Chicago and Pennsauken, New Jersey and they took over the Internet operation from the NSF on 30 April 1995. Today they run at a staggering 622Mbps.

Under the current system, sending an email to someone in another office down the road can be a long process. Usually, the email will leave your computer, travel across the Atlantic to your Internet service provider (ISP) in, say, Chicago, and back through the recipient's ISP before arriving on the

Although an exciting innovation, high-capacity fibre optics is still in development.

other person's computer. It would be more sensible to have the email carried by a localized network and to use the NAPs only when the circumstances demand it, which is now beginning to happen.

High bandwidth Metropolitan Area Ethernet (MAE) systems already exist in big cities around the world and these help to siphon traffic off the Net. The London Metropolitan Area Network connects a growing number of academic institutions. It was supplied and installed by a consortium of cable TV firms. Cable modems that can use the broader bandwidth offered by cable – rather than telephone lines – have been at breakthrough point for some time. A cable modem can give you a connection to your ISP that is about as fast as an office network.

● Network upgrade

The latest attempt to upgrade the Internet's capacity and reliability is IPv6 (Internet Protocol version 6). All the world's major companies that are interested in the Internet are involved: Cisco, Intel, Nokia, Microsoft and many others. The idea is to upgrade the network to cope with a predicted massive increase in users, in the amount of data transferred, and the need for faster, more fault-tolerant and reliable systems.

Faster processors from companies such as Intel will enable the Internet's file servers to handle more data more quickly, while new routers from companies such as Cisco will allow the data to get to its destination much faster. Only by making sure that no single link in the Internet chain is holding back the performance of the PC-to-Web-site connection will we finally see real performance gains.

Wireless Internet

IN THE UK, a company called Liberty Broadband is introducing a new wireless connection whereby data is broadcast over the airwaves rather than carried down wires. This is a fast service, transferring data at speeds from 512Kbps to 2Mbps. A roof-mounted antenna and Speedbox interface replace the dial-up or ADSL modem. However, the system isn't yet available nationwide – only when 200 customers have signed up in one area does the economy of scale make it viable for the company to install a local transceiver.

Keep up to date with wireless Internet developments by visiting Liberty Broadband's Web site (www.libertybroadband.co.uk).

ORGANIZED CHAOS

The Internet is a worldwide phenomenon encompassing both community-minded technology experts and IT companies keen to make money by developing newer technology. As a result, its development can sometimes seem a little chaotic. It's not uncommon for months of development in one area to be sidelined as a more recent breakthrough makes a leap forward. Although frustrating for the technology experts who have wasted their time, the good news for the rest of us is that this worldwide competition means that the Internet is developing faster than any other technology.

Fishing on the Net

If you're an avid angler, the Internet is a great place to learn about tackle technology developments – and everything else to do with fishing.

To the uninitiated, fishing might seem one of the simpler, less structured, sports. Some might suppose that the only tools required are a reasonably long stick, a length of line, a hook and some bait. Of course, anyone who goes fishing regularly knows that the truth is very different. Technology has not overlooked the tranquil sport of fishing and the odds are now firmly stacked against fish, as anglers employ everything from state-of-the-art composite rods and specially created bait to underwater sonar units.

● Regional variations

Just as for any other popular pastime, numerous Web sites are dedicated to the sport of fishing and related topics. However, as fishing is popular worldwide, it is necessary to dig around a little more carefully than usual to find information that relates to a given locality. Because the Internet is largely a US-dominated medium you will need to search carefully for Web sites covering popular spots in Cornwall or Scotland, as opposed to those for fishing in California or Florida.

As ever, try to narrow your search by using terms that will restrict the hits to specific places – for example, 'fly-fishing AND Scotland'. Of course, it's easy enough to spot an American fishing site simply by its content – bass and muskie are not the sort of catch to be found in rivers all over the world.

Over the next few pages we'll be looking at some of the more prominent fishing sites and the sort of information they offer. Many of the sites listed are entirely amateur, and are none the worse for that; they're produced by fishing enthusiasts in an attempt to help their fellow anglers, or simply to show off their biggest catch. But there are plenty of other sites produced by companies that organize professional fishing trips or holidays. These are worth checking out, as they can be a great way to obtain up-to-date information and discover resorts that you might not have considered otherwise.

UNUSUAL CATCHES

As rich as any one locality is in species, there is, of course, a much greater variety of fish – and fishing techniques – to be found elsewhere in the world. The Internet offers sites featuring such pursuits as ice fishing, spear fishing and deep-sea fishing, as well as pages all about species that may be unfamiliar, such as bass, muskie and walleye. These sites are easy to find and offer an interesting insight into fishing in other parts of the world. They may also give you holiday ideas – and several of them will actively help you to organize a fishing holiday.

PC TIPS

As with most hobbies, sharing tips and tricks with other enthusiasts is as much fun as fishing itself. By joining an online group dedicated to fishing, you can post messages and receive answers from other group members. There are newsgroups that you can access with Outlook Express – such as uk.rec.fishing.sea and uk.rec.fishing.coarse, but there are also many other online forums you can access with your Web browser, such as Yahoo's Groups. Search for 'fishing forums' or 'fishing chat' to find some suitable sites.

Fishing sites

There are, of course, many more fishing Web sites than we can cover here. Consider these as the bait to hook you on more Web site angling.

Fishing.co.uk
www.fishing.co.uk

This is a very professional and informative site, with something for every fishing fan, whether your interest is coarse, game, sea or whatever. There are plenty of sections that add to your knowledge and pleasure, and give practical help. You'll find articles from fishing experts that appear on a weekly or monthly basis and cover all aspects of fishing, as well as a 'trophy room' where you can display your own magnificent catch. There's also a good online interactive locator for all your fishing needs – from bait and tackle to fisheries and boat hire – and an e-shopping area where you can buy whatever you need. Alternatively, if you fancy trying some fishing abroad, the Holidays section has plenty of good ideas.

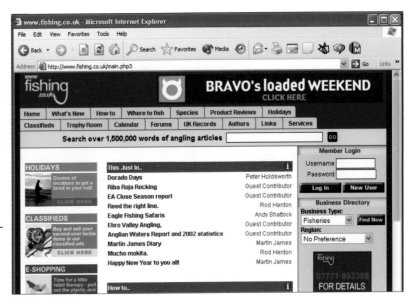

U.K. Sea Fishing FAQ
www.gorp.com/gorp/activity/saltfaq.htm

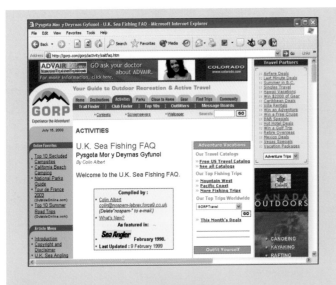

This site contains one of the few sources of information specific to sea fishing in the UK. It is organized as FAQs (Frequently Asked Questions), so there is little attempt to provide the range of features offered by the online fishing magazines. However, the FAQs provide comprehensive information and answers to all the common queries about fishing and advice which in many cases is unavailable elsewhere. The FAQ is organized into sections, the main ones being: UK Sea Angling And The Law; UK Sea Fish, Baits, Techniques, Tackle, Organisations & Clubs; and UK Sea Angling Publications & Software.

Fishing Licence Online
www.environment-agency.gov.uk/subjects/fish/246986/257338

Wherever you choose to pursue your angling in Britain, the fact is you will need a licence if you are over twelve years old – the penalty for fishing without one is £2500. From this official Environment Agency site you can purchase a one-day, eight-day, junior (12–16 year-olds) or full licence. If you buy a full licence, you will have to renew it by 31st March for each year you wish to keep it. However, do make sure that you know what type of licence you require – the price for including salmon and sea trout is considerably higher than the basic non-migratory and coarse version.

Other types of fishing licences include ones for people aged 65 and over and also the disabled, although these are not available directly through this particular Web site. The online process for purchasing a licence is relatively simple and saves the need for visiting the Post Office.

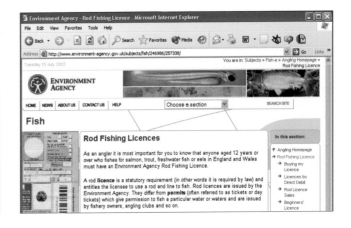

Special-interest sites

If you have a special interest in certain species, need your prize specimen preserved, or want to promote angling, here are some sites for you.

Fish & Fly

www.fishandfly.co.uk

An online-only fishing magazine, Fish & Fly is very much for the hardcore angler, specifically those who enjoy fly-fishing in the UK. This is a site created by enthusiasts for enthusiasts, and it is all the better for it. The articles are extremely detailed, but at the same time, often very entertaining. This might not be a site for fly-fishing novices, but it does have a sense of humour, and avoids being snobbish or geeky. The site is organized into various sections, such as Features, Fly Tying and Forums.

Carp Net

www.carp.net

As is obvious from its name, this site is dedicated to carp – although to a lesser extent it also embraces other freshwater fish. All the various needs of the carp fisherman are covered here, from product reviews to fishing locations. There are regular sections on bait and tackle, carp fishing articles from around the world and an excellent tactics section with diagrams. The site has a fairly basic design, but it's worth persevering because the information it contains is first class.

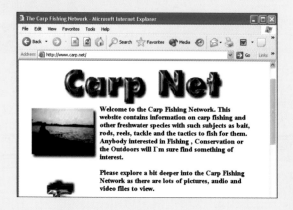

Floats Gone

www.floatsgone.btinternet.co.uk/index.html

If coarse fishing is your thing, then you could do worse than visit this charming site. Run by a passionate enthusiast, Floats Gone claims to be a complete guide to coarse fishing. It is certainly extensive – almost everything you can think of to do with coarse fishing is here and there is something for everybody, no matter what level of experience you have. As well as the usual articles, FAQs and links, there is a section on fishing for the disabled and a special children's area.

Fish taxidermy services

freespace.virgin.net/sts.northwales/intro.htm

For the less 'politically correct' anglers who prefer to keep what they catch, there are other ways to show off a fish, rather than frying it up and making it the centrepiece of a dinner party. This company deals with all animals, but specifically advertises its expertise in stuffing fish. A full wall-mounted display will cost anything from £150 to over a thousand pounds, depending on the weight of your catch.

Where To Fish

www.where-to-fish.com/

This is the Internet version of the very popular Where To Fish directory. The site boasts over 3000 pages of information, covering thousands of fishing locations in the UK and abroad. The information is split into six main areas: England, Scotland, Wales, Ireland, Northern Ireland and Abroad. The facts that you find for each individual location may, at first, seem a little basic, but all the necessary contact details are provided along with a concise listing of the fish available, fishing conditions and directions to the site.

Regional-interest Web sites

Here are some sites that cover specific areas of the British Isles.

Fly Fishing in Scotland

www.flyfishingscotland.com/subpages/index.htm

Almost everything you need to know about classic fly-fishing is included on this comprehensive site. At its core is solid and practical information about Scotland's rivers and lochs, such as when and where to fish them. And this site proves that fishing in Scotland is by no means limited to salmon and trout; whilst those fish do feature strongly, there is also plenty of information regarding other species, such as ferox and char. A good selection of pictures of flies suitable for Scotland provide a bonus – and they'll even send you tying instructions if you make a request by email. The site is still in its early stages, yet even now it contains a wealth of information.

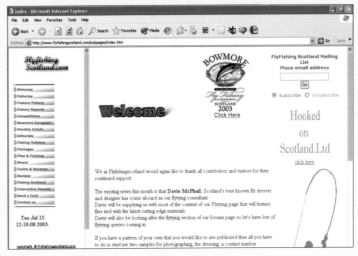

Fishing in Northern Ireland

www.interknowledge.com/northern-ireland/ukifish1.htm

It is easy to overlook Northern Ireland on a fishing trip, but this site will prove very useful for anglers. It gives detailed directions so you can find all the popular fishing locations and lists all the types of fish which can be caught there. Certain fishing areas also have disabled facilities which are detailed here.

Fishing in Wales

www.fishing-in-wales.com/

This is an extremely extensive site on fishing in Wales. It details all the best fishing areas as well as providing information on nearby shops and accommodation. There is also much general information about fishing techniques and different fish species.

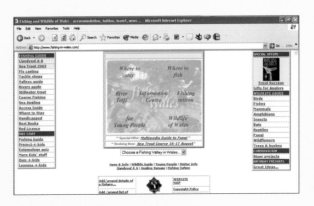

Cooking on the Internet

No matter what type of meal you are interested in preparing, or what exotic vegetable you want to include in a recipe, the Internet will almost certainly provide you with what you need.

If you want to find great recipes or new places to eat, discover more about the nutritional benefits of certain foods or find out about the different cuisines around the world, the Internet is undoubtedly the best place to look.

Food has become one of the great lifestyle pursuits of our time. We eat out more often and we're more interested than ever in cooking at home. A trip to even a modest supermarket reveals a vast array of exotic ingredients from around the world. And when we're not eating or preparing food, we might well be watching a food programme on the TV. You won't be surprised to find that this interest is matched on the Net, where food sites abound – from vast recipe databases to chatty e-zines with plenty of pictures and strong opinions.

● **A world of food**

Every culinary interest you can think of is catered for on the Web. As it's a truly global medium, the Internet is a great place to find details on your favourite ethnic cuisine and also to discover other cookery styles that you might never have otherwise encountered. It's also a good place to find recommended and specialist restaurants in your local area.

There are many sites created by enthusiasts for a particular cuisine that invite surfers to send in their views and provide a forum for exchanging ideas and recipes. And, as with any shared-interest sites, they can be a good way of making new friends. To get an idea of what's on offer, try a search for 'curry' and, even when restricted to UK sites about curry you'll find plenty of information and listings of good restaurants.

● **Healthy eating**

We are all more health-conscious these days and better informed about the health effects of the food we eat and how it is produced and prepared. The last decade has also seen many people changing to a vegetarian diet. Both healthy eating and vegetarianism are covered in many Internet food sites, and even the most difficult-to-please gourmets will find a wide range of recipes to whet their appetite. Online shopping has also boomed in recent years. Whereas in the early

Internet days, you could find only outrageously expensive luxuries for purchase online, now you can locate just about anything.

In the UK it is possible to place online orders for organic fruit and vegetables, and in many areas you can now log on to a major supermarket site, order your groceries and have them delivered to your home at a convenient time that you can specify (see Stage 4, page 153).

However you order your food, preparation remains important and to help you there is a veritable cornucopia of recipes on the Web – in fact, enough to keep you in three different square meals a day for the rest of your life. RecipeSource (see opposite), for example, is a massive database offering both search and browse facilities and which contains more than 70,000 different recipes.

Sites to visit

There is such a wealth of information on the Web for both the budding cook and experienced chef that it's difficult to know where to begin. Here, we give you a taste of some popular and unusual sites.

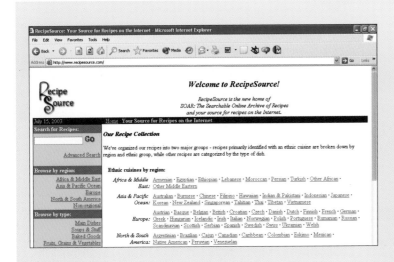

SOAR – RecipeSource

www.recipesource.com/

This online archive of recipes is an astonishing free resource for the cook. There are over 70,000 recipes in the database and all are easily searchable, so that you can quickly find something quite specific, such as recipes using tofu. If you don't feel like searching, browsing is an entertaining alternative, as the recipes are listed both by ingredient and ethnic origin. There are no frills on this site, but what you do receive is an incredible depth of information.

WeightWatchers

www.weightwatchers.co.uk

Slimming is never easy but more and more people seem to be involved in weight loss programs. The WeightWatchers Web site is busy, bright and colourful and has a wealth of features to help the potential slimmer.

In addition to all the information you'd expect to find, such as how WeightWatchers works and details of your nearest meeting, you'll find numerous slimmer-friendly recipes, together with their points values. In fact, there are over 600 recipes available, covering all tastes and courses, including desserts. There is also a message board, an online shop and a section on success stories.

THE RECIPE RING

When browsing sites devoted to cooking, you might come across links similar to those below. This is because many culinary enthusiasts have created Web sites with the sole intention of spreading their favourite recipes around the world. If you create a Web site of your own, perhaps featuring favourite family recipes, you can add it to the Recipe Ring by just following the simple instructions. You can rest assured that any site you visit via the Web ring won't be trying to sell you something, but will be the loving creation of an enthusiast and will contain lots of interesting information.

Fresh Food

www.freshfood.co.uk

This site gives you the chance to combine health and tasty eating – in the form of organic vegetables – with the ease of Internet shopping. The idea is simple and is based on what is called a box scheme. You make your order and every week or fortnight, a box of organic produce is delivered direct to your door.

Japanese Cookery

www.cookeryonline.com/Japanese/

If it is the Oriental way of cooking that interests you, then this is a good site to drop in on. This particular page is only small and its design is simple but the articles it has to offer on Japanese cookery are interesting.

There is a handy guide on how to roll sushi, a very useful dictionary of Japanese cookery terms, plenty of Japanese recipes to try out, with intriguing titles such as crab meat with wasabi mayonnaise and scallops in yuzu, and a whole host of links to other Japanese food sites. There is even a section on Japanese cooking basics to get you started if this is a new area to you.

Foodwatch

www.foodwatch.com.au

Healthy eating is the watchword of this site from Australian food broadcaster and writer Catherine Saxelby. There's a good variety of sections on offer, covering material such as the small print on labels and how to lose weight, and including a page where you enter your personal details and your weight rating is assessed. The site's recipes are very clearly and attractively presented, and there is also a comprehensive A–Z section on nutrition, which is useful for checking up on all those scientific terms.

Vegetarian Society

www.vegsoc.org/

This is the official site of the Vegetarian Society of the United Kingdom. As such, it has all sorts of information about how you can join and about vegetarianism in general. There's also plenty of useful material here about food and drink.

The site offers information on the Cordon Vert vegetarian cookery school and has over 600 recipes. You can search for a particular recipe or browse through the categories, which are divided into a large seasonal section and various other categories, such as recipes from around the world and vegetarian cooking for one. There's also an online store where you can buy books and gifts, although the site does not sell food.

BBC Food

www.bbc.co.uk/food

Given the number of cooks on TV, you would expect the BBC to offer a rich mix of cookery topics on their Web site and they do not disappoint. In fact, if you are only ever going to look at one food and cookery site, this should probably be the one. The home page is more of a portal – a collection of related sites. You can use the pull-down menu to navigate to areas for TV programmes such as *Food and Drink* and *Gary Rhodes' Classics*, where you'll find all your favourite personalities. You can also visit the Ask the Chef section for answers to all your cookery questions, information on healthy eating and, of course, recipes. There's lots of light-hearted content as well: you can send in your recipe to Jamie Oliver for a competition, or even chat with him online.

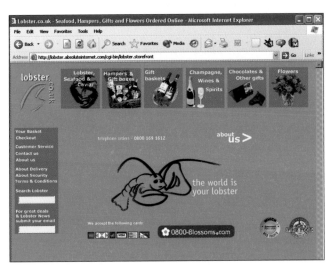

Lobster

www.lobster.co.uk

If you crave the finer things in life – such as Beluga caviar or smoked salmon – this is the site you should visit. You'll find nothing but the best on the attractively designed Lobster site, with price tags to match. You can buy individual items or select a gourmet hamper, and they offer same-day delivery in London, or next day delivery nationwide.

The Grange

www.cookery-grange.co.uk

To further stimulate your enthusiasm, and develop your cooking skills, you could take a cookery course. At this site you can peruse details of the courses offered at The Grange, a 17th-century coach house in the Somerset countryside – just one of many cookery schools around the world. For lists of schools just about anywhere in the world, try www.cookingschools.com for more options.

SITES TO VISIT

A world of food

No matter how specific your query, there'll be a site to suit. Here are some more examples of specialist food sites.

For a site dedicated to tofu try:
The World Of Tofu
http://tofu.com/

For a site dedicated to the virtues of pasta try:
The National Pasta Association
www.ilovepasta.org/

Amazing plants

If you want to find out about the more bizarre or exotic-looking species of the plant world, then the World Wide Web is the place to go.

Until gardening programmes on the TV became popular, plants and botany were not viewed as particularly interesting subjects. Now, television schedules and newsagents are packed with all kinds of gardening and nature promotions.

The subject of botany covers the physiology, structure, genetics, ecology, distribution, classification and economic importance of plants – and the Internet has abundant information concerning all of these different areas.

While you will find plenty of conventional gardening sites that help you to trim your geraniums and prune your roses, there are many others that deal with the more unusual side of plants and plant habitats. These Web pages tend to be either serious botanical sites, created by researchers and students, or ones that have been produced by amateur enthusiasts. Gardening newsgroups

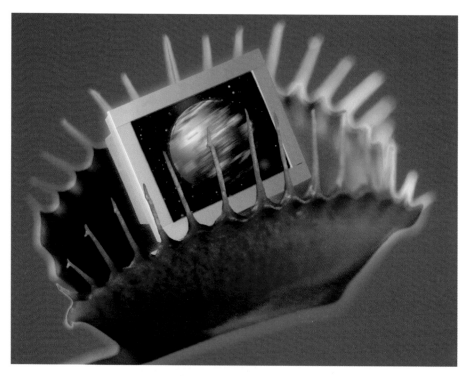

Is the Venus fly-trap really an alien? How exactly do desert plants survive? You'll find the answers to these and other unusual botanical questions – including many you never even thought to ask – on the Internet.

also abound. Whoever the author, and whatever the nature of the site, you'll find that most of these sites are well put together and totally absorbing.

● Carnivorous plants
The strangest plant that most people can think of is the Venus fly-trap. Although they are fascinating – and

there are dozens of Web sites dedicated to these weird plants – there are plenty of other bizarre and wonderful types of plant. Consider the *Rafflesia Arnoldii*, with a beautiful flower that grows up to a metre in diameter and stinks of rotting flesh – which makes it a pleasure to view but a horror to smell, unless you are a particular type of fly.

Plant life does not have to be quite so extreme in appearance, scent or behaviour to be interesting, however. Many people are just as fascinated by, for example, the 20,000-plus species of orchid in the world. With so many plants to choose from, each with their own specific horticultural needs, you require an information resource as large and versatile as the Web to keep well informed.

● Plants in the environment
Many of the plant Web sites are concerned with education, not only for school children, but also for a

ALIEN PLANTS

The idea that bacteria from passing comets and meteors might have originally 'seeded' life on earth is currently a popular theory. Some people have taken this concept a step further and suggested that there is a species of plant – specifically the Venus fly-trap – that could be of extraterrestrial origin. They argue that the fly-trap exists as only one species and grows in only one spot on Earth: a 100-mile radius around Wilmington, North Carolina. In the centre of this circle is what appears to be a series of craters from an ancient meteor shower. Drawing a parallel between the two facts has led to the belief that the fly-trap is alien in origin.

wider audience. These sites aim to promote a greater understanding of our natural environment and to draw people's attention to some of the richest plant environments in the world that are in danger of being destroyed.

The mangrove swamps of Indonesia and Australia, for example, have been gradually disappearing over the years because people considered them to be nothing more than breeding grounds for mosquitoes and crocodiles. It is only in recent years that we have become aware of the abundance of plant life they contain – and many plants that grow in these areas have never been properly researched.

Here we'll be looking at Internet sites covering many different aspects of botanical study and unusual plants. So, if you're interested in finding out more about all the different exotic species of plants, head towards one of the following sites.

LITTLE SHOP OF HORRORS

Although the Venus fly-trap is the most violent of carnivorous plants, it is not the biggest. In terms of sheer bulk, the largest meat-eating plants are those of the genus *Nepenthes* (see Borneo Exotics, below). The largest of these vine-like plants can grow up to 10 metres long. Their traps are reactive rather than proactive – animals just fall into them and die. Even so, they appear to be effective, since creatures as large as frogs and rats have been found inside the plants' traps, although the victims were probably sick or wounded when they fell into them.

Botanical sites

Whether you want to find out about rare plant species or unusual plant habitats, you'll find it all on the Internet's botanical sites.

Botany.com the Encyclopedia of Plants

www.botany.com/

It is quite rare to come across a site, such as this one, that deals with the wider world of plants in an accessible and entertaining way. The main part of this online encyclopaedia of plants lists entries in alphabetical order according to their common and botanical names.

Also included is a dictionary of botanical words and a set of links for various gardens, associations and societies. The site provides general descriptions of plants as well as information on the required methods of cultivation and propagation, and on the many different varieties and hybrids. The site lists just about every plant, from an ordinary rose bush to the most exotic species.

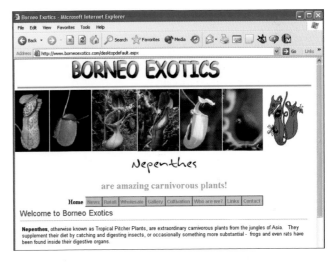

Borneo Exotics

www.borneoexotics.com/DesktopDefault.aspx

The Venus fly-trap is unique, even when compared with other carnivorous plants (see Alien plants box, opposite), but while it is in a category of its own, there exists in Borneo and other nearby islands a whole genus of insectivorous plants that capture and absorb insects. These plants are the *Nepenthes*, or more commonly known as Tropical Pitcher Plants.

Their common name comes from the oddly beautiful petals that form a pitcher-like shape in which insects are caught and killed, usually by drowning. There are currently about 90 known species of *Nepenthes*, although many of these are endangered by the destruction of their natural habitat.

This excellent site includes all kinds of information about these amazing plants, with details on how to grow them as well as how to help protect them in their natural environment.

International Aroid Society, Inc.

www.aroid.org/

Aroids are plants related to the *Araceae* family, which comprises the largest flowering plants in the world. This family includes the *Amorphophallus titanium*, or Corpse Flower, which attracts flies with its smell of rotting flesh. The Web site of the International Aroid Society provides extensive material on all aroid-related matters, ranging from numerous articles on the thousands of different species to a potted history of the Society itself. The gallery showcases plenty of fine specimens and there is also a very useful section on Latin pronunciation.

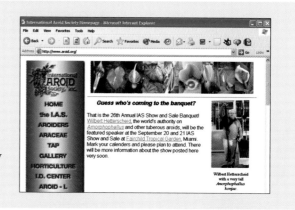

Aquatic Gardeners Association

www.aquatic-gardeners.org/

The Aquatic Gardeners Association (AGA) is an international organization of aquatic plant enthusiasts. Its Web site and journal, both called *The Aquatic Gardener*, are the only English language resources that are devoted primarily to aquatic plants. The main part of this Web site is dedicated to showing off the AGA's journal and enticing new members to join the association. The online bookstore also offers access to various books on aquatic gardening, which can be bought directly.

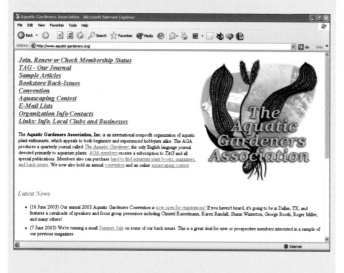

The Orchid House

retirees.uwaterloo.ca/~jerry/orchids/

The collection and cultivation of orchids was once the preserve of the rich, but an interest in orchids can now be enjoyed by anyone. A benefit of the previous exclusivity of orchid growing is that it is one of the best organized and most documented of plant hobbies. This means that information is easy to come by, but the sheer volume can make it difficult to research specific facts. The Orchid House has an excellent illustrated FAQs section that describes the basic features and needs of orchids. It also clarifies numerous false assumptions about the plants, for example, that none of the 20,000 species of orchids is a parasite.

The Silk Plant Company

www.silkplant.co.uk

Although artificial plants don't appeal to everyone, if you don't have green fingers, or if you simply haven't got the time, effort or space for a real plant, modern facsimiles do offer an interesting alternative. This is the Web site of a company dedicated to providing the most comprehensive selection of fine-quality artificial plants on the Internet. Trees and bushes seem to be the favourite type of artificial plant, but this Web site also offers a full range of other smaller plants to suit both homes and offices.

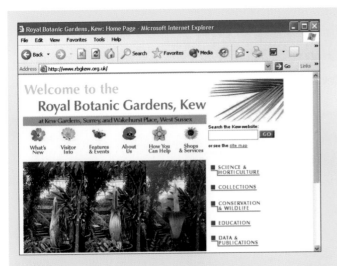

Royal Botanic Gardens, Kew

www.rbgkew.org.uk

The Royal Botanic Gardens at Kew are probably the most famous and well-stocked gardens in the world – no mean feat in the inclement climes of England. The tastefully-designed Kew Gardens Web site tells you all you need to know about the world-famous horticultural site. You can find out about everything that is going on at Kew, as well as check up on admission fees and opening times. If you are thinking of paying the gardens a visit, the Upcoming Events section will prove particularly useful.

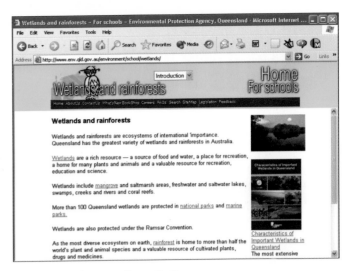

Wetlands and rainforests

www.env.qld.gov.au/environment/school/wetlands/

One of the most unusual and fascinating environments in the world is that of the mangrove swamps of Indonesia and Australia. This Web site comes from the Australian education board and, although aimed at primary and secondary school students, it is an excellent source of information for any visitor. All the information on the site's pages is split up into bite-sized chunks to ensure that young minds stay interested. The site also contains a useful list of FAQs and contact information for various Australian and worldwide authorities and organizations.

The Great Plant Escape

www.urbanext.uiuc.edu/gpe/

Botany is perhaps one of the most difficult scientific subjects to get children interested in. Luckily this site, created by the University of Illinois, has gone to admirable lengths to make the subject as interesting and fun as possible. It is aimed at primary school students, who are guided through the various pages by Detective Le Plant and his partners, Bud and Sprout. The site is organized into six sections, with titles such as 'Soiled Again!' and 'Plantenstein is the Suspect!'. Despite the awful puns, the information on the site is serious and very well presented.

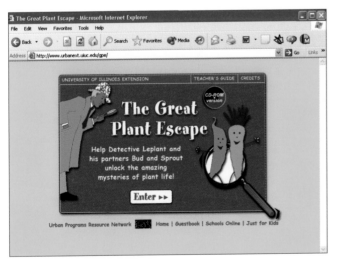

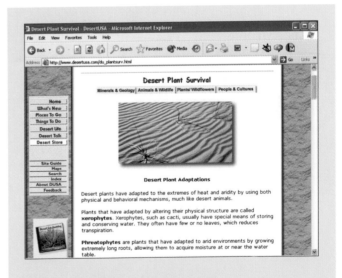

Desert Plant Survival

www.desertusa.com/du_plantsurv.html

This site, created as a teaching aid, is part of a larger Web site concerned with all aspects of American deserts. Every type of desert-dwelling plant is covered, from phraetophytes (plants that have adapted to arid conditions by growing very long roots) to ephemerals (some of which can complete an entire life cycle in a few months or even weeks). Many other fascinating facts await you at this excellent educational site, which is of interest to adults as well as students.

Charities

With charities looking at every possible way to raise money and promote their work more effectively, many are now turning to the World Wide Web.

Once Red Nose Day is over, many people assume that they have 'done their bit' as far as charitable donations go. Unfortunately, charities need a regular supply of donations or their work simply grinds to a halt. When the economy isn't doing so well, or when people think the Lottery is helping out as much as is necessary, the situation can become very bleak for charity fundraisers. As a result, most have quickly embraced the Internet as a way of getting their message across.

● Charity content
The content of the average charity's Web site is fairly standardized, and with good reason. Most people need only a quick reminder of the charity's work and those they could help before they decide to give a donation. No amount of sad stories or pictures will necessarily convince people of the

need to donate, and indeed too much 'persuasion' can easily put them off. So you'll find that many of the sites we look at over the next few pages are quite short and to the point. Added embellishments are unnecessary and a waste of the organization's hard-earned resources.

● Public education
Charity sites that offer more in the way of content are usually those where the problems they combat can be prevented more easily than they can be cured. Some obvious examples of this are the British Heart Foundation, the International Committee of the Red Cross and The World Wide Fund for Nature.

Organizations such as these have realized that by educating the public about the causes of their problems, they can reduce the need for expenditure on research or damage limitation. As a result, these three

Charity sites work well as educative resources, helping to prevent disease or disability. Straightforward appeals for money are often less effective.

charity Web sites in particular are highly educational, usually to the direct benefit of the visitor.

● Helping charity sites
Of course, not every charity can afford to maintain a Web site. Most of the sites we look at belong to the larger national or international organizations but smaller regional charities are sometimes represented on the Internet through personal Web pages.

Also, sites such as CharityNet can help you to get in touch with charities that do not yet exist in cyberspace. You might even be tempted to help these organizations make the move to the Web – something that would probably be more valuable than a donation.

● Fundraising

If your HTML skills aren't good enough for you to help a local charity with Web programming or design, most of the larger sites will suggest some sort of fundraising event as the best way to get actively involved.

Examples of previous events will be detailed on most of the sites, to give you an idea of what works and what doesn't. Of course, anything that generates money can be seen as a success, but each organization will be well aware of the best method for getting people to reach into their pockets. This might seem cynical, but with so many worthy organizations needing money, the fundraisers have to take a more professional view.

The next few pages provide details of some of the more interesting and impressive Web sites for national and international charities. Remember, though, there are a lot more organizations out there, and just because they don't appear in the following list, it doesn't mean that there isn't one doing something to raise funds in an area that is of interest to you.

INTERNET MONEY

The main obstacle to a charity's success online is the question of donations over the Internet. Despite the increasing popularity of online shopping, many people are still cautious about giving their credit card details over the Web, especially if they feel a charity site may not have the funds to spend on ensuring watertight security measures. For this reason, most sites promote their traditional phone numbers and postal addresses as the easiest, and safest, ways to donate money.

The sites

Here is a selection of the more impressive charity sites, which provide a clear message about what they do and how you can help them.

British Heart Foundation

www.bhf.org.uk

The British Heart Foundation is one of the largest and best-supported medical charities in the country. This well-designed site outlines the charity's work and how you can help it, but it also stresses the measures you should take to prevent heart disease. As the site ably points out, prevention is far better than cure.

National Society for the Prevention of Cruelty to Children (NSPCC)

www.nspcc.org.uk

The NSPCC Web site is simple but it has all the information you need. Like most charities, the NSPCC focuses on explaining what it does and how you can help. There is also plenty of detail on the NSPCC's Full Stop Campaign, and a separate Kids Zone area to tell children what the NSPCC does.

International Committee of the Red Cross (ICRC)

www.icrc.org/

The Red Cross and Red Crescent are perhaps the most famous and active charities in the world. Although there are separate Web sites for various national Red Cross organizations, this is the main international site. As you might expect, the content of the site concentrates on the work done by the charity, rather than on fundraising efforts, which are often specific to a certain region or country. This site is an interesting and well-informed resource for various humanitarian concerns.

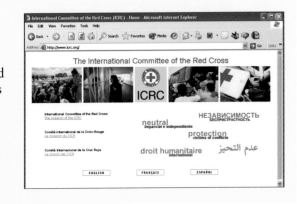

Comic Relief

www.comicrelief.com/

Comic Relief is one of the most well-known charities in the UK today and devotes itself to raising money and awareness of humanitarian problems in the UK and Africa, together with organizing self-help programmes. Its Web site is one of the most professional and attractive on the Net, and although that isn't really the point of charity Web sites, it probably helps to fire people's interest and enthusiasm.

WWF Global Network

www.panda.org/

This is the main international site for the World Wide Fund for Nature (the site at www.wwf.org lists national branches). It's an excellent site that doubles as a full-scale natural history resource. The main reason for such expansive information is to educate people, particularly children, about the damage being done to the environment, and the animals and plants currently at greatest risk. This site pulls no punches in its reporting of news stories and is openly scathing of any government that it sees as failing in its responsibility to the environment.

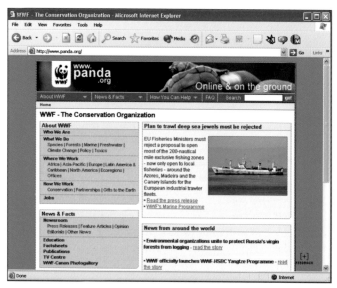

Oxfam International

www.oxfam.org/eng/

Although Oxfam started out as a British charity, since 1995 it has become international and is made up of 11 autonomous non-governmental groups. The charity's goal is to help fight global poverty. The site has been jazzed up and now reflects Oxfam's global importance, giving a thorough rundown on activities. There are numerous country-specific sites for Oxfam, of which www.oxfam.org.uk is the main British site, where you can make an online donation.

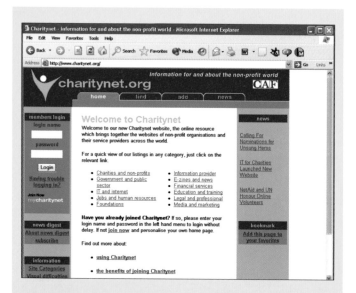

Charitynet

www.charitynet.org/

While much attention is given to the more famous and most widely supported charities, it can be easy to overlook the smaller, but no less deserving, organizations. The Charitynet site addresses this problem by providing a complete resource for information on charities around the world, with a bias towards those in the UK. For the casual surfer, the most useful section of this site is the well-stocked list of Web links. This helps you to get in contact with small and/or local charities that can't afford much publicity. If they don't have a Web site, their other contact details can be provided instead.

Royal National Lifeboat Institution (RNLI)

www.rnli.org.uk

Despite the fact that nearly everyone involved in the lifeboat service is unpaid, the Royal National Lifeboat Institution is always in need of funds – lifeboats and lifeboat stations cost a great deal of money to buy and maintain. This well-produced site explains the different ways in which you can make a contribution and outlines the services and work that the RNLI does. In addition, there's a special RNLI club for the under-16s and an extremely well-designed section entitled Safety on the Sea. This is actually a separate site aimed mostly at children, but it contains plenty of good advice for everyone.

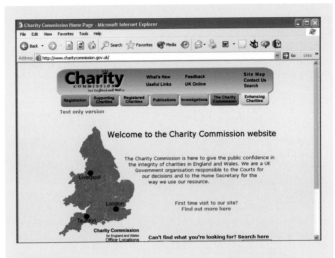

Charity Commission for England and Wales

www.charitycommission.gov.uk

To find out about a particular charity, or to set up your own, you must contact the Charity Commission. They can provide details and verify the official status of a charity, so you can be sure you are giving your money to a reputable concern. This Web site is the place to visit for advice on registering a charity and also gives details on any current investigations, as well as explaining exactly what the Commission does.

Royal National Institute for the Blind (RNIB)

www.rnib.org.uk

The RNIB doesn't just help the blind, but also the 500,000 partially sighted people in the UK. The site is constructed with the visually impaired in mind and has various built-in options for larger font sizes and easily distinguishable colours. The site has lots of information on RNIB campaigns, especially the Good Web Design Campaign to encourage site designers to make their pages accessible to the blind and partially sighted.

The Royal British Legion

www.britishlegion.org.uk

Many people assume that the Royal British Legion exists only to help veterans of the First and Second World Wars. In fact, it is dedicated to helping all ex-service men, women and their dependents. One of the best parts of its Web site is the Lost Tracks section where veterans can try to make contact with long lost comrades by entering in a few simple details. There are lots of other helpful areas too, such as a youth section to encourage younger members to the charity and also comprehensive details of upcoming events.

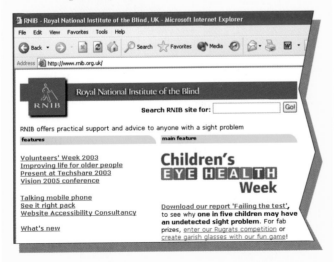

● **About the index**
Text in italics is used for cross-references within the index (as in *see also...*). Page numbers in bold type denote the main entries for a topic.

● **Acknowledgments**
Abbreviations: t = top; b = bottom;
r = right; l = left; c = centre;
bkg = background. All cartoons
are by Chris Bramley

8	Tony Stone Images/John Lund
10	Lyndon Parker/De Agostini
11bl	Courtesy IBM
14	TRH
16	Lyndon Parker/De Agostini
18	Lyndon Parker/De Agostini
20	Robert Harding
22	Superstock
24	The Stockmarket
30	Tony Stone Images
34	Lyndon Parker/De Agostini
36	Lyndon Parker/De Agostini
38	Transocean/Warner/Kobal
40	Lyndon Parker/De Agostini
42	Lyndon Parker/De Agostini
44	Lyndon Parker/De Agostini
45	Lyndon Parker/De Agostini
48	The Stockmarket
52	Lyndon Parker/De Agostini
54	Lyndon Parker/De Agostini
58	Lyndon Parker/De Agostini
62	Courtesy Hewlett Packard
64	Lyndon Parker/De Agostini

66	Tony Stone Images
70	Tony Stone Images
72	Lyndon Parker/De Agostini
76	Tony Stone Images
78	The Stock Market
82	The Stock Market
84	Lyndon Parker/De Agostini
88	Images Colour Library
92	Tony Stone Images
98	Courtesy Cybermind UK Ltd
99bl	Lyndon Parker/De Agostini
100t	Courtesy Cybermind UK Ltd
100tr	Courtesy Cybermind UK Ltd
102	Lyndon Parker/De Agostini
103tr	Lyndon Parker/De Agostini
103bl/b	Courtesy Holdan UK Ltd
106	Lyndon Parker/De Agostini
108	Corbis/Hulton Getty
109t	Courtesy Wadsworth
109bl	Courtesy APC UK
110	Courtesy Belkin
112	Cortesy Intel
113b	David Parker/Seagate Microelectronics Ltd/SPL
113(all other)	Courtesy Intel
116	Tony Stone Images/Courtesy British Airways
118	The Stock Market
119l	Lyndon Parker/De Agostini

120tr	The Stock Market
121tr	Marshall Cavendish
121bl	Marshall Cavendish
122	The Stock Market
122br	Marshall Cavendish
123bl	Courtesy Creative Technology
124	Lyndon Parker/De Agostini
125tr	Lyndon Parker/De Agostini
125bl	Lyndon Parker/De Agostini
126	Lyndon Parker/De Agostini
127	Lyndon Parker/De Agostini
134	The Stock Market
138	Lyndon Parker/De Agostini
140	Lyndon Parker/De Agostini
141	Lyndon Parker/De Agostini
142	Robert Harding Picture Library
146	Lyndon Parker/De Agostini
150(all)	Tony Stone Images
154	Lyndon Parker/De Agostini